I had been in some tight situations before, but I had no idea how I was getting out of this one…

Looking over my shoulder, I saw General Mattis, the Marine Division Commanding General, smiling at me. "Where you headed, sir," I asked, smiling back at him.

"Baghdad," he replied in his usual happy tone.

I slowly raised the collective, paying close attention to the aircraft's power available. In a four-inch hover, the instrument gauge power needles had pegged on 100%, telling me that we weren't getting off the bluff with our failing bleed air values in the heat currently consuming Tikrit.

Suddenly, with no control inputs, the tail boom began rising up as our helicopter was seemingly pushed toward the marble wall separating us from the ravine surrounding the bluff. When it became evident that the nose of the helicopter was going to strike the marble wall, I pulled up on the collective, placing more pitch in the main rotor blades that requested additional power from the struggling engines. With the low RPM horn now going off in my helmet, that small control input momentarily raised the helicopter eight feet off the ground before dropping us down onto the marble wall with an aircraft shivering impact as the skids struck the top. There was complete silence in the aircraft as we bounced off the marble wall and fell into the ravine.

Shoving the cyclic forward to keep the tail boom from hitting the wall, I found myself in the steepest dive I had ever been. With the accelerating wind whistling across the open window next to me, as a vision of our unavoidable fiery crash flashed into my mind, I glanced up to ensure there were no power lines or other obstacles in our path before yanking the cyclic back into my lap, trying to abate our steep dive. The hydraulic servos began loudly pounding beneath my feet and behind the rear bulkhead, adding more confusion to the cockpit, as once again my control inputs demanded too much from the aircraft.

On the morning of September 11, 2001, Patrick Ashtre was a happily married man with a lovely wife, three children, and a house in Arlington, Virginia. He was a good father and husband and, looking into the mirror each morning, he was happy with the reflected image—but all that was about to change.

There are events that change people forever—a friend's premonition about the future that comes true, shaking the very fibers of our beliefs about the world around us, or a traumatic episode that casts us into a sea of despair where we question mankind's true nature. These events can cause us to question our very existence. Our ability to recover from these experiences becomes even more convoluted when we stamp manmade lines of right and wrong onto the path leading back to constancy. The lucidity of those events and the rationalization as to why they occurred are normally a hazy quagmire of guesses and suppositions. But on occasion, seemingly at the darkest hour, one can come to an epiphany that allows crystal-clear clarity.

A Distant Island is the story about that moment when Patrick Ashtre began to understand his struggle with posttraumatic stress, the experiences from which it spawned, and the aspects of living a life under its influence. More than a tale about posttraumatic stress, it is the provocative story of a love affair with a former bargirl and how the rich and colorful Buddhist culture of Thailand helped Ashtre overcome a past filled with violence and death. It is a story that illustrates how sometimes the answers to our problems can come in unusual and unexpected packages. *A Distant Island* is an account of how Patrick Ashtre found his way home.

KUDOS for *A Distant Island*

In *A Distant Island* by Patrick Ashtre, Ashtre tells the story of how he got and dealt with posttraumatic stress. He details his life in the military and the effect the deaths of his close friends and colleagues had on him. Unable to deal with his life in the US after being at his desk in the Pentagon on 9/11, he flees to Thailand to start over. There he meets a Buddhist bar girl who changes his life forever, helping him to deal with his posttraumatic stress. The book is thought provoking and well written. It gives a clear picture of what posttraumatic stress is and how each person handles it differently. Even though what works for one may not work for others, Ashtre does help you to understand what it is, what causes it, and how you can come to terms with it if you have it. ~ *Taylor Jones, Reviewer*

A Distant Island by Patrick Ashtre is the story of Ashtre's journey from his life as a successful and happily married career air force officer to a desolate and unhappy man living on Thailand and struggling to overcome his posttraumatic stress. The book takes us through a week of Ashtre's life in Thailand, using flashback to his military experiences that caused his posttraumatic stress, including sitting at his desk in the Pentagon when the plane hit on 9/11. I found the book to be extremely educational, intriguing, and enlightening. It made me realize that anyone can suffer from posttraumatic stress whether we know it or not and most of us have it at some point in our lives. I highly recommend *A Distant Island*. ~ *Regan Murphy, Reviewer*

ACKNOWLEDGEMENTS

I must thank my good friends John and Kathy Shoreman, the most generous people I have ever come across in my fifty-five years. Returning from Thailand without much financial support, they lodged me in their backyard bar and each night, whether I needed or not, I was served a delicious meal.

A DISTANT ISLAND

PATRICK ASHTRE

A Black Opal Books Publication

GENRE: MEMOIRS/SELF-HELP

A DISTANT ISLAND
Copyright © 2015 by Patrick Ashtre
Cover Design by Jackson Cover Designs
All cover art copyright © 2015
All Rights Reserved
Print ISBN: 978-1-626943-42-1

First Publication: OCTOBER 2015

Published by Black Opal Books **http://www.blackopalbooks.com**

To Alison, Amelia, and Benjamin

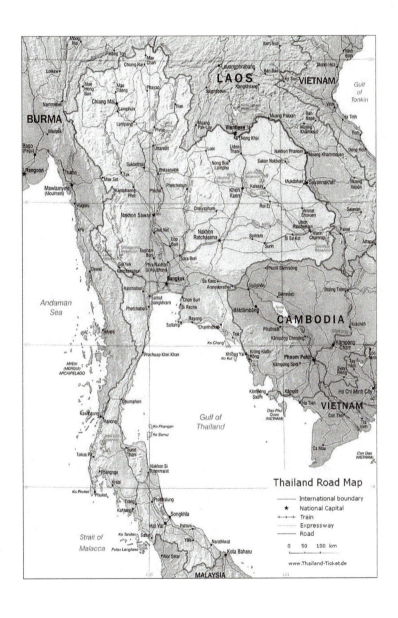

Thailand Road Map

——— International boundary
★ National Capital
+—+—+ Train
——— Expressway
——— Road

0   50   100 km

www.Thailand-Ticket.de

Every experience alters us a little,
but harrowing ones change us a lot

CHAPTER 1

The Downward Spiral

On the morning of September 11, 2001, I was a happily married man with a lovely wife, three children, and a house in Arlington, Virginia. I was a good father and husband, and looking into the mirror each morning, I was happy with the reflected image—but all that was about to change.

As a United States Marine, risk and violence were essential elements of my profession and had become inseparable aspects of my life. Except for one previous event in my career, my vocation and experiences had yet to have any discernible effect on my personality or life choices. I was able to compartmentalize those events that conflicted with an otherwise peaceful existence and keep them from affecting my life outside of the Marine Corps. But on that fateful day in 2001, I began an unwilling and dramatic transformation that would consume my life for nearly fourteen years.

In 2006, while commanding a squadron in Okinawa, Japan, after a tour in Iraq and a follow-up cruise, hunting for terrorists on the high seas, I realized that my life was completely out of control in an ever-accelerating downward spiral, affecting my job, marriage, and children. An emotion I could only describe as a feeling of hollowness had begun to overwhelm me several years earlier, and my response had been to turn to alcohol in an effort to numb the unwanted sensations. Not surprisingly, this simple act led to the feeling of more emotional hollowness and more drinking. In a state of denial, I felt confused and frustrated. Within a year, I would make the decision to retire from the Marine Corps after twenty-six years of service in a futile attempt to find some peace from my silent struggle. It was not until 2009 that I recognized I had Posttraumatic Stress, even though my ex-wife had made the claim years earlier and pleaded with me to get help.

First of all, let me clarify. I do not feel sorry for myself for being afflicted with posttraumatic stress, nor do I claim any government handout for the ailment. It was path that I knowingly chose and one for which I have accepted the consequences. In my opinion, posttraumatic stress is a personalized illness, each victim seeing, feeling, and reacting to its effects differently than other sufferers. For some, it is intolerable and never ending; for me it became manageable. For some there is a need to control every aspect of life; for me the response was exactly the opposite. Having come to the conclusion that ultimately people had no control over the events unfolding around them, I embraced the chaos. Professionally and personally, I found myself taking more risks, not concerning myself with the cost of failure or its effects on those around me.

My greatest regret has been that my children have suffered from my posttraumatic stress and the tainted choices I made while I struggled with the illness. Witnessing my struggle, they saw the man it had created and forgot the man I once was.

Having given posttraumatic stress a lot of thought in recent years, here is my personal view as to why it occurred in me and how it has affected my life. Sadly, I have come to realize that the best I can ever expect is to manage the illness because, like alcoholism, one can never be completely rid of its long-term effects.

In my case, posttraumatic stress was brought on by a career of adrenaline-surging events and violence, not just the drive north in Iraq. As a young pilot, it was not uncommon to hear of a friend's demise—some dying from super-shaft failures, some becoming disoriented during an instrument approach and auguring into the ground, and others from a multitude of other dangers we risked on a daily basis. Each had an effect on me but did not become life or personality altering. However, those events did begin to dull my emotional response to violence and death.

My first recollection of a significant experience with post-traumatic stress occurred directly after the First Gulf War when I watched a young man named Jeff Couch, along with Dan Adams, Phil Chapman, and Top Snell, die. Jeff Couch, a squadron crew chief, had a premonition about dying in a helicopter and had quit flying. Not wanting to lose the two hundred dollars a month flight pay, he came to me and asked to fly on my aircraft during a training mission to Yuma, Arizona the following day. Out of all the pilots in the squadron, Jeff chose to fly with me because he believed nothing would happen to him under my care. According to him, nothing would happen to me, therefore, he would be safe at my side. We spoke with the operations department that evening and he was placed on the draft schedule to fly with me in the lead aircraft to the Chocolate Mountains, north of Yuma, early the next morning. After we had gone home that evening the schedule writers changed the draft and placed me in the second aircraft, leaving Jeff on the lead helicopter. When we came in the next morning and saw the final schedule, Jeff and I spoke and he said he would be all right. I had flown extensively with Dan Adams, the pilot of the lead aircraft, during the First Gulf War and knew him to be an incredibly talented pilot. And I didn't believe in premonitions. In my mind, Jeff was worried about nothing and in good hands.

Two thousand feet over the fertile green farm fields of Calipatria, California, I had a front row seat to a tragedy and a lesson in premonitions. The lead helicopter's main rotor blades slowed. I watched it suddenly begin to descend as it rolled to the left. The blades continued to slow, rocking back on the mast head and cutting the tail boom from the fuselage. The mast then broke free from the transmission and, with the blades still bridled, spun through the clear blue sky like the unleashed vanes from a windmill. The final act in the tragedy was the fuselage, unencumbered by the main rotor blades or tail-boom, falling the remaining seventeen hundred feet and landing upside down onto a freshly irrigated farm field. To this day, some twenty-three years later, I can still see those events unfold with vivid clarity in my mind. I still have a hard time coming to grips with that day, even after twenty-three years.

The first three months after his death, I thought about Jeff and the accident every hour of every day. Over the next year, I thought about the crash several times every day. And twenty-three years later I still ponder that day often.

It was my first lesson in posttraumatic stress.

Many more episodes, involving close calls, violence, deadly accidents, and destruction left me numb to death and the sentimental world around me. The straw that broke the camel's back started on the fourth floor of the D ring in the Pentagon, continued through the drive north in Iraq, and ended on the high seas in Southeast Asia.

On September 11, 2001, while I was in my office at the Pentagon, a deep concussion shook the building around me. With my eardrums ringing from the blast, I was catapulted upward while sitting in a black, cushioned office chair, watching my laptop rise at arm's length on a parallel course in a ballet-like trajectory above brand-new gray office cubicles. At the apex of the flight, I watched the windows of the office fracture into a spider-web-like design on a background of fire and smoke. The next hour became a lesson in human reaction to sudden and unexpected calamity—an experience that was to become the prelude to my descent into posttraumatic stress.

It was after the drive north in Iraq that many of my friends and my wife began to say I had changed. I laughed at their analysis, claiming that their observations had been tainted by the recent re-emergence of posttraumatic stress as a popular dinnertime discussion. It took years for me to realize that I had been in denial and the war had, in fact, changed me.

If asked to attribute any one event as the culprit of my posttraumatic stress, I could not. After many hours, days, and weeks of pondering the events that unfolded around me, I have finally come to believe that the accumulation of many events over my career set the stage, and my experience during the drive north in Iraq, followed by a three month cruise in Southeast Asia, set my future in stone. During the drive north, climbing into a helicopter nearly every day and believing that day to be my last became the proverbial nails in my coffin.

In order to do the job we were tasked with, we had to take chances that the average civilian would consider incredibly foolish. And, during peacetime, they would be right. But we were at war, where waking up each morning had an associated level of risk. To take the risks we did, all in the name of patriotism and getting the job done, we had to re-adjust our belief as to our future, our goals, and our ambitions. Walter Bradford Cannon and his theory of sympathetic nervous system priming an animal for fighting or fleeing were thrown out the window. The adrenal gland could produce all the hormonal cascades it wanted to, but running away wasn't an option. The natural instinct of fight or flight had to be unnaturally reprogrammed to simply the response of fight.

I was never consumed with fear. In fact, I never recalled ever feeling afraid, but to climb into the cockpit of a helicopter during the drive north one had to understand that one's life was already over. Whatever bullet was going to kill you had already been fired, whatever act of Mother Nature that was going to disorient you and cause you to auger into the ground had already begun to form, and whatever manmade object you weren't going to see and crash into had already been built and your flight path predetermined. You were already dead. Without that mindset, it would have been impossible to strap into and fire up the aircraft before flying north.

The grand finale of my journey into posttraumatic stress occurred during a several-months-long cruise in Southeast Asia that a portion of our squadron was assigned to directly after the drive north. We had flown peacetime missions that rivaled the risk of those made during this cruise. The difference was we were in a fragile state. What many of us would have considered normal duty became the final act of establishing a future tainted by posttraumatic stress. About a month into the cruise, the unit flight surgeon came to me, claiming that none of the pilots were sleeping and they were playing cards all night.

He theorized that they all had posttraumatic stress.

I laughed at his proclamation and replied, "And we're adding more traumatic stress to the traumatic stress."

Directly after Iraq, we found ourselves flying twenty feet off the surface of the water on moonless, pitch-black nights, miles from the closest shoreline and its associated manmade illumination. For those who don't know, night vision goggles amplify light, but if there is none to be had, they become nothing but a useless weight mounted on the front of a helmet. To make matters worse, we were operating four aircraft on a deck designed for two, landing and taking off with only a few feet of clearance between blade tips on a pitching deck in the middle of the night. So shortly after getting shot at on a daily basis in Iraq, we found ourselves flying in an environment that was as equally stressful with a slightly different twist on the anxiety catalyst—someone attempting kill you had been replaced with attempting not to kill yourself. Yes, we were once again strapping into an aircraft and going flying when every fiber of our sympathetic nervous system was telling us to flee.

"We're all suffering from stress, Doc. Where have you been?" I said, continuing to chastise the flight surgeon as he stood in front of the gray metal desk in my stateroom. "And what would you recommend we should do about it? Tell the joint task force commander that we can't fly anymore and we should all go home? 'Sorry, sir, the cruise is over.'"

"But they're not sleeping," he mumbled, defeated by my laughing reprimand.

Realizing I had been too harsh on the poor doctor, I calmly replied, "Look, Doc, we're not the first pilots to ever have to deal with what's going on in our heads. But we all willingly signed up for this job and, at this point, we don't have another option. Your job is to keep us physically healthy." And then, suddenly understanding the depth of his concern by the expression on his face, I added, "If, in your opinion, someone is on the brink of mentally losing it, let me know and I'll take him off the schedule for as long as it takes."

Having quickly regained his composure from my initial scolding, he looked me in the eye. "You're all on the brink of losing it," he said, adding a hesitating and curt, "sir," before turning and walking out of my stateroom.

In 2007, after watching myself spin downward at an ever-increasing rate for nearly four years, I made a panicked and frenzied attempt to save my family from witnessing a classic case of self-destruction and a dramatic change to stop the disastrous spiral I found myself in. I took an eraser and wiped the slate of my life clean. At the age of forty-seven, I left everything behind and started over. I left my wife, my children, my country, and life as I had known it, and moved to a tropical island in the Gulf of Thailand, wrapping myself in a cocoon of Buddhism, searching for an inner peace that had eluded me for years. On that tropical island, I opened a small business on a crystal clear bay bordered by a wide ribbon of white sand and began the healing process. It was a decision twisted by fear, selfishness, and posttraumatic stress. It was a decision that I will never be proud of but one that I made nonetheless. At the time, it seemed the best of a lot of bad choices.

A second regret that I carry is my part in keeping a failed marriage going, truly believing that I would somehow heal and return to take up my marital and parental responsibilities. Even though our interactions during that time was proof that our relationship was over, I honestly believed that someday I would come home and we would resume the idyllic relationship we had before the drive north in Iraq. By the time my wife had filed for divorce and I was well on my way to some semblance of healing, I knew that too much damage had been done to ever think we could share the same bed again.

Several years ago, I was contacted by a friend who had served with me, both during the drive north in Iraq and the subsequent cruise in Southeast Asia, telling me that he was working in Bangkok and, if I were ever in the city, to give him a call. Eventually, on one of my trips to Bangkok, we met up at the Monsoon Restaurant on *Soi* Eight.

One of many oases of civility in the chaotic city, the Monsoon Restaurant has a large wooden deck that sits to one side of the *Soi* or street. Several thick tropical trees with bright green foliage-covered branches hover above and combine with a number of colorful overhead umbrellas to provide shade to eight black-lacquered wooden tables covered in white table cloths. Having been there several times over the years, I have found the Monsoon Restaurant to be a place where one can relax and drink a nice glass or bottle of wine for a reasonable price, all the while, watching the daily tumultuous Bangkok activities from several safe feet away.

My friend, his wife, and I met to get acquainted, reac-quainted, and catch up on gossip about our old military com-panions. It was a hot afternoon, but pleasant, as we sat on the deck at the Monsoon Restaurant, sweat building on our brows and condensation beading on our wineglasses. We watched the tourists wandering up and down the *Soi*, the local merchants peddling their wares, and bargirls coming and going from sev-eral nearby hotels or bars. Most of our conversation focused on common military friends and the cruise we took directly after Iraq, hunting for terrorists on the high seas in Southeast Asia, veering away from anything about the drive north.

As the conversation began to wane, my friend looked over at me and asked, "Do you ever think about the war?"

Hearing the question, his wife politely turned her attention elsewhere, knowing and respecting that the next few minutes of conversation were to be private.

Trying to describe posttraumatic stress to someone who has never been a victim is like trying to describe blue to someone who is blind and has never seen the color. You know what it is, you can see it in front of your face, but you can't describe how it looks in any fashion that would make sense to the blind person. Surprisingly, from my experience, two people who have shared the same risks and dangers that created posttrau-matic stress see it and feel its effects slightly differently as well. Posed with his question, I immediately realized that the color blue to me would not necessarily be the color blue to my friend.

As we sat under the trees and vibrant umbrellas, all provid-ing shade from the unrelenting heat of the afternoon, I thought about Jeff Couch, the Pentagon, Iraq, and the Southeast Asian cruise. Wondering how to put all those memories into a coherent response to my friend's question, I sat silent for several minutes before answering.

With a career of violent experiences swirling through my head, I finally responded, "I used to think about it a lot."

"You don't anymore?"

"Not nearly as much as I used to, but I still think about it often."

"I still think about it a lot," he admitted in a somber tone.

Looking down at my wineglass, with condensation dripping from its sides making a damp ring on the white table cloth, I explained, "Directly after the war I used to tell people it was an experience that I was glad I had because it gave me a level of understanding about human nature that most people never discover or understand. That understanding somehow made it worthwhile. Later, as I began to understand the implications of what the war had done to me, I began saying that it was an experience that I was glad I had but it did me no good as a human being." After a few more moments of silence, I looked up from my wineglass and added, "But my whole perspective on the war and those experiences has continued to slowly develop and change over the years."

"What do you mean?" he asked, glancing over at his wife, who was watching the activity on the *Soi*.

"I was in Pattaya not too long afterward—after Iraq, I mean. I'm not sure why I was there but I remember a conversation I had with a complete stranger in some bar."

"What did you talk about?"

"He saw my haircut and figured I was in the military, and asked if I had been in Iraq," I replied before taking a sip of wine. "When he found out I had been in the war he asked if I had any regrets."

"What did you tell him?"

"I think he was expecting me to say I was sorry I participated in what went on and that I was against the war." I chuckled. "Boy, was he in for the shock of his life."

"What'd you tell him?" my friend asked again, breaking into an understanding grin.

It was my turn to glance over at his wife and see that she

was still focused on the *Soi*, before saying, "Remember that time when we were flying over An Nasiriyah and we saw all those men coming in from the farm fields outside the city? We were only a couple of days into the drive north, and they were waving and smiling at us. I thought they could be men coming home after a hard day's work in the fields, and I was trying so hard to not to kill innocent people that I forced myself to believe they were farmers."

His smile disappearing, my friend added, "Yeah, we found out later that they were Iraqi soldiers dressed in civilian clothes making their way to the local hospital to pick up weapons to use against us."

"Had that occurred a couple of days later," I continued. "I wouldn't have hesitated. I would have killed them without any remorse."

With his lips warping back into a grin, my friend asked, "But what did you say to that guy in the bar?"

"I was still beating myself up so much over that farm field incident that I looked the guy in the eye and told him that my biggest regret was that I didn't kill enough of them."

His smile breaking into a full-fledged grin, he laughed. "What did he say?"

"Nothing. He was so shocked at my answer that he looked at me with this dumbfounded expression and then, after a few minutes, walked away."

"I think I went through the same rollercoaster of emotions right afterward," my friend responded, still smiling. "But you say you don't think about it as much? Why? What changed in you?"

"I don't know. I feel like I'm slowly coming to terms with it all, I guess." Then looking him in the eyes, I asked, "And you still think about it a lot?"

His grin quickly vanishing, replaced by a reflective solemn expression, he answered, "It's like a huge hole in me that's always there—a profound sadness that won't go away. It's hard to explain to people."

Looking out at the *Soi*, watching two bargirls walk down the street, one in a skimpy black and neon blue outfit, the oth-

er in a short bright red dress, I offered, "It was a loss of innocence. I used to really believe it was an experience I was glad
I had because it gave me a level of understanding about humanity that most people never achieve. And that was so far
from the truth."

"And what do you think now?"

"It was an experience I wish I never had," I confessed. "It
was loss of innocence that did me no good as a human being. I
think to be truly happy in life you need to maintain a certain
level of naiveté. You need to believe in the Easter Bunny and
Santa Claus. You need to believe that good things happen to
good people. When you lose that innocence, happiness becomes an evasive and unachievable objective."

"Did your loss of innocence drive you to Thailand?" he
asked, before taking another sip from his wineglass.

"Whether by subconscious design or accident, I came to a
country and buried myself in a culture that is all about not
judging the people around you for their failures, and making
merit for the next life. I have slowly built a life here that actually has restored a small bit of that innocence. I almost feel at
peace at times."

Thailand had restored some of my innocence, but I have also come to realize that I will never be the man I would have
been had I never joined the Marine Corps and witnessed the
violence and death that's associated with that profession. I
may have a deeper understanding of humanity but that education came with a cost. My emotional reactions have been
dulled; my smile is not as wide or as genuine; and there will
always be a hole in my soul that can never be entirely filled. I
will never be the happy and content man I was on the morning
of September the 11, 2001 looking into that bathroom mirror.

The following story is true and takes place over the course
of one week, April 10th through April 17th, 2014, accurately
summarizing the beginning of my awakening from posttraumatic stress. While I have never been one to keep a journal or
record of my daily activities or life, I choose to write about
this week because it epitomized the sudden clarity that one
sees the world around them as they emerge from a difficult

struggle. The lessons seemed to suddenly be condensed; the experiences suddenly seemed to be focused on the issue at hand. Everything that happened during that seven-day span seemed to be precisely designed to aid me in surviving the remaining days of my life without the heavy yoke of post-traumatic stress.

CHAPTER 2

Past Lives ~ 10 April 2014

Scurrying crowds and scooters encircled us as Supattra and I sat in the front seat of our idling black Toyota four-door pickup, looking out across a horizon of bluish-green water. We were parked in a long line of cars, trucks, and trailers on the Koh PhaNgan pier. A white haze obscured the surrounding islands and a cool breeze blew from the vents on the dash in a fog-like mist, two good indicators that humidity was high that afternoon.

At the end of the long concrete jetty, an international crowd of forty or fifty colorfully clad tourists sat or milled around two shaded seating areas with faded blue tiled roofs while waiting for one of the high speed transit boats destined for *Koh Samui*, the next island south and only one in the archipelago with an airport. Several fishing boats and two long banana-shaped cargo boats, all wooden and brightly painted, bobbed next to the pier adding a unique Southeast Asian flair to the scene. *See Langs*, with their tubular steel sidecars, and stainless steel rolling kitchens, pushed by merchants, moved up and down the dock, delivering more passengers and cargo or hunting for hungry travelers.

A rabble of scooters twisted through a crowd of travelers as they pulled their wheeled luggage across the concrete-surfaced dock. In the distance, we watched an old blue ferry plowing its way through the semi-calm water with white foam churning at its flat bow. Sitting back in the passenger seat, watching the old, oversized ferry move closer, I attempted to estimate how much longer it would take for it to make its way to the pier.

Having ridden the ferry multiple times over the years, I should have found it an easy task.

"How long do you think?" Supattra asked for the second time in as many minutes.

"Fifteen minutes," I said, giving her my best guess while trying to sound confident in my answer.

"Only ten," she retorted, looking over at me with flashing dark brown eyes.

"Fifteen, give or take five minutes," I said, restating my approximation with a smile. Then, in as innocent a tone as I could conjure, I asked, "Are you sure you want to drive the truck onto the ferry?"

She parried my question with one of her own, flashing her dark brown eyes in my direction again. "You don't think I can drive it onto the ferry?"

"I never said that," I calmly replied, suddenly finding myself on the defensive. "I just asked if you were sure you wanted to pull the truck onto the boat. You know how close they park the cars next to each other."

"I can drive it onto the ferry," she responded in such a way that I knew the discussion should be over.

"I'm just offering," I said, pressing the issue because, in actuality, I was not confident in her abilities.

Without looking at me, she said, "Pat, shut up."

"Just offering."

"Shut up."

A frenzy of activity erupted at the end of the pier as a white, motorized catamaran, with a wide red and blue stripe running down its sides, pulled up to load on the Koh Samui bound passengers. The colorfully dressed tourists popped up from their seats like blooming flowers and their suitcases appeared from seemingly nowhere like an army of ants emerging from the ground amongst the shaded seating area.

Ignoring the vibrant disorder, we waited patiently as the oversized metal ferry continue to push its way through the calm water, for our destination was not the next island south but Donsak on the mainland, where we planned on driving to Supattra's hometown near the city of Kalasin in Isaan and the annual Songkran celebration. Songkran, the water festival or Thai New Year, is celebrated throughout Thailand but it has special significance in Isaan, located in the northeast corner of the country, where the annual festival lasts a full three days. Droves of Isaan people flock back to their country farms from low paying jobs in Bangkok and elsewhere to celebrate family and life.

The celebration is not unlike the American Thanksgiving holiday except for it being a hyper-drive version. The two days prior to Songkran, the Thai road network leading north is jam packed with bumper to bumper traffic. Small pickups with their beds crammed full of people, luggage, and cargo; buses loaded with more people and luggage; and cars, packed with the same, ascend at a snail's pace from south and central Thailand to the Northeast Khorat Plateau and rice country.

Drunkenness is acceptable and expected during the three-day celebration. The drinking starts at sunrise and ends when the last man (or woman) passes out in the early hours of the next day, all to resume again when the sun comes up. The food is regional and, to foreigners, many times distasteful. Bugs and organs that have never seen a Western tabletop are prevalent; Leo Beer on Ice, and whiskey in any form mixed with soda water and coke are the norm; the music is all whiny Isaan songs, telling tales of broken promises and hearts; and a drenching in water followed by a dousing of talcum powder is tradition and a form of respect. It is a celebration unlike any other in the world.

The oversized ferry finally reached the pier, groaning and grunting as the captain maneuvered it between two large, rusted, blue-steel cylindrical girders supported by concrete pylons. As it came to a growling halt, men began running around throwing lines and shouting instructions. Finally, in a metal-screeching cacophony, the bow began to slowly lower onto the pier until a loud clang indicated it was ready to offload its interior cargo.

More running and shouting, and a hundred people and twenty scooters erupted from the bow, followed by a small traffic jam of cars and trucks.

Once the interior had been purged, the travelers standing on the pier destined for Donsak began pouring across the lowered bow and disappearing into the bowels of the ferry, followed by ten or fifteen scooters. Once the scooters had been stowed and the people seated in the passenger area on the third deck, our long line of vehicles, one by one, slowly moved onto the ferry, stopping at the bow just long enough to hand a man with a crooked nose and dressed in green coveralls a ticket showing we had paid our way. With Supattra at the wheel, our black truck bounced across thick worn ropes formally used to harness ships to piers that had been laid out to protect cars from the leading edge of the ferry's lowered bow. With the guidance of a young man who didn't seem interested in his job, Supattra moved to within a foot of a large truck filled with a towering cargo of coconuts held in place by a massive net. Another man, seemingly more attentive to his duties, appeared from between two cars and slipped several chocks under the wheels of our pickup, kicking each twice to ensure they were adequately wedged into place.

I sighed in relief when the entire procedure had been completed and we had successfully parked the truck in the ferry's hold without incident. After trudging up a narrow set of metal stairs to one side of the hold, its handrail warped from bulging corrosion that had been painted over in high gloss white paint numerous times and dirty from a thousand greasy palms, we momentarily stopped at the railing overlooking the docks below. Turning to me, Supattra asked me where we should sit and I nodded to the heavily worn, blue vinyl chairs in the second class seating area.

"Why not the air conditioning?" she asked.

"The one thing I look forward to on this trip is the sea breeze," I offered as an explanation, to which she nodded in agreement.

Supattra followed as I wandered down the warped steel-floored aisle to the second to last row of seats, knowing from experience that the televisions in the front aired either bad Thai comedy programs or static. Closing my eyes, I slipped down onto one of the chairs and could feel its cracked vinyl rubbing across my jeans. Sensing my entire body relaxing as I slid down onto the old, worn chair, I could feel a slight bump as small swells moved and shifted the ferry tied up against the pier. I could smell the diesel exhaust from the ship's idling engines. I could hear the rubbing of the metal hull against a hundred rubber tires hanging from the blue cylindrical steel girders and concrete pylons. The anticipation of the next two-and-a-half-hour journey, with its accompanying sea breeze and undulating motion excited me, as I have never made the trip without at least an hour of sleep brought on by its serene environmental conditions.

With a smattering of Thais chatting around us, I could hear the crew unlashing ropes and the engines stirring in the lower depths of the ferry as background noise. With my eyes still closed, I prepared for the inevitable sleep that was about to overtake me when Supattra reached out and took my hand into hers, her skin soft and warm. It was the perfect venue. It is why I love this journey across the lower Gulf of Thailand to the docks of Donsak, just east of the city of Surratthani on the mainland.

"You came too early," Supattra whispered.

Keeping my eyes closed, I immediately knew what the conversation would entail over the next few minutes and sighed. Not a sigh of frustration or one of relief, but an emotional murmur of knowing who you have chosen to spend your time with and how that relationship is predictable and unpredictable all at the same time.

"Or you waited too long," I said, teasing her.

"No, you came too early," she explained. "Something delayed me and you came too early."

"I'll try and wait next time."

"That is why you were lost for so long," she added.

"I know. I was looking for you."

"But you didn't wait and you became lost."

"You and I both know that we are like infants when we come back and know nothing," I calmly replied. "It took time for me to see that I was looking for someone and even then I was uncertain who it was. I made some mistakes."

"I knew the minute I saw you."

"I did too. The second I saw you I knew."

Of course, we were talking of our past lives and this one. We were talking Buddhism. It was typically a bi-annual discussion that normally preluded my departure for the US or some other stressful event in our relationship. Early in our friendship Supattra explained to me that we have had many lives together, and that I came back to this world too early on this occasion. I should have waited.

I have sometimes joked with friends that in my past life I was a dog, moving from bitch to bitch based on the simplicity of a scent. Of course, I save that joke for *farangs* (how Thais refer to light-skinned foreigners) for no Thai, and especially not Supattra, would find the witticism the least bit amusing, but it does make sense of my past in Buddhist terms.

But according to the lovely Thai woman I have chosen to spend my time with, I came back too early and looked for the one I belonged with but she was nowhere to be found. I was lost without her.

That, of course, explained the two ex-wives.

The *farang* in me tells me this is her way of dealing with our age difference and the two former wives before I met her. My dog theory only covers one of those issues. After living in Thailand for many years and having spent that time with the same Buddhist woman, I now see some merit in her explanation. I have become open to the teachings of Buddha.

I shifted in the blue chair, the cracked vinyl scratching at my jeans again, as I tried to find the perfect position while waiting for the last of the conversation to play out. Based on previous discussions concerning this topic, I knew we would go through a banter session prior to the finale.

"Part of the problem is that you came back *farang*," she explained, as she always does during this conversation. "*Farangs* are so self-absorbed. They can't see beyond their own selfish desires."

"I know a few selfish Thais," I muttered in response.

"That is true. There are selfish Thais," she answered, "and they will pay for selfishness in their next life."

"But so will all the selfish *farangs*."

"Yes, but they have an excuse," Supattra replied in the midst of a massive yawn. "They don't know better."

"And Buddhism takes that into account?" I asked, finally opening my eyes and raising one eyebrow in disbelief.

"Buddhism takes everything into account. It would be unfair to hold someone to the same rules who has never been placed on the path."

Chuckling, I close my eyes again and say, "Thank God for that. I'm safe from all my misdeeds; past, present, and future."

Patting me on the knee, Supattra shook her head. "You've been placed on the path."

"How come I don't remember being placed on the path?"

"The first day I took you to the temple in Pattaya and the monk blessed you, you were placed on the path and began the process of becoming Buddhist."

"You should have warned me."

Running her fingers through my hair, she gave me a *hom noi* (Thai kiss or a sniff) on the cheek. "You came back too early, but I still love you."

Using my traditional response at the conclusion of this particular discussion, I said, "I'll wait next time," before slipping off into deep slumber.

Sleeping soundly in the blue vinyl chair, a vision of my first wife floated into my dreams, like some wispy translucent apparition. Her face filled with both strength and sadness. An uncanny feeling came over me that she was attempting to tell me that "it was time." When I asked, "Time for what?" the specter quickly faded, leaving me with an unsettling emotion.

The best of friends, my first wife and I were too much alike to have ever been married. We immaturely equated a deep friendship with love. Two things that I would learn are not mutually exclusive but neither do they guarantee a harmonious relationship. Head strong, slightly impulsive, and highly ambitious, she had personal traits that were difficult to successfully mesh into the hectic life as a marine's wife. She would tell me later that she had considered divorce as early as my flight school training days, even before our first anniversary. Rather than face the ugly truth, we stayed together, hurting each other as if we were playing a game of tennis—tit for tat. Rarely arguing, by the end of our marriage we were playing like professionals, balls of pain screaming across the low slung net at astounding speeds. We did manage to create a beautiful baby girl in the midst of our endless mental wrestling match. The end of our marriage came after a quick succession of three six-month deployments and the Jeff Couch incident. Sitting in my quarters at Marine Corps Air Station Futemna on Okinawa during my third six-month deployment in less than three years, she called me one night and simply asked, "Is it time we went our separate ways?"

Besieged with the realities of our situation and still struggling with the memories of the helicopter disintegrating in the clear blue skies over Calipatria, California, I replied with an equally simple, "Yes."

Being the woman she was, we went about separating our lives in an unemotional and professional manner. She would move back to our home state and finally begin working at a job worthy of her skills. Within several years her once-a-year bonus would eclipse my accumulated annual pay. Each of us finding a second spouse rather quickly, throughout the years I think we both regretted our inability to find a solution to the difficulties that plagued us as we realized that our friendship could never be duplicated.

My last conversation with my first wife occurred just before I climbed onto yet another navy ship to deploy to Kuwait and the eventual drive north in Iraq. She had struggled with breast cancer for years, and I asked if she was going to be okay. She confidently replied yes, but knowing her as well as I did, I could hear a fear her in voice that had never been there before. She died as the fleet of ships I was sailing with passed by the Hawaiian Islands. Learning of her death over a satellite phone in the ship's communication center one night, its red overhead lights creating an ominous scene, I solemnly walked down to my stateroom and pulled a hidden bottle of Irish whiskey from my sea bag. Maneuvering my way through the ship's narrow passageways, I stopped at the first door where I heard voices and knocked. Inside, surrounded by the younger pilots working for me, I passed the bottle around the room, each filling a glass with a shot of liquor. Raising my glass, surrounded by the crowd of young men in flight suits headed for the unknown, I toasted, "To the passing of a friend and strong woman. The world will miss her. I will miss her," before tossing the whiskey down my throat. I will never forget the emotions swelling inside of me as I drank that whiskey— regret and loss, mixing with happiness that her suffering had finally ended.

My second wife attended the funeral, making arrangements for my first daughter to move to our home California. For my oldest daughter, it would become a case of "out of the frying pan and into the fire," as she would endure yet another bout of my failed marriages. Fortunately, my oldest daughter had inherited her mother's strength and, as a young adult, freshly graduated from the University of Colorado, she has risen above it all. As a young woman, I know she struggles in her relationship with me as I am the man who abandoned her—not once, but twice.

Two and a half hours later, as I was snoozing while leaning sideways on the blue vinyl chair, Supattra gave me another *hom noi* on the cheek and whispered in my ear that we were nearly there. I groggily opened one eye and looked up at her oval-shaped face and half-cloaked dark brown eyes smiling down at me. Sitting up, I looked to my right and saw the An Thong National Marine Park on the horizon in the distance as we glided across flat green water. Looking left, I saw the concrete piers of Donsak slipping by with people running around another large ferry that was obviously in the final stages of launching.

The engines rumbled under us, and the ferry began slowing. The oversized steel vessel turned and began moaning and grunting as the captain guided it backward up against a long misshapen concrete pier. As the ferry came to a groaning halt, men began running around, throwing lines, and shouting instructions. Finally, with a loud metal shriek, the stern begin to slowly lower onto the pier until a loud clang announced it was ready to offload its cargo. Standing above me, holding her imitation Gucci handbag under one arm, Supattra beckoned with her free hand, silently signaling for me to get my lazy ass moving. Looking at the beautiful Thai woman standing above me, I couldn't shake the vision of my first wife, telling me it was time.

Time for what?

CHAPTER 3

I have yet to describe the Thai woman I hang out with and who is a main character in this story. At twenty-eight years old, Supattra is tall for a Thai woman, standing at a whopping five-foot-four. With golden skin, an oval-shaped face, large, half-cloaked dark brown eyes, full lips, and a rounded Thai nose. She has thick black hair that drops below her shoulder blades and an athletically toned body. Supattra is exotically beautiful and wickedly intelligent. Most Thais will agree that Supattra has a captivating personality or charisma. On the other hand, most *farangs* will disagree with that description concerning her personality. I account this disparity to the fact that Supattra is not your typical submissive Southeast Asian chick. She is smart, stubborn, and independent.

Years ago, just after we had become friends, I invited Supattra to meet me in Kuala Lumpur, Malaysia, as I would be there on business. The only issue with the invitation was that Supattra had never flown in an airplane before, much less left the confines of Thailand. While I thought the trip might be a bit daunting for her, she immediately agreed to the plan. At the time, her English skills were wanting and there was still a considerable language barrier between us. Long story short, she made the trip.

The only glitch was that once off the airplane in Kuala Lumpur she had no idea that she needed to go through customs and was stuck in the international transit area for a considerable amount of time. Having taken a taxi to the airport to meet her, I stood in the terminal waiting, not knowing whether she had made the trip or backed out at the last moment. Two hours later, I had nearly given up when my phone rang and it was Supattra. Between her being upset and the language barrier, I had no idea where she was until I heard an announcement over the public address system above my head that echoed through the phone's speaker telling me that she was in the same airport. Fortunately a kind *farang* woman had seen that Supattra was upset and bought a Malaysian SIM card for her phone so she could call me. Thirty minutes later she emerged from the International transit area and we had a great weekend together.

As I am a fairly undemanding boyfriend, her time with me has only strengthened that independent spirit. This self-sufficient characteristic is apparently considered a redeeming quality among Thais, as she has been accepted among the business elite on Koh PhaNgan and has become a prominent member of several island women's organizations. In some ways, a Western university-educated man has ridden a third world Southeast Asian high school graduate's coat tails when it comes to island society circles.

After driving the black Toyota pickup off the ferry at Donsak, Supattra turned and told me that she would like to try a seafood restaurant near Surratthani, recommended by several friends, before checking into the hotel.

When I asked if she knew where the restaurant was located, she silently pulled the pickup over to the side of the road and took her cell out of her handbag, typing the restaurant name into a Google Maps app. Still without a word, she handed me the phone, put the truck back into gear, and began driving down the narrow road leading away from the Donsak piers, toward Surratthani.

Checking out the map on the phone's small screen, I loaded in the location into another Google Maps app and the cell immediately announced, "Continue straight."

"What's that," Supattra asked, looking over at her cell in my hand.

"Bitch'n Betty," I replied, immediately realizing that I might have made a language-based mistake.

Over the years, Supattra's English skills have improved dramatically since our Kuala Lumpur adventure and, thanks to me, she knows the meaning of nearly every profane word in the language.

However, she thinks of those words in literal form, so I typically avoid their use.

"Bitch?" She asked, "The voice is a bitch?"

"No, it's just a joke," I attempted to explain. "Before the military put voice warnings into cockpits they did a study that found pilots were more apt to listen to a woman's voice—hence the name Bitch'n Betty."

"A bitch is a girl dog or a bad woman," she dictated the short definitions of the word, ignoring my explanation.

"It's just a joke," I repeated. "A woman who complains a lot is called a bitch in the west. It's slang. When the military put a woman's voice in cockpits to remind or warn pilots, they began to call her Bitch'n Betty. It was a joke because the pilots claimed the woman's voice was complaining each time it announced a warning."

"Because the lady's voice reminds pilots when they need to do something?"

"It's a joke," I calmly repeated for the third time.

After a moment of silence, she said, "The military had to do a study to find that out? I think it is common sense that men listen to women more than other men."

The narrow road, bracketed by a thick lush jungle of tall grass and flowering bushes crowding a sea of palm trees came to an end at a wide four-lane highway. As we pulled up to the stop sign, Bitch'n Betty announced, "Turn right."

I repeated Bitch'n Betty's instructions. "Turn right."

Looking back over to her cell phone in my hand, Supattra shook her head and, with a hint of frustration in her voice, said, "I'm not sure I like the lady's voice."

"I wonder if the military studied the effects of a woman's voice on a woman pilot," I teased.

Glancing at me, and in a perfectly serious tone, she stated, "Women listen to women more than men," before accelerating onto the highway.

The Google Maps app remained silent as we raced down the four-lane highway, passing large, colorful, double-decker tourists buses and a sporadic crowd of new vehicles mixed with late model cars. Continuing west, the road twisted between high emerald-green-covered finger-like peaks and plantations filled with young, thin, white-barked rubber trees. Leaning back in passenger seat, watching the tropical scenery pass through the window next to me as Supattra chatted about seeing her family. Catching glimpses of the Gulf of Thailand in the distance, I began thinking about my first cruise on a helicopter assault ship as an aviator and young lieutenant in the Marine Corps.

Prompted by the distant sparkling water and nothing at all, I recalled a night sortie off the coast of Southern California just prior to my first six-month deployment.

∽∾∾

There had been a thick overcast layer of clouds, or marine layer, hanging over the coast that was normal for that time of year, but the light from all the homes and businesses in San Clemente, Oceanside, and places north and south, reflecting off the clouds would provide ample illumination for our night-vision goggles. Sitting in the ready room, preparing for the night's multi-aircraft training mission, the weather briefer claimed that he wasn't sure how high the ceiling was and, given the rules at the time, we weren't allowed to fly unless it was above twelve hundred feet.

At some point, the squadron commander decided to send one helicopter up for a weather check, to see just how high that overcast layer really was. The task fell onto the lone Huey assigned to the mission, the aircraft I was to co-pilot that night. A fellow marine aviator, Mike Lueck, and I sauntered up the metal ladder leading to the flight deck. Stepping out onto the large flattop, we could smell a briny aroma in the air that had mixed with a fine mist hanging over the ship, creating halos around each white light. As we walked across the flight deck and climbed into the aircraft, the brininess was quickly replaced with distinct and familiar smell of hydraulic fluid and aviation fuel. We sat side by side, our shoulders pressed by the armor plating mounted on the sides of the seat. I opened a small blue binder and began calling out items on the checklist as we methodically began to start the helicopter.

Sporting the call-sign of "Lurch," Mike Lueck was a big man of Swedish descent, with wide shoulders, pinkish skin, and wavy, white blond hair that was beginning to bald on top. He was not one to smile too quickly, as if he needed time to ponder and ensure something was actually humorous before he gave it his jovial approval. He was several years senior to me. We had flown quite a few missions together by this time and I trusted him implicitly at the controls of a helicopter. I looked at the big Swede as a mentor.

After we started up the helicopter, with the main rotor blades spinning overhead, the engines howling behind us, and our seats jiggling in cadence with the mechanical madness, our light attack detachment commander jumped in, joining the lone crew chief in the cargo area behind us. The air boss or head air traffic controller, situated in a windowed room high on the superstructure next to the flight deck, announced that the ship was turning off its lights, and the flight deck plunged into a bluish glow. Lowering our night-vision goggles turned everything into a greenish grainy scene. Mike gave the flight director standing in front of us a thumbs up, indicating we were ready to takeoff.

At the same moment, I passed the same information over the radio to the air boss. "Sea-Elk 43 ready for takeoff."

After the blue-shirted sailors had removed the chains strapping the helicopter to the metal flight deck, the air boss gave us clearance to takeoff, and the yellow-shirted flight director raised his arms, confirming that clearance. Mike looked over at me and asked if I was ready to go.

After my smiling "Giddy-up," he raised the collective while shifting the cyclic to the left, guiding the helicopter over the edge of the flight deck.

With our seats rattling in tune with the turning overhead blades, it was an eerie setting as we flew through several small clouds, echoing the lights along the coast between San Diego and Los Angles, tinted gritty green by our night-vision goggles. With shimmering dark water below and the occasional pelting of heavy rain, we climbed through the night, trying to find the base of marine layer above. Reaching the overcast layer five minutes later, with wispy fingers and ridges reaching downward, it was difficult to determine its exact altitude, but we all agreed that it was hovering around 800 feet, well below the 1,200 foot limit. The detachment commander behind us attempted to contact the ship on a radio mounted to the cabin floor but was unable, so I began switching one of the cockpit radios to the correct frequency. Since I was having difficulty accomplishing this simple task, Mike began helping me dial in the correct frequency, before we realized the radio wasn't working. Inoperable radios in Hueys weren't an unusual occurrence in those days and we immediately began the standard troubleshooting steps, pounding on the radio and turning it off and then on.

At some point during the process, as we were trying to get the radio to operate and accept the new frequency, I felt oddly uncomfortable and looked up. I wasn't sure what it was but I felt as if something was wrong or out of place as I looked out the windscreen in front of me. Then it struck me, the lights glowing from the coast were too high on the windscreen and the helicopter's nose was pitched downward. Looking down at the instrument panel, I saw the vertical speed indicator was nearly pinned at the bottom of the gauge, before I quickly glanced at the altimeter which showed that we were passing through seventy feet.

Adrenaline surged into my veins, but before panic and fear could cloud my reflexes, I reached down and grabbed the controls, jerking the collective upward while pulling back on the cyclic. Feeling the controls yanked in his hands, Mike looked up and quickly realized what was going on, joining me in leveling the aircraft out as the crew chief, screamed "Altitude!"

In retrospect, I think I must have heard or felt the helicopter speeding up as it descended. Whatever it was that drew my attention away from the malfunctioning radio that night saved our lives as I was able to stop our descent at the last moment.

Having skimmed across the waves at the bottom of our dive, Mike climbed the helicopter up to a reasonable altitude and we made our way back to the ship in near silence, only communicating essential flight information. Mike and I would have many more flights together over the course of the subsequent six-month cruise across the Pacific, visiting ports and flying training missions in numerous countries.

Among other things, he would teach me to become a maintenance test pilot, checking out aircraft that had just had one repair procedure or another performed. During one of those training flights for my maintenance pilot qualification, several miles east of Pattaya Beach and sixty miles southeast of Bangkok, he would instruct me to pull into a hover at two thousand feet, an exceedingly difficult task, given there are no stationary references to monitor at that altitude. Just as I established the helicopter into a precarious hover, Mike rolled the throttles down to idle and held them in place, looking over at me with a crooked smile. Lifting out of my seat as the helicopter began dropping through the clear blue sky, endless hours of training took over, and I pushed the collective down to take the pitch out of the blades and cyclic forward to gain some airspeed. Once again feeling adrenaline surge into my veins, I went through the standard procedures to put the helicopter into an autorotation. He would explain later that day over a beer that he had done it to show me that the charts in our manuals were correct. According to the Height-Velocity Diagram in the UH-1N NATOPS manual it was supposed to take 800 feet, which was about the same altitude I had lost before the helicopter could be established in a stable autorotation from a hover. It was through flights like those that the more experienced pilots began to teach me something even more important—how to control my fear and never allow it to consume me during stressful events. But if ever asked what I remembered the most from my first cruise as a young lieutenant, I would easily point to a night flight off the coast of Southern California when we nearly crashed into the ocean while trying to tune a frequency on an inoperable radio.

‿ↄ℮ↄ

As the highway took us down a wide sloping meadow, next to a flat-topped bluff with gray rocky sides and a spiked green top, leading to a large intersection ahead, Bitch'n Betty announced, "Turn right in 800 meters," interrupting my memories of that Southern California flight.

I translated the Google Maps instructions, pushing the visions of that first cruise to the back of my mind. "Turn right at the intersection."

Ignoring my directions, Supattra said, "I've been talking to you but you weren't listening. You were thinking too much again."

"I was just recalling something that happened when I was a young pilot."

"Did we miss the turn off for the restaurant?"

Sensing her frustration, I calmly replied, "No, we still have twenty kilometers."

"My friend told me that we turned just after Donsak."

"The restaurant is another twenty kilometers down the road," I answered for the second time.

"Are you sure the lady's voice is right?"

"Trust your gauges," I articulated an old aviation rule of thumb.

"I don't trust the voice," she softly declared, stopping under a red light at the intersection.

"I do," I said, realizing that I would likely never be able to alleviate Supattra's concerns about the Google app. "We have another twenty kilometers."

"I don't trust the lady's voice," she said slightly louder, turning right under the now green light onto another perpendicular situated four-lane highway.

Sixteen kilometers down the road, Bitch'n Betty announced another right turn, and Supattra obediently followed the app's instructions without hesitation or complaint. Quickly consumed in heavy traffic along a narrow village street, Supattra negotiated around darting motorcycles and maneuvered passed double-parked cars. Coming to halt behind a three wheeled *See lang*, filled with passengers and large brown cardboard boxes, we patiently waited for it to make a U-turn before continuing toward our destination. The cultural and customary aroma of fried chilies and garlic found its way into the truck cab and mixed with the coolness being blow from the dashboard air vents.

"I don't trust the voice," Supattra proclaimed for a third time as she slowed to allow the opposing traffic through a narrow section of the street.

"Trust Bitch'n Betty, she'll get us there," I promised.

"But what if the lady's voice is wrong?" Supattra retorted.

"I'm looking at the map. She's right. We've got another four point three kilometers."

"But I was told it was not far from the main road."

"You were also told it was just after Donsak," I replied, trying not to show my building frustration. "We aren't far from the main road. We've been slowed down by the traffic. We have another four kilometers."

We finally broke out from the village traffic into a coastal countryside scene with wide open green fields, broken up thin twisting inlets bracketed in tall wispy tropical trees, and Bitch'n Betty instructed us to continue straight at a fork in the road.

"Follow the main road," I explained.

"But she said to go straight. We can't go straight."

"Take the main road, beautiful. Trust me."

"I trust you but I do not trust her," Supattra replied as she steered the truck passed the fork along the main road.

Just past the fork the road began paralleling a brackish river surrounded by tall sea grass, and then made a sharp turn, passing over a bridge. On the far side of the bridge, we rounded another corner and the road came to an abrupt halt in a small seaside village. One side of the road was lined with narrow, weather-stained, two-story concrete buildings housing small businesses; on the other was a large parking lot.

Spotting a faded overhead banner, advertising something in Thai, at the far end of the parking lot, I asked, "What's that say?"

Pulling into the parking lot, she replied in a slightly defeated tone, "That's the restaurant. We're here."

As we stepped from the truck, I immediately realized that there was another motive to our early dinner at the recommended restaurant.

Walking under the faded overhead banner, we passed through a maze of open shops selling multiple forms of fresh and dried seafood.

Knowing her for as long as I have, I recognized that Supattra was looking for a reason to come here in order to purchase and take gifts home to Kalasin, to include much-prized dried seafood.

Following a warped wooden planked pathway that passed over a dark marshy area filled swamp trees, we emerged onto a sizeable covered deck overlooking a wide inlet. Taking a seat at a rickety wooden table, we looked out over the inlet's calm brown waters lined with stilted homes and bobbing long-tail boats tied up next their docks. With the musty scent of brackish water hanging in the air and small waves gently slapping against the pylons below the deck, Supattra asked me what I wanted to drink.

"Water," I responded.

"No beer?"

"Just water," I repeated.

After translating my order into Thai for the waitress, she looked at me. "You don't drink as much as you use to."

"I haven't for quite some time—and you always say that."

The waitress quickly delivered a Singha Beer for Supattra and a plastic bottle of water for me, both sweating with condensation. Filling two glasses with ice from a small silver bucket, the waitress poured the Singha beer into Supattra's and water into mine.

Looking at me with her large brown eyes, Supattra reached across the table and took my hand, before asking, "Do you believe in Buddha?"

"I am fascinated with Buddha and his teachings," I replied as a long-tail boat sputtered past the deck, its passengers looking at the rare *farang* sitting in the restaurant.

The waitress stepped up to the table again and Supattra ordered our dinner before asking, "What do you mean?"

"I like what Buddha has done for Thailand," I explained. "The Thai people aren't perfect but they aren't nearly as narrow-minded as Westerners. As you pointed out on the ferry, *farangs* are selfish and that's true. Material things are not as nearly as important to Thais as they are in the Western world. Thais realize that the things they do in this life have implications in their standing in the next. They know that everything they do—every decision is important. Material things become meaningless with that mindset."

"Material things?"

"New cars, trucks, big houses—that kind of stuff."

"Thais like new cars and big houses."

"That's true, but those things have a different significance to Thais," I replied. "Thais do things in moderation. Westerners aren't like that."

"But do you believe in Buddha?" she asked again.

After a few moments thinking about her question, I answered, "I believe in the way of life that Buddhism teaches."

"Do you believe in your God?"

"When I was in the military, I never went to church," I began explaining. "If asked whether I believed in God, I would say I believed in something but wasn't sure what. I had been taught as a boy that atheists were evil and I didn't want to admit that I might be one.

"An atheist?"

"Someone who doesn't believe in any God," I replied.

"You didn't believe in any God?" she asked, looking at me with a puzzled expression.

"I knew I didn't want to be an atheist, but I didn't know what I believed." I sighed. "If pressed on the subject, I would hem and haw and then say that I believe in a higher power. I just didn't know what that higher power was. I think I wanted to believe but everything going on around me pointed to there being no God. I watched bad things happen to good people and good things happen to bad people."

"Bad things happen to good people because they make mistakes. They are still learning how to be good," she said. "No one is perfect and everyone must suffer. It is a part of finding enlightenment."

"My father used to harp that life wasn't fair," I said, as the waitress delivered a silver tray filled with palm size oysters on the half shell. "As many times as he told me that life wasn't fair, it became obvious that he felt it was an important lesson to pass on to his children."

"So you don't believe in your God?"

"I had deep reservations about the existence of God when I was a young marine."

While spooning a spicy green sauce on the top of one of the oysters, Supattra asked, "But that has changed?"

"Sort of. Or maybe I've come to terms with my confusion," I replied, while watching Supattra heap fried red onions over the spicy green sauce topped oyster. "During the drive north in Iraq, I witnessed good people die and bad people survive, which added to my doubt as to whether there was a God or not. But even with my growing reservations, I began saying a prayer every time I climbed into a helicopter."

Picking up the onion and spicy sauce laden oyster, Supattra asked, "What did you say to your God?"

"I asked God to take care of the people I loved if something were to happen to me."

Slurping the oyster out of the shell, Supattra took a quick swig of beer from her ice-filled glass before asking, "So you began believing in God during your war?"

"I guess that, even though I was completely confused as to whether there was God or not, I needed to believe that there was something more to survival than just dumb-luck. I needed to grasp onto something that made sense of everything going on around me."

Pouring more spicy sauce and heaping more red onions on top another oyster, she asked again, "So you began to believe in God?"

"I needed to believe there was an order to the chaos around me. I needed to believe that there was something or some plan, even one that I couldn't intellectually understand, that made sense of the madness. So I turned to what I had been raised to believe in—God. Even now, I don't know if there is a God or not, but I still say that same prayer to this day, every time I climb on an airplane or find myself in a potentially life-threatening situation."

"But you don't know whether you believe in your God?" she asked, looking baffled while handing me the oyster she had just prepared.

I answered, "In the midst of all the bedlam during the drive north, there were several times that I didn't understand how I survived. There were several times I should have died. I had an experience before the war when I watched several friends die and I should have been with them."

I sucked the oyster covered in spicy sauce and red onions off its shell, into my mouth.

"You mean the Jeff man," she interrupted.

Coughing from the heavy spice on the oyster, I choked, "Yes, Jeff Couch."

She giggled, watching my face turn red and sweat break out on my forehead. "It's spicy."

After taking a long drink of cold water, I continued, "I should have been on that aircraft with Jeff but, for some reason, I was moved to the other helicopter," I replied. "I should have died that day with Jeff Couch and Dan Adams. The only way I have been able to make sense of all my close calls over the years was to believe that I had been saved by some higher power or by some universal plan."

"You believe but don't believe?"

"I believe there is something that we are unable to intellectually understand."

"So you believe in something, and you also believe in Buddha…or just this higher thing?"

"I believe in both," I said, smiling at Supattra as she prepared a third oyster. "In many ways Buddhism makes more sense to me than Christianity, but even Buddhism doesn't account for the experience I had in Iraq."

"Buddha helps us find enlightenment by placing us in difficult situations. The decisions we make trying find our way out of those situations will either move us farther along the path, or not. Life is a struggle and suffering is a part of walking the path."

Chuckling, I said, "Maybe my father was a Buddhist. Life isn't fair."

"Do you believe that we've been together in past lives?" she asked, before sucking the oyster loaded with spice and fried onions into her mouth.

Watching her golden face turn red, I replied, "Because of my relationship with you, I want to believe. You saved my life when no one else could and you are a Buddhist. I was a mental mess when I met you."

"I remember," she whispered. "But you saved my life, too."

"I was in an emotional freefall," I continued. "I didn't understand what was happening to me. There was a dark hole in my soul. I was lost and you accepted me anyway. You looked past my torment and took me into your life without asking for anything in return. You nurtured me back from certain self-destruction."

"You saved my life, too. If I had stayed in Pattaya much longer, I would have been lost in that bad world. I would never have been able to better myself. You looked past what I was doing for a living and saw the good in me. You saw who I really was."

"We saved each other," I said, reaching out and taking her hands into mine. "I want to believe that there is something guiding us, and we are and have been together in the same struggle for many lives. I want to believe that there is an order to the chaos that I am intellectually unable to understand. I know that you and Buddhism stopped my emotional freefall and saved my life."

"We saved each other's lives."

Looking out onto the inlet, I asked, "Do you ever question your belief in Buddha?"

"Never," she unhesitatingly replied.

"But do you ever wonder why Buddha would place you in

such hard conditions as a child and then require you to sell your body in order to survive?"

"Buddha placed you in a war to prepare you for enlightenment. He placed me in Isaan for the same reason. There was a reason my life started in that village, but I made the decision to go to Pattaya. I didn't know what else to do. I was blinded by my situation. I am trying to be a better person in this life so I won't have to endure the same hardship in my next life, but the decision to go to Pattaya may have ruined my chances."

Looking at the beautiful woman across the table from me, I asked, "But if we were together and loved each other in the last life, why would Buddha make me a *farang* and have you grow up in Isaan?"

"He was teaching us," she said matter-of-factly. "Our place in this life was created because of our decisions in our last life. We both were good people but we needed different circumstances to move towards enlightenment."

Smiling, I said, "Buddha did bring us together again," as I raised my water-filled glass up for a toast.

"Our lives are intertwined and we will always be together," Supattra replied, touching my water glass with her glass filled with golden Singha beer and ice. "We are like two hooves on the same buffalo moving along a common trail. We will always suffer together. We will always be partners until the day our candles are blown out when we have reached perfect enlightenment."

"What about after perfect enlightenment? Can't we still hang out together?"

As our discussion came to an end, the waitress delivered a plate of large steaming prawns, an enormous lone crab, and a sour southern fish soup that rivaled the spiciness of the oysters. Each time our drinking glasses drew down to the midway mark, the waitress dutifully stepped up to the table to fill them with more ice and liquid.

After paying our bill at the end of the meal, I patted my stomach and looked at Supattra who was silently watching me. Reaching out, she caressed my cheek with the back of her hand and smiled. Wordlessly we stood and retraced our route along the warped wooden pathway, past the dark marsh, into the market area selling seafood. After Supattra picked out an assortment of dried fish and a large plastic bag of shrimp paste, an old frail woman wearing tattered clothes with a basket tucked under one arm approached her. A short conversation later, the old woman pulled two plastic bags filled with small anchovy-sized fish from the basket and handed them to Supattra.

She handed the old woman a seemingly large amount of money and the old woman thanked her, moving off to seek out another customer.

"What's that?" I asked, gesturing toward the plastic bag filled with the fish.

"Just small fish."

"And they're good?"

"I don't know," she said, smiling at me. "I just felt sorry for the old woman. She told me that she has no family to take care of her and she has to sell these fish to survive."

I chuckled, thinking that the old woman's story was a brilliant marketing technique. "And you believed her?"

Looking at me quizzically, Supattra replied, "Why should I not believe her?"

Quickly realizing that this was one of those moments when our cultures collided, I said, "You're right. There was no reason not to believe her."

With me now behind the steering wheel of our pickup, we drove back along the road paralleling the narrow, brackish river and, as we approached the fork in the road, Bitch'n Betty announced, "Continue straight."

Looking over at Supattra, I saw her spellbound by the navigation graphics on her cell phone.

She repeated Bitch'n Betty's instructions. "Continue straight."

We passed the bright green fields with thin twisting inlets and tall tropical trees. We drove through the busy village with the narrow street. As we approached the intersection with the four-lane highway, Bitch'n Betty announced, "Turn right in one hundred meters."

"Turn right in one hundred meters," Supattra repeated again.

Glancing over at Supattra again, I said, "I thought you didn't trust Bitch'n Betty."

Looking over at me with a wide smile on her face, she replied, "I like the lady's voice. It's very accurate. We should use her all the way to Kalasin."

CHAPTER 4

Movies, Ghosts, and Fear ~ 10 April 2014

Supattra and I have stayed in Surratthani many times and, over the years, have found a hotel that we both are comfortable with called "The One Hundred Islands," a named coined from the number of islands in the Samui Archipelago. A three star hotel by Western standards, The One Hundred Islands Hotel is a four-story structure that wraps around an enormous pond with a small waterfall flowing from a twenty-foot stack of large boulders at one end. A stunningly beautiful pond with slightly green water, fallen leaves, and other garden debris floating on top, surrounded by lush gardens and tropical trees, it took me several stays in the hotel to realize that it was not a water feature at all but a swimming pool.

The silent consensus that we will always stay at the hotel is based on the facts that the rooms are large and clean and—this was before we bought the pickup—it's within easy walking distance of several good restaurants and a Tesco Lotus shopping center with a movie theater. While the availability of a hot shower has to do with several obscure factors, none of which I have ever figured out, and cold beer could only be purchased in the lobby at the front desk, these are simply minor inconveniences. After all, hot water and cold beer are never considered a given in Thailand. Other determining perks included that the hotel has never raised their price ($30 per night) and we have never had to reserve a room because there was always one available, no matter what time of year we visited.

During the forty-five minute journey from the seaside restaurant to Surratthani and The Hundred Islands Hotel, Supattra
recommended that we go to the newly opened Central Plaza
Shopping Center to see a movie. After I agreed to the plan, we
checked in, dropping our luggage in our room, before making
the short drive to the new shopping center. I had known there
would be a trip to the Central Plaza long before we left Koh
PhaNgan. While the plan to see a movie at the mall's theater
was legitimate, the island we live on has a very limited selection of ladies' fashions. So every time we come to the mainland, I know that a shopping center will be at the top of the list
of places to visit so Supattra can update her wardrobe.

There are two problems with going to a movie theater in
Thailand. First of all, the best Thai movie would be considered
a bad B movie in the Western Hemisphere and, secondly, you
rarely know, when you're stepping into a Western-produced
film, whether it has been dubbed into Thai or not. The first
problem is a cultural issue. Thais love goofy slapstick comedies, and all the male actors have unnaturally deep voices and
the actresses have unusually high-pitched nasally voices. This
makes Thai movies painful to sit through. Combining goofy
slapstick comedies with bizarre voices creates an agonizing
theater experience. As for dubbed Western-produced movies,
one could ask the ticket office about the soundtrack but that
tactic is far too calculating in a country where foreigners come
to escape the logical methodology of dealing with the western
world.

Several months ago, Supattra and I went to a theater and
watched *Elysium* starring Matt Damon and, unsurprisingly, I
ended up spending two hours listening to the star in an unnaturally gruff and poorly timed Thai voice. While it was interesting to watch a movie and only understand about a third of
what was being said, after a while, I began to simply study the
visuals. From that prospective, observing Matt Damon stum-
bling through the *Elysium* storyline, it seemed like a pretty
lame movie. At the end of the film, as we were walking down
the red carpeted stairway toward the side door exit, I asked
Supattra about the movie. With a solemn expression, she

shook her head and told me it was awful. A poor review is one thing but when the critic is a resident of a country that enjoys bad B movies, that assessment places it in a special category. From my perspective, I learned you don't always need to understand the dialog to be an accurate critic.

The movie theater in the Central Plaza is particularly nice, providing information on whether the film had been dubbed or not, and whether subtitles are available (i.e. Thai movies with English subtitles, or dubbed Western-produced movies) on the film directory. As we scrutinized the promotion billboard for the movies currently showing, Supattra asked me what we should see and, in the midst of a soul searching moment, I recommended a Thai comedy with English subtitles. Knowing that Supattra loves cheap slapstick, I knew the offer would make her happy. I also figured that maybe a Thai movie with English subtitles would help me understand a little more about the culture I had chosen to spend my time surrounded by. With a large smile on her face, Supattra bought our tickets and then we decided to roam the mall, waiting for the movie to begin. In short order, Supattra had headed off, allegedly to buy more gifts for her family, and I began to explore the shopping center to see what types of books they offered for my downtime in Kalasin.

After an hour of searching for English books in five different Thai bookstores, and failing, I met Supattra back at the entrance to the theater. Carrying a solitary shopping bag, she gave me a *hom noi* on the cheek and I asked what she bought.

"A purse."

When I asked her who the purse was for, she replied, "My sister, if I decide I don't like it."

"You're thinking about keeping it for yourself? I thought you were shopping for your family?"

"It was on sale," she replied in a tone that made her answer to my question sound perfectly logical.

Quickly realizing that pressing this issue wouldn't be worth the possibility of upsetting our night out, I pointed out that we still had thirty minutes before the movie began.

Smiling, likely because I avoided the purse issue, Supattra

suggested we get a coffee at a Starbucks on the lower level.

With the aroma of freshly brewed coffee drifting over our table, I sat across from Supattra watching her sip a café mocha and fiddle with her cell phone, posting something on Facebook. A television over Supattra's shoulder, mounted on the wall in the corner of the room, caught my attention as a newscast airing a report about some insurgency group that had spawned in Syria during the Arab Spring and the country's civil war that had begun moving across into Iraq, threatening some of the same cities the marines had captured years earlier, flickered across the screen. The faces of the civilians in the background exuded emotions that I had witnessed many times during my career as a marine—fear, panic, and terror. Sitting across from the beautiful and innocent woman I had spent the last eight years with, I began thinking about an experience that had taken place nearly twenty-four years earlier, vividly recalling the incident. It was an experience I hadn't thought of in over two decades and one I had never considered as harbinger of my posttraumatic stress.

☙❦❧

It was my third cruise on a helicopter assault ship—a miniature aircraft carrier with a flat top and tall superstructure to one side—as we journeyed south, across the Western Pacific Ocean during a deployment workup. While not assigned to the later deployment, I had been tasked with training those UH-1N pilots that had been assigned to the composite squadron that would take part in the follow-up cruise.

The ship had made its way from Okinawa, Japan to the Mariana Trench, where I was assigned to fly with two other aviators in what we called the unaided night bounce pattern—teaching them how of takeoff and land on the ship at night without the use of night-vision goggles. On a clear night with a big moon it would have been an easy flight but not a lot of fun. The flight was based on a simple racetrack configuration to one side of the ship, which we would share with five or six other helicopters of various makes and models, just like the standard pattern at any airport. Takeoff, fly the pattern, and land. We would repeat that process for however long the schedule writers had deemed necessary—usually forty-five minutes to an hour and a half.

It would have been an easy flight, except the weather was really foul that night. There was an overcast sky, so no moon. The ship was miles from any land mass, so there would be no manmade illumination, except what the ship projected. And the seas were rough, rolling the ship side to side and pitching it fore and aft. The weather had taken what could have been a fairly boring and routine sortie and turned it into a hair-raising experience because, in order to hover a helicopter, you need stable external references and a visual horizon. If you don't have those references, all you have are the gauges on your air-craft's instrument panel: a gyro and vertical and horizontal speed indicators, to name a few. Those instruments are great for flying, but lousy for taking-off and landing. With night-vision goggles, we would have likely picked up the horizon and that would have given us something, but without them, there would be nothing. To make matters slightly worse, at the time, I was flying the smallest of those in the composite squadron on the ship, so we inevitably were assigned a spot near the front of the flight deck. The minute we took off, every reference would vanish and the pilot would have to immedi-ately go to the gauges—a difficult transition as you're building up speed and altitude from a dead stop.

Having just returned from the First Gulf War and a previ-ous six-month cruise on another helicopter assault ship before deploying onto this one, I knew what was in store for us that night and could feel the stress building long before stepping into the ready room for the preflight brief. But during my short tenure as a marine aviator, I had honed my skill at controlling that stress so it never reached the next incapacitating level—fear. On the other hand, the two pilots I was flying with had never flown unaided night bounces and had no idea what was in store for them. Undoubtedly, being junior and having served less time in the marines, they had yet to sharpen the essential skill of controlling anxiety and consternation.

When I walked into the ready room, the two young pilots I was to fly with that night were laughing and joking around, excited about upcoming sortie. I walked directly up to them and, in no uncertain terms, explained that they may be thrilled and excited by the prospects of the impending night flight in the ready room but when they stepped from the helicopter and walked down the ladder leading from the flight deck after it was over, they would be scared. I told them that this would be the most hair-raising flight they had experienced to date in their short Marine Corps careers.

After a relatively solemn flight brief, I and the first pilot to fly found our way up the ladder to the flight deck and climbed into the aircraft. The brightly lit flight deck was rolling side to side and there were sailors in various colored vests running around, getting ready for the night's sorties to begin. The heavy smell of hydraulic fluid and aviation fuel mixed with the brininess of the ocean, swirling inside the cockpit as a stiff breeze blew across the deck. Looking over at the pilot next to me, I could see he was wide-eyed and his was mouth contorted into a grimace as the implications of my earlier ready room proclamation began coming into focus. A smattering of rain fell across the windscreen as we began the startup checklist, but I hesitated turning the windshield wipers on because the added distraction of them swinging back and forth as we launched into the dark abyss might further disorient the pilot next to me.

Given the hand signal that we could start by the plane director in a yellow shirt standing in front of the aircraft, we went through the final stages of the checklist. The engines roared to life behind us and main rotor blades began slowly accelerating above. The blue shirts, the sailors assigned to unleash our helicopter from the deck by removing the chains, scurried in and out from under the turning blades. The yellow shirt silently nodded his head to a command he had received through the radio on his hip before raising his arms to indicate that we were cleared to pick up into a hover. Simultaneously, we received a call over one of the helicopter's radios telling us the same.

The pilot sitting next to me pulled up into a hover on the pitching deck, attempting to use the undulating ship as a reference, and immediately began drifting toward the superstructure. I took the controls, jerking the cyclic to the left and pulling the collective up, flying off the deck into the black hole that seemed to be consuming the ship. Keeping my eyes glued to the gauges, I flew the same course that the ship had been cruising until we reached an altitude of 800 feet, at which time I began to make a standard rate turn to the left. As I made the turn to downwind leg of the pattern, the ship came into view, looking as if it was child's illuminated toy boat that someone was waving in the darkness. There was no visual difference between the sky and water. All we had was the illuminated and pitching flight deck. I gave the pilot duties back to my shocked co-pilot, now that we had the visual reference of the deck below and to our left. He hesitatingly took the controls. The rain began to strike the windscreen slightly harder. I reached down to the console between us and turned the windshield wipers on, their slapping motion adding more tension to the stress-filled cockpit. Glancing over at the pilot next to me, having just experienced his first unaided night takeoff in bad weather, I could see the terror on his face. I could hear the fear in his voice as he called abeam the ship. And I could feel the simmering anxiety growing in my belly.

We turned toward the flight deck and began making the approach for our first landing. The rain began to come down even harder, water building on the windscreen as fast as the wipers could whisk it away. Having been assigned Spot 2 by the air boss, the closest to the bow of the ship, the pilot next to me jockeyed the controls in a failed attempt to stay on a glide path to our landing point. When your only reference point is a rocking ship, your position will vacillate from below to above glide path as the deck swings side to side. This minor disorientation isn't a problem during the day when you have other references, but in a black hole, where the water is the same color as the sky and a rolling deck is your only orientation, it's frightening. As we approached the edge of the pitching deck, the young pilot asked me to take control, which I promptly and happily did, pulling the helicopter over our spot. As the deck swung through a semi-level position, ignoring the disgruntled yellow shirt waving his arms and shaking his head, I dropped the collective and the helicopter plunged onto the spot with a loud metallic clang as the aircraft skids struck the flight deck.

I let out a long sigh of relief. Over the radio through the speakers in my helmet, I could hear fright and panic in the voices of the pilots flying in the pattern with us as they approached and attempted to land behind us. Most called for a wave off, unable to land on the rolling deck that first time around, and took another turn in the pitch-black pattern.

It took several more turns in the pattern for the other aircraft to get everyone back onto their spots and then we started the process all over again, taking off one by one into the void from the pitching deck. The events of the second turn in the pattern played out nearly identically, except during the approach, pilot next to me was able to get the helicopter over the spot before he let the helicopter drift toward the superstructure again, requiring me to take the controls and land. We waited patiently for all the other aircraft to land, taking another four tries by several of the helicopters. A scheduled forty-five minute flight only allowed four of five takeoffs and landings due to the time it took to get everyone back onto the ship. By the time the first flight was over and we were chained back to the flight deck, the first pilot to fly with me had only been able to takeoff from the deck into the darkness one time without forcing me to take control. He had, however, been able to land several times after a few words of advice.

"Pay no attention to the yellow shirt, just position the helicopter over the spot and drop the collective the first time the deck straightens out."

"But we're not supposed to land until given clearance by the flight director."

"The yellow shirt has never been on an unaided night bounce in bad weather. He's going to go through the same rigid routine he's been taught before giving us clearance to land in his usual methodical pace. Trying to hover over a pitching deck in complete darkness while that guy goes through his routine is impossible—just drop the collective the first time the deck is semi-level. Ignore him."

As the first pilot unstrapped his harness, with the engines still howling behind us, the main rotor blades spinning overhead softly bumping our seats from side to side, and with the smell of the ocean's brininess mixing with hydraulic fluid and aviation fuel in the air, he looked across the cockpit with the clear expression of relief, mumbling, "Thanks, and good luck," before disconnecting his helmet from the inter-cockpit communication system. In his way, he had just told me that I had been correct. He was scared. It had been the most hair-raising flight he had ever experienced.

The second pilot climbed in and an exact replica of the previous forty-five minutes unfolded. The evening of torment ended suddenly when the Navy Search and Rescue helicopter that had been flying in the pattern with us failed to call abeam or respond to numerous calls from the air boss. It was one of those nights we really shouldn't have been flying without goggles, but no one wanted to be the first pilot to tell the king that he had no clothes, informing the squadron commander that he should cancel the unaided night flights. It was just a matter of time before the pilots in one aircraft or another became disoriented and augered into the water.

I had learned over the years that fear is the consequence of two basic types of scenarios—the surprising and unpredictable, and that which can be anticipated. While one's reaction to a surprising incident that produces panic or fright is difficult to control, predictable events allow one to prepare for the onslaught of trepidation and restrain one's emotions. I knew before we began that flight that the other two pilots flying with me were talented aviators but they had not yet learned how to control the fright elicited by predictable and recognizable stressful situations. The lessons I had learned during my previous cruises were unfamiliar to them. Having been trained to take my fear and wad it up like a lump of black coal, I could feel it throughout the entire flight burning in my belly, but knew if I had released it, we could have very well been the aircraft to crash into the water that night. Controlling one's fear was a valuable skill and essential in our profession, a lesson that those two pilots I had flown with that night began to learn and understand. But I sometimes wonder whether that kind of fear, the type you prepare for, is not more damaging to the human psyche than a sudden and surprising terror.

In the end, directly over the Mariana Trench on a night that we shouldn't have been flying, we lost one aircraft and an aircrew of four. Having experienced numerous similar events in the few short years I had been a marine helicopter pilot, I easily fell asleep, not giving the incident or the lost aircrew as much as a second thought.

ꞔꞩꞔꞩ

Suddenly, I realized that Supattra was glaring at me from across the table and I instinctive asked, "What?"

Shaking her head, she said, "I was talking to you and you weren't listening."

"I was just thinking about something that happened long ago," I replied, reaching out and touching her hand.

"It's time we go back to the theater," she informed me, pushing her chair out from the table, adding, "You think too much," as she stood up.

As we rode the escalators up to the top floor, I contemplated the memory of the unaided night flight over the Mariana Trench and wondered why the television had provoked its return. By the time we arrived at the movie theater, I had decided it was simply the looks of terror on the civilians, prompting a memory of seeing fear and panic on another face.

Thais believe in ghosts. We recently had run in with a ghost at our house on Koh PhaNgan. Headed for Surratthani several months ago, we got up at 3:30 a.m. to catch the 5:00 a.m. ferry to Donsak. I had showered and walked out on our back deck for a morning smoke in time to see an old and frail gray-haired lady standing next to the home's spirit house. The hairs on my head and arms stood up, and then the old woman seemed to dissolve into the darkness. With the hairs on my body at rigid attention, I peered at the spirit house, wondering what had just happened. Having survived several wars and numerous skirmishes around the world, I was not going to let my imagination get the best of me, so I walked over to the spirit house. Standing next to the small shrine in the darkness of the morning, I could still feel the old lady's presence. Taking a deep breath, I walked back into bedroom and told Supattra what I had seen.

She calmly looked over at me, closing her suitcase. "It's the woman who used to live here."

I scratched my head, trying to take in her revelation. "How do you know?"

"My friend Pen's daughter, Kow-Fung, saw her and talked with the old lady about two months ago. The woman told her that she was upset because I wasn't leaving enough food at the spirit house each week. Kow-Fung got ill after she talked with the old lady so Pen doesn't want her to come back to our house."

"The old lady is evil? And she made Kow-Fung ill?"

"No, no. The neighbors have seen her many times early in the morning too. They say she is good and will protect the house, but Pen is still worried because of the timing of Kow-Fung's illness. The neighbors were the ones that told me she was the former owner and that she protects the house."

"I thought this building used to be a brothel for the Thai fishermen?"

"Yes, many years ago, but even after the house stopped selling women to the fishermen, she lived here before dying about twenty years ago. No one else lived in this house until we bought the building."

"So we own a former brothel and the ghost of the former pimp lives with us."

"What's a pimp?"

"The head bargirl...the mamasan."

"She was never a bargirl," Supattra coolly replied as she snapped the latches on her suitcase shut. "She never slept with the fishermen. It was her husband's business."

As I carried our luggage out to the truck, Supattra stepped

over to our neighbor's shop, which opened at 4:00 a.m. to sell donuts and sweet drinks to the returning fisherman each morning. Standing next to the driver's side door, I watched as she had what appeared to be a serious discussion with the couple. Giving our neighbors a Thai style farewell, a *Wai* or pressing her hands together in front of her face in steeple like position, she walked back over to the pickup and silently climbed into the passenger seat.

Climbing in the driver's seat next to her, I looked over and asked, "What'd they say?"

"I asked if they had seen the old lady this morning."

"Had they seen her?"

"No, but they're not surprised she was there. The old lady is a quite active."

Back to the Central Plaza—I had chosen a movie based on an old Thai story about a husband and pregnant wife who are separated when the man must go off to war, presented in a comedy format. The wife and child die during birthing process while he is gone, but she loves her husband so much she comes back as a ghost and acts as if she never died. The village is terrified and when the husband comes home, he has no idea his wife is a ghost. Any villager that finds the courage to tell the husband about the state of his wife meets an untimely death. In the end, an elderly monk comes with his young apprentice and talks with the couple. Unbeknownst to the couple, the husband was dead as well, killed during the war, but wanted to be with his wife so badly that he too became a ghost. The story ends when they agree to meet in the next life.

When the film was finished, as we were walking out, Supattra looked up at me and asked if I liked the movie. I told her that I loved the movie because it helped me understand her and her culture a little better. She reached out and took my hand as we walked to the elevator. The funny thing was that the subtitles had made a difference and I had enjoyed the movie. It had also given me an insight into Thai culture that I had never experienced before, bolstering the fact that the Thais believed in spirits, forgiveness, and multiple lives.

And then there was that pesky vision of my first wife, telling me it was time. I hadn't been able to shake the memory of her apparition all day, even thinking about it as the movie came to a close. Hoping that my first wife's ghost wasn't coming back to haunt me for my past misdeeds, I drove Supattra back to the hotel.

Back at the hotel, I took a cold shower and climbed into bed to watch a little international news. After her shower, Supattra, wrapped in a towel, walked over next to me. Standing next to the bed, she looked down with a crooked grin, while I looked up at with a quizzical expression.

With her wide grin still in place, she pulled the towel loose and let it drop to the floor, revealing her slim naked body. "There is no privacy in Kalasin."

Repeating her words, I said, "There is no privacy in Kalasin," and began smiling myself as I reached out and took her hand, pulling her down onto the bed.

There is no privacy in Kalasin and Supattra realized that we had better take care of the intimate side of our relationship before we got there. In other words, she didn't want me pawing at her when her family would know exactly what was going on.

CHAPTER 5

The Problems with Living in Thailand ~ 11 April 2014

Waking early the next morning, pressed up next to Supattra's bare back with my arms around her shoulders, I yawned and stroked her thick black hair before whispering, "Good morning, beautiful."

Turning her head without opening her eyes, she mumbled, "Good morning, sweetheart. You did not sleep, again."

"I got a few hours."

Reaching up with her golden hands, she rubbed her closed eyes. "You haven't slept well since you stopped drinking."

"That was a reason I was drinking," I whispered, placing my right hand on her naked hip under the sheets, adding, "I couldn't sleep without a few nightcaps," before realizing that I had just used an English phrase she had not heard before.

"Nightcaps?"

"A drink before sleep," I clarified.

"More than one drinks. You used to have many more than one drinks before you came to bed."

I have always been amazed at the way countless *farangs* living in Thailand communicate with the locals. Many of the ex-pats living on the island of PhaNgan speak simplified English, leaving out grammatical articles and adverbs when talking to Thais, believing that this abbreviated version of our language somehow is the panacea to better communication.

I can't count the number of times I've watched a Thai quietly look at the ground (their version of rolling one's eyes) during a conversation with one of those ex-pats speaking this version of Pidgin English. On the other hand, I have always used proper English when speaking to Supattra and corrected her when she said a grammatically incorrect sentence, no matter how small the mistake. I'm also convinced that Supattra's English is excellent because of this habit. I also realize that there are certain nuances that she will never master and those same errors remind me why I am in this country and with Supattra.

At this stage in our relationship, I rarely correct her English.

"That was a double plural," I uncharacteristically commented, knowing she understood the term from the numerous times I've used it to correct her over the years.

She clarified her comment. "You used to have many more than one drink before you went to bed. Do you think too much and cannot sleep?"

"No, actually I don't think at all, I just can't sleep."

"That makes no sense."

"I know, but it's a fact." I yawned. "I didn't dream for many years after the war—or at least remember my dreams. They say you always dream whether you remember or not. I'm not sure how they know, but that's what they say."

"I dream every night," she said quietly, her eyes still closed.

"If the experts hadn't figured out that I was dreaming, I would have had no idea. I would have said that I wasn't."

"How do they know that people always dream?"

"Maybe brain activity or something," I replied. "Maybe they hook up electrodes to people's heads while they sleep and can see something going on."

"Electrodes? Brain activity?"

Ignoring her definition questions, I continued. "All I know is that I didn't dream and it was relatively disturbing. Dreams are an important part of our lives and living without them is troubling. Or maybe the troubling part was that I didn't know why I wasn't dreaming."

"Why weren't you dreaming?"

"I don't know, and that was troubling part. I just wasn't and that was upsetting."

"The reason you were not dreaming was upsetting?"

"Exactly."

"But you don't know why?"

"Exactly."

"That makes no sense."

"That is exactly how I felt."

Hesitating for a moment, likely trying to take in our cryptic conversation, she groggily asked, "Do you dream when you sleep now?"

"I do. I slowly started dreaming again about two years ago, but I quit sleeping when I stopped drinking, and that's when I began dreaming again."

"That makes no sense," she said for a third time.

"I typically fall asleep around four in the morning and wake up for a few minutes every hour, but there's a lot of good dreaming going on in those short periods. Eight is the witching hour and I normally can't fall back to sleep, so I get up."

"You don't sleep but you dream. That does not makes sense." She sighed sleepily before asking, "Are you going to breakfast?"

Softly, I responded, "Yes, I'm going to hit the morning buffet while the food is still fresh," and even though I already knew the answer, I asked, "You want to come with me?"

I don't mean to indict the culture or to stereotype an entire ethnic group, but the Thais I know enjoy their sleep and the more they get the better. No matter what time Supattra goes to bed at night, if there is no crucial reason to rise the next morning, she can easily sleep 'til noon the following day. I'm not sure if this is learned due to the intense heat of the day, or some Southeast Asian genetic trait, but it seems to be widespread amongst the Thais I consider friends. So when I asked Supattra whether she wanted to come to breakfast, while we're off island and on vacation, I already knew the answer and was not surprised at her response.

"You go, sweetheart, I want to sleep a bit longer."

"We have a long drive today," I responded, dislodging my arms from the warmth of her body, before sitting up and placing my bare feet on the cool hardwood floor. "You can't sleep too late."

"Just a little while more, please," she answered, rolling over and wrapping her soft and warm arms around my waist. "What time is it?"

The bedcover had slipped off her when she rolled over and I looked down at her naked frame, running my hand up her thigh and over her hip, before bending down and kissing her forehead. Tempted to slide back down next to her, I forced myself to pick up my cell phone from the side table and look at the time.

It was just after seven in the morning. "Let's plan on leaving around nine," I said.

"Okay, nine o'clock," she muttered in response. "Thank you, sweetheart."

Then in as innocent voice as I could conjure, so as not to imply that I was questioning her ability to wake herself and get ready, I asked, "Do you want me to wake you?"

Farangs who live in Thailand and many tourists, no doubt, understand that time in this country is nothing more than a general guideline and deferential to many tangible and intangible factors. My general rule of thumb is, whether in regards to Supattra, my lawyer, or even the staff working in our business—when given a length of time, multiply that number by three and then add an adequate extension for preparation. When given a specific time during the day, consider the actual appointment or engagement to be plus or minus two hours from that scheduled meeting. While this was one of the more difficult cultural adjustments I was required to undergo after moving to the country, I am now at perfect ease with their sense of time.

"Please. I need twenty minutes to get ready."

Making the cultural adjustment, I concluded that I needed to triple her estimated time to get ready and then add an addition twenty minutes in order for us to make my self-imposed timeline. After a quick calculation, I determined that I needed to wake her at 7:40 a.m. to make the nine o'clock deadline.

Then, reconsidering my Western shrewdness, I shrugged

my shoulders. "Okay, I'll wake you at 8:40," recognizing that the one hour delay wouldn't really make a difference.

As I stood from the bed and began making my way to the bathroom, it dawned on me that I had been in Thailand too long. My lack of appreciation for an entire hour was not in keeping with my Western heritage.

After a hot shower I walked down to the breakfast buffet. Piling a mixture of Western and Thai food on my plate, I found a small table in the corner of the hotel's restaurant and began eating my breakfast. Taking a bite of a sausage before nibbling at the green curry, checking its spice level, my thoughts wandered across memories of the conflicts I had found myself over the years. As I dug my fork into a pile of fried rice, I began thinking about the First Gulf War, the least threatening in terms of someone shooting at me. It nonetheless had its own challenges and dangers and, sitting at that corner table, I began recalling those first few days of the ground war.

ℰ⁄ℑℰ⁄ℑ

At the time, I was still a Lieutenant and assigned to fly in the wingman position for one of the less experienced captains in the squadron. Later, I would learn that assignment had been made because, having proven myself on my previous deployment overseas, the command decided that adding me to his flight would eliminate their concern that the captain would get himself into trouble during the scheduled one-day mission, supporting one of the front line infantry units as they pushed their way into Kuwait City.

The air was thick with dark smoke from the burning oil wells as we flew our helicopter at twenty feet and no more than sixty knots across the dreary flat desert landscape of Kuwait. Even though my watch said it was just after noon, the sky was dark from the dense smoke, making it looked like it was the middle of the night. Tucked in fifty feet behind and to the left of the lead aircraft, flown by the inexperienced captain, our the two armed UH-1N helicopter gunships were following a road that allegedly would lead us to a forward refueling point located at the abandoned military airfield of Al Jaber, south of Kuwait City. The flames of two burning well heads on our left, and one on our right, shot upward like powerful fountains and easily cut through the gloom. I remembered feeling the heat from the burning wells through the open windows and cargo doors of our helicopter, even though the closest was over a hundred yards away. Other than the fiery cascades, we could see no more than a hundred feet ahead of our aircraft. As the acidic smell from the burning oil quickly gave me a headache, I remembered thinking that all the smoke couldn't be good for my respiratory system.

Passing the flaming well heads, we flew our helicopters over one long shadowy trench line after another, littered with an assortment of weapons, the former inhabitants discarding their arms before abandoning their position in face of the approaching marines. The occasional remains of a Russian-made T-54 tank would appear in the gloom on the side of the road, burnt and broken.

The barely visible road finally led us to a tall chain link fence with a concrete guard shack next to a gate. Bumping the helicopters over the top of the gate, we continued following the road until we saw the shadow of a building emerge from the darkness. Skirting around the building, we suddenly found ourselves over a tarmac and, as we traversed across the airfield, I saw the remains of several shattered A-4 Skyhawk aircraft with a Kuwaiti flag painted on their broken wings.

The scene was eerie. Each concrete hangar along the flight line had a single hole in the roof—created from a direct hit by precision guided munitions—all shrouded in an oily gloom. The sun, barely visible, looked like a faint orange basketball hovering above.

"Switch the radio over to the fueling point frequency," I casually requested of my co-pilot.

"Lead hasn't told us to switch yet," he replied. "We're supposed to wait until he calls for the switch."

"He forgot. Just switch the radio."

As he tuned our radio to the correct frequency, we caught the last of the lead aircraft's discussion with a ground controller at the forward fueling point, as he was explaining to our section leader where on the airfield they were located. Following the lead aircraft through the abandoned airbase, we finally saw two fuel trucks with several armed marines posted around its edges, providing security. The lead aircraft lined up to land and I mimicked his approach on the left.

Flying over a dirt strip between the tarmac and a taxiway, a muffled explosion shook our aircraft. Watching as a strobe-like flash, that threw out a gray mist of shrapnel and dirt, erupted under the lead aircraft's belly, bumping the helicopter up ten or fifteen feet from its approach, I quickly realized that the downdraft of his blades had set off a land mine, or maybe one of the unexploded munitions from a coalition force cluster bomb.

The small explosion was followed by the ground controller calling over the radio, "There are minefields all over the base!"

Pulling up on the collective, I turned away from our intended landing point, going around for another attempt after the dust settled, flying over the safety of a concrete taxi way the second time. After an uneventful landing, we inspected the bottom of the lead helicopter for damage. Finding none, we refueled and continued our journey north, breaking out of the smoke several miles north of the airfield, searching out the unit we were to assist. Discovering the infantry unit we had been tasked to support ten miles south of the city, the rest of day had been filled with missions reconnoitering small enclaves of buildings on the outskirts of Kuwait City, during which we were only challenged twice by small groups of Iraqis. Each of those incidents the enemy forces quickly capitulated.

While we had been instructed to return to our base, south of the smoke-filled oil fields, we received a message to remain overnight with the infantry unit. Apparently the gloom had become denser and the section of helicopters assigned to relieve us had been unable to penetrate the oily darkness. That night we sat on the top of our Huey, leaning back against the cushions placed in the intakes, watching the fixed wing attack aircraft destroy every vehicle attempting to escape into Iraq along a highway some twenty miles north. It was like watching a Fourth of July fireworks display—the night sky flashing, followed by an endless procession of thunderous claps. Across the world, in the United States, that same section of road would soon become known as the "Highway of Death."

The next morning, we left the infantry unit to return to the abandoned airbase of Al Jaber but found the greasy murkiness had indeed become denser and our section leader decided to hunt down a new a source of fuel. Haphazardly searching for fuel, we finally came across a long line of twenty or thirty fuel trucks headed north along dirt road in the desert west of the city. Flying just off the desert floor next to the speeding caravan, I asked the crew chief to tell me what it said on the side of the tanker trucks. When he replied A1, I knew we were in luck.

Continuing to flying low to the ground next to the racing tanker trucks, not knowing what frequency they were monitoring, I instructed the crew chief to give the drivers the hand and arm signal for needing fuel, bobbing his hand back and forth next to his face with his thumb extended. Several minutes later, one of the driver's midway down the long line of tankers abruptly pulled over to the side of the road, stopping the entire back half of the line of fuel trucks.

Landing in front of the stationary truck, blocking the back half of the long caravan, I watched its driver hastily putting his gas mask on and asked the crew chief what signal he had given.

"They didn't seem to know the signal for needing fuel," the crew chief explained behind me over the inter-cockpit communication system.

Looking over my shoulder into the cabin behind me, I asked again, "What did you do?"

"I just gestured him like this," he replied as he repeatedly swung his open hands down onto his shoulders.

Laughing, I said, "You just gave these guys the signal for a gas attack."

Having only lost one friend during the entire operation, I

smiled at the memories of that picnic of a war, realizing that the most life-threatening event of the entire episode had been an incident when I inadvertently put the helicopter I was flying into a phenomenon called Vortex Ring State, losing all lift while in a steep descent. As the helicopter fell through its own downwash, I was sure our plunge could only end in a catastrophic fiery ball. Once again feeling adrenalin pump into my veins, I wrapped my fear up into a tight ball before lowering the collective, placing the aircraft in an autorotation profile. Just before our inevitable impact with the desert floor, I pulled an arm full of collective, dramatically increasing the pitch in the overhead blades. With the low RPM horn singing in my helmet, indicating the engines could not provide the power requested, miraculously the helicopter groaned and shuddered, flying out of the occurrence several feet above the ground. Releasing the tight ball of fear, it immediately warped into giddiness and I jokingly told my co-pilot I had simply been giving him a lesson in the how not to avoid Vortex Ring State.

∽∾∽

At 9:52 a.m. Supattra and I dropped our key with the front desk and stepped out of the hotel carrying our luggage. Supattra was in a particularly good mood, likely because our next stop would be Bangkok where we were to pick up her sister— a sister that she hadn't seen in over a year.

"Who's driving?" I asked, as she clicked the button on the key chain to disengage the door locks twenty yards from the truck.

"I'll drive first," she said without hesitation. "You drove from the restaurant to the hotel. It's my turn."

Feeling a slight rise in my blood pressure, I responded, "The road from Surratthani to the freeway north is pretty busy."

Supattra is a great driver but she has very little experience. Early in our relationship, I had taught her the basics of driving when we rented a car in Kalasin during one of our visits to her family farm, and we would occasionally rent a truck to make visa runs, where she would drive some of the less challenging segments of the trip. Then, two years ago, even though we had no car or truck at the time, she decided that she needed her driver's license. She sought out a driving instructor on the island and, for a month, spent two days a week learning to drive. At the end of the course, the driving instructor accompanied her to Koh Samui, cheering her on while she took the written and driving test. Easily passing the written exam, she failed her first attempt during the practical application of the parallel parking test. The next week she returned to Koh Samui without her driving instructor and passed. On the other hand, her middle sister Aae, without training, took and failed both the written and driving test. Rather than go home without a license, she simply paid the government official managing the testing center a bribe and was issued the same license as Supattra.

Since receiving her license, Supattra has met my recommendations, as to when she should and should not drive, with stubbornness. My logical approach to this obstinacy is to point out that I bought my first car when I was sixteen and at the ripe old age of fifty-five I have many more hours of experience. Her reaction is to dig her heels in and ask me if I think she's a bad driver. With this in mind, when we purchased the pickup, I signed us up for "first class insurance" that will pay for any damage, no questions asked.

Walking across The One Hundred Island Hotel parking lot, flashing her dark brown eyes at me, she asked, "Do you think I'm a bad driver?"

"No, no, you're a great driver," I answered.

"Then why can I not drive the road to the highway?"

"It's just a really difficult and dangerous part of the trip."

"Would you rather have me drive in Bangkok?"

After a very brief hesitation, considering the implications of her remark, I quickly gave in. "You can drive the first segment," I said, knowing that Bangkok is a far more hectic and risky place to be behind the wheel of a moving vehicle.

With the Google Maps app armed and talking, we began driving down the narrow two-lane road, cutting through a scenic tropical coastal area, linking Surratthani with the artery that leads up the Thai peninsula to Bangkok. This particular section of road is deadly. Slow-moving sixteen wheelers (which Supattra refers to as "giants"), speed-limit-abiding families, and fast-moving high rollers determined to arrive at their destination as quickly as possible even with the threat of bodily injury or death, all sharing a single lane, with the same demographic replica sharing the opposing lane. Did I tell you that Thailand has the second highest traffic fatality rate in the world? It might be third, but they fall within the top three deadliest places to drive around the globe.

To take my mind off of the mayhem occurring on the highway around us, I asked Supattra about the Thai writing on the license plates.

"It tells where the car is from," she said as she swung our truck out into the opposing lane to pass two cars, likely law-abiding families, droning along behind a giant struggling down the road.

Estimating we had about ten seconds to pass the two cars before a massive head-on collision with a red Mercedes, I asked, "Where's that car from?" Pointing to the small white Toyota sedan we were passing.

"Hat Yai," she calmly responded as she swung our pickup truck in front of the two law-abiding family cars and behind the giant, before the fast moving red Mercedes that threatened the head-on shot by in the opposite direction.

"What about that Mercedes—the one that we nearly collided with?" I asked sarcastically.

"Bangkok."

Laughing in disbelief, I asked, "You were able to read the license plate of the Mercedes?"

"Bangkok." She pulled the truck out several feet into the opposing lane to see if anyone of was coming. "Thais like others to know where they are from," she calmly remarked before hastily swinging back in behind the giant just as two speeding cars careened by in the opposite direction. "People from Kalasin like Kalasin plates, people from Bangkok want others to know they are from Bangkok. It's a pride thing," she added as she pulled the truck back out again to see if it clear to pass the giant yet.

As she abruptly swung back in behind the giant again to avoid another collision with a law-abiding family, I commented, "But our truck says Surratthani and you're from Kalasin," as I felt my blood pressure rise to life-threatening levels.

"I am South now," she explained as she pulled our pickup truck out into the opposing lane and began passing the giant. "I have lived here for seven years, I have a South identification, and my name is registered with our house in Chaloklum."

"You feel more southern Thai than Isaan?" I asked, wondering who would claim my body if I were to die on this road in a head on collision.

"The old women in the village call me daughter and tell me I look more South than Isaan," she replied as she swung back over into our lane in front of the giant. "They tell me my skin is dark like a South Thai."

"But you feel more South than Isaan?" I asked again, feeling a momentary drop in blood pressure. "You were very proud to be from Isaan when I met you."

"I am still proud to be from Isaan but I am South now."

"How many languages do you speak now?" I asked, wondering if she had picked up the southern dialect and not told me.

"Four."

"Isaan, Thai, English, and South?"

"Yes."

"Do you speak South when on the island?" I had never heard her utter a word of South, a very clipped and grunting language.

"Never," she replied, as she reached out and patted my right thigh, never taking her eyes off the road as we raced toward the next slow moving group of vehicles ahead.

"Why?"

"Because I am Isaan and if I were to try and communicate with south people in their language they would think me a fake."

"But they call you daughter and tell you that you look more

South than Isaan," I remarked, somewhat confused. "They have accepted you as one of their own, but you don't want to speak their language?"

"You are not Thai and don't understand. If you moved to England would you talk with an English accent even though you speak American English? They might accept you and like you but they would then think you a fake if you tried to speak with their accent."

"But South is an entirely different language," I responded. "If I were to move to France and knew the language, I would speak their language."

"It is different in Thailand. We have the common language of Thai. I understand the South language and that is enough. If I were to speak South they would think me a fake. I am Isaan."

As we sped down the narrow two-lane highway that cut through serene tropical meadows with water buffalos grazing on tall green grass and men fishing from small wooden boats floating on narrow finger like inlets, I considered her logic and realized that it would be foolish for me to use my Western reasoning in an attempt to unravel the mysteries of Thailand. Thailand is a Buddhist country that is proud of its non-colonial heritage. It is a country where making merit for the next life is as important as making money for this life. It is a country where applying Western values and logic would be like trying to put a square peg into a round hole. I am not Thai and I don't understand half the things that go on in this country, even though I have been here for nearly eight years. But I would also submit that most Thais don't understand half their own culture, either.

Forty-five white-knuckled minutes later, I recognized the intersection with the freeway that led north, up the Thai peninsula, in the distance and quietly sighed in relief. We had survived the first stage of our trip to Bangkok. Coming to a halt behind a small row of cars and trucks waiting for the light, Supattra looked over at me, smiling with a clear expression of conquest. Looking back, I returned her smile and shrugged my shoulders.

When the light turned green, she pulled out onto the highway and accelerated to where we were keeping up with the final demographic, the fast-moving high rollers.

Thai freeways are unique for several reasons. First, the preferred lane for both slow- and fast-moving traffic is the inner or fast lane. While there might be regulations concerning truck weights, weigh-stations are nearly non-existent in the country and those that exist are rarely open. Transport companies have taken advantage of this oversight and load their trucks with as many goods as possible. As a result, the pavement in the outer or slow lane has been compressed from years of use by overweight sixteen wheelers, becoming rough and full of potholes. Driving in the outer slow lane, from a pilot's perspective, is a lot like flying through moderate turbulence. While some drivers are courteous and move to the outer lane when overtaken by faster vehicles, many times to pass a slow moving car or truck on the highway one must use the rough outer lane. Careening across jagged pothole-laden pavement is uncomfortable, to say the least.

The second reason driving on Thai freeways is unique is because Thai drivers like to use both lanes at the same time. Several times I have asked Supattra, as she was driving down the line separating the two lanes, why Thais do this, and each and every time she looked at me with a confused expression and asked what I was talking about. In other words, I think Thais are oblivious to this habit.

Thais have different standards when it comes to rules and regulations. In my opinion, the uniqueness of driving on Thai highways is symbolic of their culture. Rules have a wider gray area in a country where its main religion teaches its followers to live a life based on common sense, not getting hung up on the little things, and that everyone is on a personal journey whose actions should not be judged from someone not traveling that same path. Buddhism has cultivated a culture of people who have become unaware that their neighbors aren't abiding to the exact limits of the rules, regulations, and laws because everyone's path in unique and private, and, by ignoring these small distractions, they are making merit for their next life. Driving in the smoothest lane is common sense, and everyone does it, so it's not worth worrying about. Placing as much as possible on a truck transporting goods is common sense and makes their businesses more profitable. Objecting to it lacks importance in the bigger scheme of life. And it really doesn't matter if you use one or both lanes at the same time. It's not worth the time and effort to even recognize such a small thing. Their culture has given Thais a perspective on life that not only cultivates a laissez-faire lifestyle, but also low blood pressure.

Several hours of maneuvering through the building Songkran traffic and bouncing down the outer lane in order to pass giants and law-abiding families on the freeway had worn Supattra down. Tired of driving, she looked over at me stretched out on the passenger seat and asked if I was ready to take the wheel. The timing could not have been more perfect because I needed to use the restroom, partially due to bouncing down the outer lane. We agreed to stop at the next gas station to use the amenities and swap positions.

Passing groves that resembled aspen trees, we could see several large signs advertising petrol stations in the distance. Near the coastal city of Lang Suan we selected one of the gas stations and Supattra pulled our pickup in.

CHAPTER 6

Fear and Corruption ~ 11 April 2014

When Supattra pulled up to the gas pump, I stepped from our pickup truck and told her that I would be right back as she was instructing the gas attendant, a young woman wearing a gray shirt with red piping, to fill the truck up.

The gas station was busy with most of the travelers headed home for the Songkran celebration. Walking across the parking lot toward the restroom surrounded by clay pots bursting with flowering tropical plants, I attracted some attention, the lone *farang* mixed in with a predominately Thai crowd. Some Thais gawked, but most smiled at me as I walked by.

Arriving at the restroom, I peeked into the first stall and my heart sank. I found myself looking down at the standard Thai squatting toilet. Finishing my business, I sauntered back to our pickup, now parked in front of a Seven Eleven and found Supattra leaning up against the hood, licking a chocolate ice cream cone.

With a mouth full of ice cream, she mumbled, "They didn't have *farang* toilets."

"How'd you know?"

"The back of your pants are wet." She giggled before taking another bite.

"I'd ask for lessons but that seems a bit creepy at the age of fifty-five."

"If you haven't figured it out in the eight years you've been living here," she said before licking her ice cream cone again, "I think you are lost and hopeless."

"Lost and hopeless is a pretty brutal description for the man you've chosen to hang out with."

"Only lost and hopeless when it comes to going *chee-chong*," she replied, using the Thai word for urination.

"*Chee-chong* isn't the issue, it's the procedure for taking a *men-men* in this country that kicks my butt," I responded, using the Thai word for foul smell, as I opened the driver's door and climbed into the truck, adding, "More specifically, it's the fact that I lost the flexibility and balance required to complete the procedure with any semblance of gracefulness a long time ago," before closing the door.

Driving down the freeway through a lush tropical forest filled with silver-barked trees and tall flowering bushes, we rode in silence, Supattra checking out Facebook on her cell phone while I kept my attention on the road. Pulling the truck into the slow lane, we bounced across the rough pavement, passing two lumbering giants, before I accelerated to 140 kph once back in the fast lane, focusing on the next group of slow moving vehicles in the distance.

"The day the airplanes flew into the buildings," Supattra said, out of the blue. "You were a part of that?"

"Yeah," I replied, feeling strangely calm when presented with her question about my military past. "I was at the Pentagon."

"What happened?"

"I was sitting at my desk and an airplane hit the building."

Flashing her dark brown eyes at me, as if she knew I was holding back, she asked, "Do you think I will not understand because I am Thai?"

"No." I chuckled at her correct perception. "What do you want to know?"

Looking over at me, she said, "I want to know what happened."

"The twin towers in New York had already been hit," I began to explain. "We were all watching it on a small television that sat on a tan filing tan cabinet in one of the cubicles in the office. I'll never forget, as we watched the towers, with black smoke pouring from these big gaping holes on their sides,

someone in the crowd offhandedly asked why they struck civilian buildings and not a military target like the Pentagon.
Another person, a civilian contract worker, jokingly replied
that they wouldn't hit us. We were on their side because of
how long it takes the Pentagon to accomplish anything."

Looking at me with a quizzical look, she asked, "Was that
funny when all those people had just died?"

"Of course not. It was just a bad joke."

"And then the airplane flew into your building?"

"I walked back to my desk and sat down. It was still relatively early and I had just put my uniform on. My wallet, cell
phone, and car keys were sitting on the top of my desk—
anyway, I sat down and, a few minutes later, we were hit. The
impact launched me upward. I'll never forget watching everything on my desk rise straight up into the air. I could have
reached out and grabbed anyone of them. My laptop, wallet,
cell phone, keys—everything. As I hovered over the cubicles,
I can remember seeing the windows had cracked and there
was fire and smoke on the other side."

"What happened then?"

"Next thing I knew I was back on the floor, still sitting in
my office chair. The only difference was that I was in a complete state of panic."

"And?"

"Someone shouted we needed to get out of there and we all
raced from the office. Another thing I won't forget was that
there was a civilian holding the office door open for all the
terrified fleeing military personal. We were on the fourth floor
of D ring, and pretty far down the corridor from the courtyard.
The Pentagon has a massive courtyard at its center."

"Did you run to this courtyard?"

"I ran toward it. With everyone else I ran down the corridor
in a state of panic. The hallway was filled with people running. It was pure pandemonium. At the end of the corridor
there were two brand new escalators; one up and one down
escalator. Both were at a dead stop but no one was using the
up escalator to run down. It was as if we were trained to use
only the down escalator to go down, whether they were oper-

ating or not. Well, anyway, I ran down the down the escalator with everyone else but on the third floor, the next floor down, I stopped. I was as panicked as I had ever been and as I ran down that escalator I knew I needed to calm down. I needed to take the fear consuming me and wrap it up in a little ball, and tuck it away so it wouldn't effect what I was thinking or doing. So I stopped and leaned up against a wall, trying to get my wits about me. Standing next to the wall, watching the frightened and shocked throngs of people racing passed me and down the escalators, I suddenly realized that my wallet and keys were on my desk."

"What did you do?"

"I took several deep breaths and walked up empty up escalator to the fourth floor, all the while watching this mass of people continue to pour down the down escalator, trying to escape the building. By this time the corridor I had just fled from was nearly empty and I walked back toward my office."

"You went back to your office?" Supattra asked with an astonished expression. "Why would you go back to your office?"

"I didn't have a spare set of keys for my car and it would be a huge pain in the ass replacing my driver's license, military identification, and credit cards—all in my wallet. But I never actually made it back to my office. I was stopped about halfway down the corridor by a thick wall of black smoke. There was another civilian standing there."

"But it was not smart to try and go back to your office," she insisted. "You could have been killed."

Glancing over at her, I replied, "If you had ever had to replace you license and credit cards, you wouldn't say that."

Likely wanting to avoid getting sidetracked in an argument about my past safety before hearing the entire story, she asked, "What happened at the wall of smoke?"

"There was a woman calling for help. She was well beyond the wall of smoke, someplace down the corridor and obviously in distress."

"Did you save her?"

"I stuck my hand and arm into the smoke and it disappeared. I could smell aviation fuel and feel heat radiating from the floor under me, telling me that there was a massive fire someplace below. I knew right then that an airplane had flown into the Pentagon. We yelled at the woman trying to guide her to us, but we both knew that if we had gone into the smoke, we would have been quickly overcome by the fumes and never make it back. At some point the lights went out, replaced by flashing overhead strobe lights, and these sliver fire doors at the end of the hallway clattered closed, adding an eeriness to the whole setting."

"Were you afraid?"

"It was like being in a creepy discothèque—strobe-lights flashing in a dimly-lit smoke-filled space. The only thing missing was some 1970s era disco song, but I wasn't afraid. I had learned a long time ago how to control my fear. The woman eventually quit responding to our calls and I walked away."

"How long did you wait?"

"I was probably at the wall of smoke, yelling at the lady, for ten minutes after she had quit calling for help. I can only imagine that she had been overcome by the thick smoke."

"Did she die?"

"Probably." I sighed, remembering the moment when I realized she was probably dead.

"And you left?"

"I did. I walked away. I jogged down to the courtyard. Half the people around me were crying, the other half were looking around as if they didn't know what was going on."

"Why?"

"Because it's a big building. People on the far side of the Pentagon hadn't felt the impact and didn't really know what was going on. They were looking at the smoke billowing from the outside of the building and heard the news of what had happened, but they hadn't been blown off the floor when it hit the building. Their response was more of curiosity; not panic."

Cocking her head to one side, Supattra asked, "Why was that?"

Watching her scrutiny out of the corner of my eyes, I replied, "It's a funny thing. When I went to war or to a conflict, I felt the stress but never the fear. I figure it because I was given time to prepare myself and was able to establish a state of mind that somehow controlled my emotional reactions to danger. But that day in the Pentagon, I initially felt fear. No one expected that plane to plow into the side of the building and, without having been given the opportunity to prepare themselves, fear became a common emotion. The people who felt the full impact of the airplane were afraid. Those who worked far enough away to not feel fear, never had that surge of adrenalin pumped into their veins. They only felt simple curiosity. Standing against the wall of the third floor, before venturing back down the corridor toward my office, I had taken my fear and bound it up. I had prepared myself, from that moment on, for anything."

"What did you do then?"

In the middle of my description of what occurred at the Pentagon, my thoughts floated across time and space, and I suddenly began thinking about the night I learned of my first wife's death. Suddenly the vision of me entering the stateroom filled with young pilots carrying the bottle of whiskey fluttered across my mind, and I lost my train of thought.

Supattra punched me in the shoulder. "I hate it when you do that."

"Do what?"

"Stop talking or listening in the middle of a conversation. It's like you go someplace else and forget who you're with or what you're doing. You do it quite often."

"Sorry," I replied before continuing the story. "At some point they announced that there was another airplane inbound and we needed to evacuate the building, so I walked to the entrance or exit I used every day, the one that led to the parking lot where my car was sitting—a car I had no keys for. As I was walking down the wide hallway that led to the exit, hearing for a second or third time from the overhead speaker that another plane was inbound, suddenly there was a rush of frantic people running up the corridor back toward me and the courtyard. Calmly—far calmer than I had been when the airplane hit the building, I thought my life was over. I thought the people running toward me had seen the second airplane flying into the side of the building that I was exiting. I imagined the fire and heat from the impact blowing up through the corridor I was attempting to exit from as it hit the building. With a clear mind, I stepped behind a large concrete structural pylon, and waited for the blast, knowing that it couldn't possibly protect me."

"What happened?"

"The people running by were followed by a several medical attendants with stretchers—and then I remembered that the medical clinic was at the end of the corridor, next to the exit. When the stretcher bearers began running up the corridor into the Pentagon to the aid of the injured, they created a stampede. The people exiting in front of me saw the stretcher bearers running and thought the same thing I had, an airplane was flying into that side of the building."

Reaching out and placing her hand on my thigh, she asked, "And you finally made it out?"

"I did."

"And what was it like?"

"There were thousands of people loitering around the edges of the parking lot. My first thought was to call my wife and tell her I was okay, but I had left my cell phone on my desk."

"Did you borrow one?"

"I tried, but all the cell lines were busy. The whole town had gone crazy with the news that airplanes had flown into the twin towers and Pentagon, and there was another one likely headed for DC. Everyone in Washington DC was on their cell phone and the lines were clobbered. Or maybe the government had shut the cell towers down. You couldn't get a line out. So, after about thirty minutes of trying to figure out what to do, I began walking toward Rosslyn, just up the road and along the route to where I lived. When I arrived in Rosslyn, it was like a set from a global disaster movie—a meteor or nuclear missile headed for DC. It was almost worse than the Pentagon, filled with frightened people trying to get out of the city. The streets were jam packed with cars and the sidewalks with people.

Every phone booth had lines of people trying to make calls because their cell phones didn't work. I walked all the way to a place called Claridon before I found a phone booth that had a short line."

"And you made a call to your wife?"

"I got in line and the guy in front of me turned around, seeing my smoke-stained uniform, asked if I had been in the Pentagon. The minute I said yes, he let me in front of him. The person in front of him heard me and let me in front of him, and so on. Next thing I knew I was standing at the phone and called my wife."

"Was she glad to hear from you?"

"Yeah, she was pretty upset but happy I called. The funny thing is, when I got off the phone, I walked down to Washington Boulevard, a major intersecting street in North Arlington, and stuck my thumb out, hitching a ride," I explained. "I had these black dress shoes on that were really uncomfortable. I couldn't imagine walking all the way home in those shoes, even though it was only a mile away."

"Hitching?"

"Hitchhiking means you stick your thumb out, gesturing for a ride from passing cars. You have to understand that Washington DC is the last place you would never expect to be picked up as a hitchhiker, and the first car that passed by, a jeep actually, saw my uniform and picked me up. The woman drove me all the way home."

The pickup truck was oddly quiet as we drove down the road in silence while Supattra digested my account of the Pentagon. As usual, I found that I had become tense as I told the story and tried to think about something else in order to relax. Nonetheless, I grimly sat in the driver's seat, poised to take follow-up questions.

Several miles down the road, she said, "There are a lot of new cars on the highway," changing the subject and breaking the anxious silence in our truck.

Relieved that she wasn't going to question me further about the Pentagon, I said, "It's the emerging middle class."

"Middle class?"

As she glanced over at me with a quizzical expression, I realized that I had never used that term in a conversation with her before. Spending a moment considering the best way to define middle class, I finally said, "The people between the rich and poor. Beginning in early 2000, as Thailand's industrial nation status solidified, a middle class began to emerge. Slow at the beginning, but now Thailand's middle class is growing quite fast."

"Why?"

Hesitating again, attempting to figure out the best way to describe what was happening in Thailand, I said, "Because people are being paid more money for their work. The lower class is shrinking as the middle class is growing. This new middle class can afford more things, like new cars. When they buy new cars, more money is pumped into the economy which in turn creates more better-paying jobs, creating more middle class."

After eight years of friendship with Supattra, I am no longer amazed when she listens to a fairly complex statement and then makes an obscure connection during a conversation. Given a Southeast Asian topic, my high school-educated girlfriend could contend with any of my college-educated pals. So when she said, "They are the Yellow Shirts," I was not surprised.

The Yellow and Red Shirts are two politically opposed factions in Thailand. The two groups can be identified regionally, with the Red Shirts spawning from Isaan and Yellow Shirts from Bangkok and areas south. Generally speaking, the Red Shirts represent the poorer segment of the country and the Yellow Shirts are made up by the emerging middle class. While it is a bit complicated to explain, with multiple levels of disagreement, the primary gripe between the two political factions is that the Yellow Shirts are tired of the corrupt government officials that the populous Red Shirts tend to elect into office, largely because of timely bribes or illicit payments prior to the casting of votes.

When I first met Supattra, she considered herself a Red Shirt, mostly due to the region where she had grown up. As time passed, listening to other views on the issue, she slowly became a Yellow Shirt. When I asked her why she had made the change, she explained that the leader of the Red Shirts, Thaksin Shinawatra, is a bad Thai and, even in self-imposed exile, he has created an atmosphere in which Thais hurt Thais. Simmering under the surface of Thaksin's tinkering with Thai politics, and unbeknownst to most, is that this disposed prime minister wants to see the Thai monarchy go away and for Thailand to become strictly a democratic nation.

This might make sense to a Western-educated person, but one of the first things you learn when you come to Thailand, whether as a tourist or to live, is that Thais love their king, Bhumibol Adulyadej (Rama IX). This love teeters on the verge of fanaticism and is nearly universal in this small country. It's okay to call the prime minister and his cabinet all crooks and liars, but call the Rama IX anything but a benevolent leader, and you'll find yourself with a one-way ticket out of the country with no return invitation. The fact that Rama IX is a compassionate leader makes their enthusiastic devotion easy to understand. While I haven't given it much thought, I'm sure, like nearly everything else in Thailand, this fervent love has something to do with their religion and history.

"Yes. The Yellow Shirts are primarily made up of the new middle class," I replied, pulling into the rough lane again, to pass a line of four law-abiding families. "And they will be the force that cracks down on corruption in the government and the police," I continued in a garbled voice as we bounced across the ruts.

"No one will ever make the police good," Supattra retorted, shaking her head.

"It will eventually happen," I countered. "In the past, the poor couldn't afford to call for changes and the rich didn't want change, because the corruption mostly benefitted them. The Yellow Shirts have the required financial resources and it's advantageous for them to crack down on corruption. As their numbers grow, their voice will, too, and the government and police will lose their power over the people."

"Like the Shutdown Bangkok mob," Supattra said.

Unlike the West, the use of the term "mob" does not have a

detrimental connotation in Thailand, and most Thais use that word to describe any organized protest with a large crowd.

"The Shutdown Bangkok mob was Yellow Shirts," I agreed, "and they were protesting government corruption. That's just the beginning and what they do will be good for Thailand. Thailand's reputation for corruption and what happened in Bangkok during the mob may seem bad to outsiders, but in some ways this country is well ahead of its neighbors politically. Malaysia has corruption but none of its citizens have ever stood up and called for change. Burma, Lao, and Cambodia are all up to their ears in corruption, but only Thailand is in the midst of changing, of fighting it in a transparent atmosphere."

Looking out the window at the passing scenery for a moment, she asked, "Did America ever have these problems? Did they ever have the problems we have?"

Taken back by this question because most Thais, Supattra included, believe what they see in movies, I silently sniggered. To Thais, America is a crazy place where the police are in cahoots with criminal elements and gun battles on the streets of New York and Los Angeles are not an uncommon sight.

Trying to keep a humorous tone from my voice so she wouldn't think I thought her question was unintelligent, I replied, "I think our ancestors in sixteenth-century Europe worked out a lot of the low-level Thai-style corruption."

Turning her attention from the passing scenery to me again, she asked, "What do you mean?"

"Every country has corruption, but in different forms. Your sister buying her driver's license was a form of Thai style corruption—"

"She's a horrible driver," Supattra interrupted.

"America was the home of European immigrants," I continued. "The French Enlightenment, and the growth of the well-structured English legal system destroyed the basis of low-level transparent corruption. We still have corruption, but it's well hidden and not evident to the average citizen."

"So Thailand will be more like America when the middle class stops the corruption?"

"Yes. The Yellow Shirts will destroy low-level transparent corruption, but both America and Thailand suffer from a more complex and hidden version."

"But many of the Thai police are bad, and that's not good any place."

"You're right, that needs to go away," I agreed. "The issue in every developed nation is a deeper and more sinister corruption. For example, we elect politician to make critical decisions about our country, yet we also allow for lobbyists to wine and dine those same elected officials in support of one cause or another. In my mind that is an institutionalized type of corruption that perverts the entire system. And I imagine that same type of corruption exists in Thailand."

"What is a lobbyist?"

"Someone hired to convince politicians to vote one way or another."

"That doesn't seem like corruption to me."

"In its basic form, no. There's nothing wrong with someone trying to speak on behalf of one issue or another, but the profession of lobbying has become so powerful and institutionalized with gifts and favors, that it has warped into corruption. That's what I mean by hidden and complex corruption. You can't fix it without throwing the baby out with the bathwater, and undermining basic freedoms."

"You can't fix that kind of corruption?"

"I don't know." I laughed, surprised she didn't ask me to define the "baby out with the bathwater" comment. "I've never given it much thought. After all, there's nothing wrong with someone speaking on behalf of one issue or another."

After a moment of silence, with the rhythmic sound of the pickup's tires rolling across the pavement, Supattra asked, "Was corruption the reason for your war?"

Somewhat shocked at her question, I asked, "Why would you ask that?"

"Many *farangs* living on our island think George Bush was bad and misled America when they went to war. I have heard them tell you that you were wrong for fighting for George Bush."

She was right. I had been questioned and reprimanded numerous times over the years by Europeans living on Koh PhaNgan, telling me that I was wrong for participating in George Bush's war. While I have never hidden my past from other islanders, I learned very quickly as an American and former marine in that environment, the best course of action was to avoid all political discussions and the reasons we went to war in Iraq.

While I may have been affected by posttraumatic stress and struggled over what I saw and did, I have never questioned my presence in the wars and conflicts I found myself in. When pressed on Iraq by disapproving Europeans, in an attempt to defuse the situation, I would respond that I was a firefighter. When told where the fire was, I would go and fight. It was not my job to determine the how it had started, the validity, or the severity of the fire. And while some might think that answer was a cop-out, it was as simple as that in my mind. Someone needed to go and, eventually, would go. I would rather it be me than my children years down the road when the problem was far worse than it was when I could have participated.

"I don't believe our war with Iraq was corrupt," I began, as I pulled the pickup truck back into the slow lane to pass two more giants. Then in a slightly jumbled tone as we careened across all the potholes, I said, "I believe we are in a world war—a war of religions or between civilizations—I don't know which. It's even occurring here in Thailand between the Muslims and Buddhists down south near Hat Yai. We can ignore it today but if we do, we will fight it tomorrow. As a young marine I was taught the best defense is a good offense. History will have its way with George Bush, one way or the other, but I will never feel as if I participated in anything less than an offensive operation against a growing threat."

CHAPTER 7

The lush southern jungles gave way to open fields and the traffic continued to build as we closed in on Bangkok. We found ourselves traveling in the rough lane more and more, passing a crescendo of slower-moving law-abiding families and giants. Bitch'n Betty remained silent and Supattra napped while I followed the same highway north for the next two hours.

Waking up and stretching in the seat next to me, Supattra asked, "What time is it?"

Looking at the clock on the dashboard, I answered, "Two-thirty. We should get into Bangkok in about an hour or so."

"My sister doesn't get off work until five o'clock. Let's go to dinner. My friend told me where there's a good seafood restaurant on the water."

Smiling, I asked, "Are all your friends restaurant critics specializing in seafood?"

"Wasn't the restaurant in Donsak good?"

"It wasn't in Donsak like your friends told you. It wasn't even close to Donsak."

"Wasn't it good?" she snapped.

"Yes, it was good."

"Then let's go and try the restaurant my friend told me about in Bangkok."

I was concerned that my next comment might cause an argument, but I finally gave into my impulse. "The words fresh seafood and Bangkok always seemed a bit like antonyms to me."

"What's an antonym?"

"Opposites."

"Bangkok has good seafood," she retorted, flashing her dark brown eyes in my direction.

"As long as the fish aren't caught in and around the city, that's probably true."

Looking at me with a suspicious expression and tightly knitted eyebrows, she asked, "Why?"

"Just look at the waters flowing through the rivers in Bangkok." I laughed. "Just look at the waters flowing out of Bangkok. They're a disgusting brownish-green all the way down to Pattaya, and that's sixty miles south."

She silently glared at me for a few moments. "My friend told me where there's a good seafood restaurant on the water. Let's go eat before we pick up my sister and her husband."

I realized her request for an early dinner was threatening to escalate into a match of wills between two stubborn people who'd shared the same cramped cab of a pickup truck for at least six hours, so I gave in. "Okay, punch it into Bitch'n Betty, but if I get sick from some strange and exotic fish virus, I'm blaming you."

Out of the corner of my eye, I watched Supattra silently shake her head as she typed the restaurant's name into the Google Maps app. She tended to be grumpy when she first woke up so, doing what any all-American boyfriend would do, I ignored her.

Traffic intensified and Bitch'n Betty warned us of an up-coming turn as we rode along in silence. The overhead signs didn't indicate on which side of the highway the exit was on and it was not intuitive. Remaining silent, Supattra sat in the passenger seat looking directly ahead as our scheduled turn approached. I stubbornly did not ask her for help and, making an assumption, pulled into the right-most lane.

Four hundred meters before our turn the Google app finally announced that we needed to be in the left lane. With just enough traffic to make changing lanes difficult, I began to maneuver the pickup truck to the other side of the freeway. While Thais spend their days trying to give to those in need and not judging their neighbors, seeking merit for the next life, I have learned that none of these traits takes place on the Thailand's roadway system. Had Buddhism not instilled an unusual amount of patience and the sense to let bygones be bygones into the country's population, road rage would probably be the number one cause of death in this small nation. With Bitch'n Betty screaming about the approaching unqualified disaster of missing our exit, I managed to get myself into the center lane without much difficulty, but the cars traveling bumper to bumper in the left-most lane were not interested in letting us in. In Thai fashion, I adjusted the steering wheel so that our truck's trajectory was in a slow collision course with the car blocking me from reaching the left lane, giving that driver a choice of slowing down or to moving onto the shoulder and letting me in. Of course, his other option would be colliding with the big black Toyota pickup truck bearing down on him. Thankfully, the windows of our truck were tinted and driver of the other car could not see a *farang* at the wheel, as that would have undoubtedly created an international showdown—colonist versus a citizen of the only country in Southeast Asia to have never been colonized. The other driver finally surrendered his position, slowing and allowing us to slip in front of him. We made the exit onto the ramp leading to the intersecting highway that Bitch'n Betty was jabbering about, but it wasn't a pretty sight.

"You shouldn't have done that," Supattra snapped from the passenger seat, as we looped under the highway onto another four lane freeway headed for the suburbs of southern Bangkok.

"My co-pilot was playing head games and didn't tell me which side of the highway I needed to be on."

"You told your co-pilot that her capital city was dirty."

"I said the waters flowing through her capital city were dirty. I made no such claim about the city itself."

"It's the same thing."

"No, it's not," I could feel her simmering anger.

"Yes, it is," she spat.

Sometimes I have to remind myself that I am living with a

woman half my age and need think back to when I was that young. This is not to say that Supattra is immature, because she is not. She is simply half my age and has not learned all the life lessons I have. My favorite lesson, and one that I have tried to instill in my children, is that the word sorry is free and easy to use. Not to mention, using sorry has minimal ramifications on future discussions. Therefore, I use the word frequently.

"Sorry, I didn't mean to call your capital city dirty," I replied in as a genuine tone as I could summon. "I love Bangkok and think it's a clean place."

The other positive characteristic of saying sorry is that it is like a yawn. When one person says it, others find themselves instinctively repeating it.

"I am sorry, too, sweetheart," she replied, her angry tone all but gone. "I should have told you which side of the road to be on."

Everyone has at least one talent and I learned long ago that most of mine are all centered on a distinctive spatial awareness. I was a natural pilot, easily able to determine what kind of control input was required for any maneuver. Without measuring, I can immediately tell if something is going to fit into a container. At a glance, I can compare dimensions of two similar objects and tell you which is larger. And, with one glimpse at a map, I can find my way along a semi-complicated route to a desired destination. While this is not a highly sought after skill in the international job market, I'm still very proud of this aptitude and, even though I have never advertised this talent, simply using it for my own benefit, Supattra quickly picked up on my ability. She learned early in our relationship that trying to give me verbal directions was a waste of time when all she had to do was to let me peek at the map.

Thirty minutes down the new highway, with the Bangkok skyscrapers coming into view on a hazy horizon, I asked, "So where is this place?"

Pulling the map up, she handed me her cell phone and said, "There."

I quickly saw that we needed to pass over one bridge, take

the second left, and hook back on a frontage road before passing under the freeway. We then needed to drive over a small bridge before turning left again, onto a street that paralleled the coast. The route now engraved into my mind, I silently handed the phone back to Supattra and nodded my head. One of the many things I love about Supattra is that she never questions the things she believes in, Buddhism being one good example and my skill at navigation another.

While most people would be questioning each other over the correct route to a specific destination, she remained silent as we passed over the bridge, made the hooking left turn onto the frontage road, and then passed under the freeway bridge, the Google Maps app verifying every turn. The issue with navigating to the seafood restaurant in Bangkok came at the very end of the route, after we passed over the small bridge and turned onto the street that paralleled the coast.

"It's on the left someplace around here," I commented.

"It's on the right," she countered.

I felt a sense of triumph when the Google app announced to turn left in 200 meters, and said, "I told you it was on the left," as I searched for the road leading to the restaurant.

"It's on the right," Supattra repeated in a disappointed tone, as if I had failed a basic navigation test.

"Left, beautiful," I replied, feeling my frustration building. "Didn't you hear Bitch'n Betty?"

"On the right sweetheart," she replied again, now challenging both me and the Google Maps app.

"Left," I said, slowing the truck and looking for the entrance to the restaurant.

"Pat, I'm looking at the restaurant and it's on the right."

Looking over to the right side of the road, I saw an enormous restaurant overlooking the Gulf of Thailand with a large sign advertising something in Thai. "How did you know it was on the right?"

"There was a sign back near the small bridge we drove over. It said the restaurant would be on the right, next to the water."

"Why didn't you say so?" I asked.

"I did. I told you it was on the right."

Silently rolling my eyes, I turned into the restaurant's parking area and found an empty space near the entrance. After locking the pickup truck, we strolled out over a faded woodplank pathway, crossing a marshy area—much like the restaurant we ate at the day before—and onto a gigantic deck on the water. A small plump waitress in a baggy faded floral dress under a dirty white apron met us halfway across the deck and led us to a table at its edge.

The calm waters reflected a golden hue and a briny aroma scented the slightly turbulent air around our table. Bamboo fencing surrounded the waters around the deck, separating it from the open gulf. I speculated that the bamboo was in place to keep a fresh stock of fish from swimming off into the Gulf of Thailand.

With a light gusting breeze ruffling our hair and threatening to blow the small pink paper napkins from the table, Supattra ordered us drinks, and I leaned back in my chair, stretching the long drive out of the muscles in my back. The waitress quickly delivered a beer for Supattra and a plastic bottle of water for me, pouring both into ice-laden glasses.

Looking out across the gulf, Supattra causally commented, "You seem different from when we first met," before taking a sip from her iced beer.

"People change," I causally replied, focusing on spinning my glass while trying to keep the ice cubes stationary inside. "We're always changing. The trick is to change together."

"It's something different," she said, shaking her head. "You were never really happy before, but lately you seem different."

"I was never really happy?" I laughed. "If I was never happy, why did you hang out with me?"

"You rarely smiled and always had a very serious look on your face, like you were thinking of something other than what was going on around you." She paused. "Do you ever think of the war?"

"I used to think about it quite often, but not anymore."

I still concentrated on spinning my water glass while wondering what she was trying to say or where she was trying lead our discussion.

"When did you stop thinking about it?"

"I didn't just stop thinking about it." I looked at her. "The need to think about it just sort of faded away. Do you think about growing up poor a lot?"

A solemn expression crossed on her face. "All the time."

Examining the beautiful woman across the table from me, I considered her experience of growing up in Isaan. Having been to her village numerous times, I can attest to its poverty—homes falling apart, a village plumbing system that only provides water for several hours each day, and the constant and frenzied pursuit for money to buy food and other essentials. After my first visit to her home, she cried as we drove back to the hotel that evening. When I asked why she was upset, she said that she was embarrassed to have me see her house—to see the circumstances in which she grew up. I was surprised at her reaction because. While her house was in pretty poor condition, it was clean. And while her family was not rich, they were kind and generous with what little they had.

My thoughts then shifted to my ex-wife's experience during the drive north in Iraq. During one of the few times we discussed the war, she related a story about driving home one day to see a white government type van parked out in front of our house in Oceanside, California. At the time, she was attending a memorial service at least once or twice a week for fallen marines, including some friends, and she was aware that the standard notification procedures included a visit by several marine officers and a navy chaplain. Each time a doorbell was rung on a marine's home in Oceanside during the drive north, heart rates would accelerate and breaths would shorten until it was determined that the person standing on the doorstep was not a marine officer in uniform, preparing to notify them of the death of their spouse.

When she pulled onto our street that day, seeing a white government type van sitting in front of the house, predictably she thought it was the notification team. She sat in the car, down the block from our home, for a full hour before a plumber finally came out of the neighbor's house and began to stow his tools into the white van.

The war had damaged my ex-wife, not unlike it had harmed me, forever changing her. Prior to the war, she had been a happy-go-lucky and easy going woman with a good sense of humor. Upon my return, I found an uptight and controlling stranger sharing my bed. In hindsight, she was as affected by posttraumatic stress as I, but her reaction to the illness was exactly opposite of mine. Her lack of control over the events that had unfolded around her during the war had created an urgent need to influence and dominate everything with relentless precision. Just as I had, she had seen bad things happen to good people and lost her innocence. Just as I, my ex-wife had found herself in a self-destructive downward spiral.

I can still recall a day, not too long after I had returned from Iraq, that my ex-wife looked at me and admitted that she didn't know who she was anymore. It was a shocking admission and, at that moment, I knew I had lost her forever. On the other hand, I was in complete denial and believed that the war hadn't altered my personality even the slightest. I was the same man who had deployed a year earlier and it was her problem, not mine. What was once the perfectly matched couple became the perfect mismatch. She could no more help me realize that I had posttraumatic stress and help me through my struggles than I could convince her that she struggled from the same and help her through hers.

With my thoughts returning to Supattra, I suddenly realized that posttraumatic stress was not limited to those who had witnessed wars or other life threatening events. It was like a sudden brilliant light. Posttraumatic stress had a far wider range of victims than I had ever realized prior to that moment. Supattra had lived a through an experience that had driven her into a bar in Pattaya Beach to sell her body. Having not experienced the trials of her youth and, until that moment, never understanding the daily stress she must have endured, I had had no idea. I had been so busy trying to come to terms with my own past that I had been oblivious to the struggles of the woman I had fallen in love with. The beautiful woman across from me was suffering from the same ailment as I. She had her own form of posttraumatic stress.

As this illumination cascaded across my consciousness, it suddenly dawned on me that her acceptance of a broken man had been because she had seen herself in me, and the ease at which I had fallen in love with a woman who was selling her body to make ends meet had been because I had seen the same in myself. The shared malady of posttraumatic stress had been the catalyst behind our acceptance of one another, and the love that had emerged had been because we dealt with aftermath in the same manner. Our shared posttraumatic stress experience had become the cornerstone to our relationship.

Sitting at that table across from Supattra, I quickly realized that my loss of love for one sufferer, only to fall in love with another, had simply been based on our reactions to the effects of the same ailment. My ex-wife had become controlling and intolerable to change while I strove to avoid control. My ex-wife couldn't understand my reaction to posttraumatic stress, and I couldn't understand hers. Those opposite reactions had made us incapable of helping each other. On the other hand, Supattra's experience, much like my own, had driven her to embrace the chaos of life, and its intrinsic injustice. Supattra understood firsthand the inherent unfairness of life that I witnessed over my career, and that commonality led us to understand one another, allowing us to help each other through the struggle.

The difference between us was that I had begun to heal, but clearly, she was still struggling. Sitting at our table with my water glass still in my hand, I wondered if that was because of the length of the posttraumatic stress catalyst. While I had spent a career in and out of highly stressful situations, Supattra had spent her entire youth in her own private never-ending hell. While each intense event in my career had a follow-up intermission or time in which I could relax, Supattra's was one long terrifying experience, lasting years.

"Why does it bother you?" I asked her, even though I already knew the answer. "You've found happiness."

"I think I am mad at the way I grew up and sad about the decisions I made." She sighed. "I am so sorry you found me in a bar. I am embarrassed about my past. I am also embarrassed for you."

"Why are you embarrassed for me?"

"Your friends know our past—my past."

"We don't tell them how we met. We tell them that story we made up."

"They know. It is easy to see through the story. It is easy to see that our story is not the truth."

"I could care less what they think of us or why they think we're together. I love only you and have never had second thoughts about who I should spend the rest of my life with."

"I'm mad I had to grow up in that poor village and sad about by my choices."

"You told me yesterday that Buddha placed you there to help lead you to enlightenment." I pushed my water glass aside and reached out, taking her hands into mine. "If that is true, it might not have been easy, but it was for a good thing in the end."

"Buddha placed me in a rice village in Isaan and I failed his test. I made a choice to work in a bar and damaged my chances of moving closer to enlightenment."

Watching her eyes fill with tears, I asked, "But isn't that what the entire struggle is about? No one is perfect. You made decisions that placed you in a bar and I made decisions that placed me in a war. We made those choices and then changed our lives with new decisions. During our next life, hopefully we will have learned from that experience and not make the same mistakes."

"You did not sell yourself—sell your pride."

"I did, but in a different way. I selfishly sought glory and cloaked it in the notion of patriotism. I wanted to prove I was a courageous man when I should have been happy proving that I was a good man—a good father."

"You are healing and I am not," she said, outwardly asserting for the first time that I had begun to come to terms with my past.

Realizing that our roles had been reversed and I was now professing the wisdom of Buddha, which was likely tainted by my Christian upbringing, I replied, "Neither of us will ever be completely healed until the day we reach perfect enlightenment and our candles are blown out, and we will reach that moment at the same time, together."

Releasing my hand and wiping a tear from her left eye, she giggled, "Only if you wait for me next time."

A comfortable silence followed our short conversation, and when the waitress arrived carrying our meal, we both dug in with ferocity. The meal was nearly identical to the food we had the day before, except the oysters were a fraction of the size and the southern fish soup had been replaced with Razor Back Clams fried in chilies, garlic, and basil—a delicacy that I had never enjoyed before.

After we had eaten, Supattra stood up and moved to a chair on my side of the table, smiling as she sat down next to me. Draping my arm over her shoulder, we looked out on the golden hued waters of the gulf.

After a few moments of silence, taking in the serene scene, I looked over and asked, "Are you okay?"

"Yes, and thank you for listening to me," she replied, placing her right hand on my thigh and leaning over, giving me a *hom noi* on the cheek.

"I wish I could help." I looked into her dark brown eyes, knowing from experience that the journey she was on was a private one and, as she did for me, all I could offer was my support and understanding. "I wish I could make it all go away."

"I am better than when we first met. I was always so angry when we first met."

"I never noticed," I lied, reaching over with my free hand and wiping a tear from her cheek.

"You're lying," she said, smiling at my fib. "You saw it. When we first met I would become angry over very small things. My friends told me that you were perfect for me because my anger never upset you. You just ignored it."

"I was too busy thinking about myself to believe your an-

ger was very important—and those were small moments that
you quickly recovered from."

"You weren't thinking about yourself. You were thinking
about life's struggle. I could see it, because I felt the same
way."

"Why didn't I see you were struggling, too?"

"Your heart did, but your consciousness was too busy because your struggle was fresh and mine was old."

"You knew we were suffering together?"

"We have been suffering together for many lifetimes," she
explained. "I don't know how, but I knew who you were the
first day you walked into my bar. My heart was so full of joy
that day because I knew we would be together again. I knew
you would save me even before we talked for the first time. I
didn't tell my friends but I knew, even before they told me,
you were the one I had been waiting for."

"I am sorry I didn't see your suffering."

"You saw it in your heart."

"I wish you would have given my consciousness a hint, because my heart didn't share the information."

Silence took hold of us for several minutes before she said,
"I think I am worried that you seem so happy and don't think
about your past as much. I am worried that you won't need me
anymore. I am still full of anger and still struggling. You are
almost free."

"Time is the only thing that will heal your suffering. My
struggle was different. Mine was dished out in small episodes
and punctuated in one stressful year, during which I had to
readjust my expectations. You spent your entire youth struggling with something that was a flash in the pan for me."

She laid her head on my shoulder. "Please don't ever leave
me. I don't think I could heal without you."

Kissing the top of her head, I said, "I will always be with
you," and then, smiling I added, "And I'll wait for you next
time."

CHAPTER 8

After another thirty minutes of looking out over the gulf, we silently agreed it was time to leave, paying our bill to the small plump woman in the faded floral dress and dirty white apron. By the time we climbed into the pickup truck, Supattra had already loaded her sister's address into Google app, and she showed me the map.

"Whoa, that looks like a jigsaw puzzle." I laughed. "Where does your sister live?"

"She lives west of Bangkok in an area called Thawi Watthana." she replied, looking at me with a concerned expression. "What is the problem?"

"I was being facetious." I laughed again. "The route is pretty complex. Lots of turns onto small roads in a pretty heavy urban area. I'm going to need some help on this one."

After backtracking to the highway, Bitch'n Betty took over the navigation responsibilities, Supattra repeated the instructions, and I obediently followed those directions. The route took us directly through several subdivisions west of Bangkok, down narrow streets, and through tightly knitted city centers, maneuvering through heavy rush hour traffic. Lush vegetation sprang from empty lots and any space large enough to support a root system.

As I snaked my way through heavily congested small communities just outside of Bangkok, mechanically following Supattra's instructions, my mind began drifting and I found myself thinking of my ex-wife and the demise of our marriage. It had been a shocking turn in our relationship. One day we had an incredible love that seemed is if it would last a lifetime, the next our marriage became a broken relationship that hobbled along for years and should have been put out of its misery long before a death blow finally ended our suffering.

ↄﬗↄ

Shortly after the incident at the Pentagon, my wife and I sat in our living room, discussing our future options with the Marine Corps as it was nearly time for us to rotate to a new duty station. On one hand, enjoying the relative quiet life that Washington DC and Headquarters Marine Corps had to offer, I had made a tentative deal to swap positions with another marine officer at Patuxent River Naval Air Station in southern Maryland where many of the aviation program offices were housed. On the other hand, I missed the excitement of Fleet Marine Force.

Sitting across from one another on our matching sofa and loveseat set, gold with a delicate red and blue paisley pattern, in our small North Arlington living room, the evening news as background noise, I said, "I don't know what to do and the Marine Corps is going to demand an answer. And if I don't tell them where we want to go, some guy at Headquarters Marine Corps is going make the decision for us."

Sipping on glass of wine, her big brown eyes sparkling across the room at me, with a knowing smile, my wife said, "Honey, you and I both know that you can't get a squadron command by working in Pax River, and you will always regret it if you don't go back to the fleet and try."

As a scream erupted in the back bedroom from one our children, I knew she was right and responded with a simple, "Yeah."

While a leisurely evening with my family each night was satisfying, I missed the exhilaration of flying in countries around the globe and I would always regret not trying for a squadron command. "You do realize that, based on what is going on in the world right now, I could be shipped off the minute we arrive in California, for God knows how long."

"We'll be okay," she replied in her usual easygoing, confident tone, not knowing just how wrong she would be, and, indeed, upon our arrival in California, I was immediately assigned the executive officer position in a light attack squadron and shipped off within a matter of months.

Returning from Iraq, it was not a slow building feeling that my wife and I had somehow shifted out of sync from one another. While it was to be a short reunion before I was to be redeployed overseas and the awaiting Southeast Asia cruise, within several days I realized that the woman who met me at the airport was not the same person I had left on the docks of San Diego some months before.

The adventurous, easygoing woman, who had convinced me that returning to the fleet was the next logical choice, had suddenly become incredibly controlling and lacked any tolerance to the unknown or risk, complaining about each inadvertent infraction from her rigid schedule of expectations. Small things, like taking the trash out to the curb once a week had to be completed on demand, coming home late from work as the squadron prepared for our quick redeployment overseas was met with a tsunami of pointed questions as to my tardiness, and my interactions with our children became her studied experiment as to a failing father.

She was not the only one to blame. I became critical of her questionable housekeeping. While she had never been the tidiest or most organized of people, upon my return I decided that my stay-at-home wife was lethargic when it came cleaning the house or completing even the simplest of chores. After a full day's work, I felt as if I was suddenly picking up the slack, wondering what she had done all day as I washed the prior evening's dinner dishes and pots, cleaned the children's rooms, and made our bed. It wasn't as if I had graduated from some mythical cleanliness college during my absence, spending the first month using water bottles to shower as we drove north in Iraq. I decided that it was obvious that she was not spending her days really doing anything, when in reality, nothing had changed. She had always been that way.

Several weeks into my return, having just been reprimanded for some issue concerning what I wanted for dinner while we stood in an Oceanside grocery store, she turned to me and said, "I'm sorry. I don't know who I am anymore—and I don't really like myself."

Having completed that cutthroat acquisition tour at the Pentagon before being sent off to Iraq, I knew from experience that when you lose something of value you never get it all back. At that moment, I knew the woman I had left before deploying overseas would never completely return and, eventually, a new norm would be established in our relationship—a new standard that would not benefit either of its participants.

In retrospect, I think her sudden need to control created an environment where she couldn't control anything. The harder she tried, the more influence she lost on the events around her. Her response to this loss of control was to try to manage her surroundings with even more strict precision. The results could have been anticipated by anyone standing on the sidelines. She lost even more authority over her life and blamed on the closest target she could find—me. In my post-Iraq state of mind, I revolted, silently not giving inch.

I found my position in the midst of this relationship upheaval to be easy. Having become completely numb to emotions, I handled my complaints the same way had I learned to deal with the news of fallen comrades throughout my career with the marines. While stubbornly not giving in, I filed those grievances with my wife away in a corner of my subconscious and, in her case, feigned tolerance. I compartmentalized my objections and began letting those feelings of discontent brew. The sad aspect to the entire situation was that, while I spent countless joyous hours with my children during this same period, my most vivid memories are of the difficulties of living with the angry woman who claimed to be my wife.

Returning from Southeast Asia some eight months later, I knew through correspondence what to expect. She had become comfortable in her new persona and I was prepared, thinking somehow our former affection for one another would allow me to overcome my unhappiness and understand this new woman.

After all, I was linked to her through an enormous past love and, of course, marital vows.

I was given command of an operation support airlift squadron, and we suddenly found ourselves, as a family, headed for Okinawa, Japan. What I would have expected to be a festive occasion—the thought of three years on a sunny Asian tropical island and the obvious kudos of selection for one of the Marine Corps few aviation commands—became an immediate nightmare. She had no desire to leave the States and her concerns seemed to transcend any logical argument.

While I watched her take solace in organizing the daily pre-deployment tasks, required elements of a family overseas tour, it appeared to me as if she was incapable of completing any of them without help. She seemed to be happy with coordinating but the act of executing eluded her in her distracted state. Balancing the executive officer's duties of the squadron I was currently assigned, I stepped in and completed those tasks normally performed by the wife: passports, determining what household items were to be shipped overseas and what was to be stored, and arranging for family lodging prior to our departure to name a few.

Our children were enthralled with the sunny island of Okinawa but my wife became even more distant and distracted upon our arrival. Initially, we ended up on a small base strictly used for housing American families, and she became critical of every one of our neighbors. While we sat on our deck in the evening, watching our children happily climb an enormous banyan tree in our backyard, weaving in and out of its numerous thick branches, she would describe to me each of her issues with those other families living around us. When it finally became intolerable, I offered to move off base to any house of her choosing.

I was an absolute emotional thug. She could have told me that the sky was falling and I would have calmly looked at her and told her that I would support any decision she made while, in reality, I was the least supportive person at her side. Once again, her plight became like my fallen comrades, I didn't let it sink in deep enough to allow me to feel any emotion.

A long story short, she found a beautiful house next to a large baseball field in the small Japanese village of Kitanakagusuku. With numerous balconies and porches, and natural light flowing into each room, and a large courtyard out back, the kids and I loved that house. Most afternoons we could hear the Okinawans pounding away on drums while the local team played baseball. The house was also on the edge of a large sugar cane field, and the kids and I would frequently take walks or ride bicycles along its narrow winding roads. Within the several days of our moving to the house, my middle daughter and I drove down to the local pet store and bought a rabbit for the courtyard. The naming of the rabbit became a huge event, and Captain Wooblar, a black-and-brown-striped Japanese rabbit, became an official member of the family. During the same period, my oldest daughter began taking horseback riding lessons at a stable that overlooked the Pacific Ocean. I would sit in the stands on weekends watching her ride on an immense background of sparkling dark blue water hugging a brilliant blue sky while a warm gentle breeze drifted across the stables. It was stunningly beautiful. Within a year of our arrival in Kitanakagusuku, my son would look up at me and make a perfectly pronounced request in Japanese that he had picked up from the local Okinawan boys. I remember laughing when I had to tell my five-year-old that he needed to speak English to me. It was like a breath of fresh air, living amongst the Okinawans, enjoying our unique surroundings, and learning the Japanese culture and customs.

Sadly, my wife's reaction was that I had driven her off base and she was now isolated from her friends—not to mention the rabbit was eating all her plants. My reminder, that it had been her decision to leave the comforts of the base and she had chosen the house, were lost on deaf ears. What could have been an incredible time in our lives once again became a living hell. While loving my time with my children, I began taking each and every flight that would take me away from the nightly confrontation with my wife.

Two years into the nightmare I met Supattra.

While posttraumatic stress had clearly been the primary

catalyst behind the slow and painful eradication of our marital vows, what I neglected to keep in mind was that my second wife suffered from bouts of depression throughout our marriage. Occasionally, she would go through periods during which whatever chemical change occurs in those afflicted from depression had its way with her.

During those events, I attempted to care for her as best I could. Substantiating my new emotionless thug persona, in the midst of my personal struggle, I had ceased recognizing my ex-wife's fight with depression and discontinued supporting her through those periods as I had faithfully done in the past. While I had assumed she was simply suffering from posttraumatic stress upon my return from that final Southeast Asia cruise, she had actually been struggling with an overwhelming mixture of both depression and posttraumatic stress. In retrospect, she was far less capable of overcoming the events unfolding in our household, placing the demise of our marriage squarely on my back.

ℰ ℑ ℰ ℑ

The sun had begun to drop below the horizon but still provided an overhead glow as Supattra and I traveled down a narrow two-lane road with tall shadowy bamboo foliage to one side and three-story weather-stained buildings on the other.

Suddenly Supattra looked up from the map. "I recognize this area. We are close."

"Can we turn off Bitch'n Betty?"

"Yes, yes, yes. Turn left up there." She pointed to a wide dirt path that accessed a long rectangular open field paralleling the road that was filled with and illuminated by numerous small wooden business stalls and rolling kitchens. The far side of the field was lined with three- and four-story buildings, housing more businesses on their ground floors.

The dirt turn-off was packed with parked late model cars and scooters, with hundreds of people milling around the stalls that were selling everything from food to clothes to kitchenware. More people congregated around the rolling kitchens that were advertising a wide assortment of local delicacies. A brightly lit "Seven-Eleven" sign hanging on a building just beyond the swarm of shoppers announced the convenience store location. Animated, Supattra pointed to a street-like corridor between the buildings, lined with more shops on their ground floors. I edged the pickup past the parked cars and scooters, trying hard not hit people focused on the merchandise offered in the stalls and kitchens, into the shop-lined corridor.

At the end of the block, Supattra, eager to see her sister, pointed to the right. "There, there, there."

"Where? Where? Where?" I teased her.

"Turn there, to the right again," she directed me, complete oblivious to my jest.

Turning down another intersecting side street, we found ourselves surrounded by townhouse-type buildings packed next to each other with fingerlike stains on their walls, created from the mixture of ever-present population and frequent downpours. With just enough room for the pickup to maneuver passed the parked cars along the narrow lane, Supattra rolled her window down and enthusiastically thrust the fingers of her right hand at a weathered pink home with dirty white trim. Each townhouse seemed to overflow with pots filled with colorful tropical plants blooming from windows and exploding from small courtyards. Spindly Doctor Seuss-looking trees sprouted from buckets, boxes, and any other type of containers capable of holding soil, each resident seemingly doing their part in camouflaging their stark concrete jungle.

As I came to a halt next to the pink townhouse, Supattra jumped from the truck, rushing into the home's small courtyard, which was filled with a disarray of odds and ends, and through the home's open door. Looking around, I realized that our pickup truck was blocking any other traffic attempting to travel down the narrow street and saw an open parking spot behind me. Backing up and parking the truck, I stepped from the driver's side in time to see Supattra appear from the pink townhouse carrying two small bags.

Behind her, Supattra's older sister Yii stepped from her

house, carrying two more bags. Dressed in bright green shorts, looking as if they had been purchased from a store specializing in 1950s outfits, and a white blouse with light blue piping, Yii had a much paler complexion than either of her sisters, and her hair, in the right light, looked brown. I have often speculated that Supattra's mother had a short fling with a *farang*, tainting Yii's blood with Western genes. Of course, I would never admit that to Supattra.

Sakchai, Yii's husband, was the next to step from the weathered pink townhouse, closing and locking the door behind him. Sakchai, a short, stout man, was slightly younger than his wife and had wavy dark hair, innocent brown eyes, and a perpetual smile on his face. He waved when he saw me walking toward the townhouse. I could tell he was excited about the trip north and, no doubt, the prospect of not having to ride a cramped public bus that would have surely added an additional six hours to the journey.

As I took the bags from Yii, it was apparent that she had dressed in her nicest clothes and made her best effort at makeup, not wanting to be upstaged by Supattra too much. Sadly that effort fell far short of its objective. Having lived amongst *farangs* on the island of *PhaNagan* for nearly eight years, Supattra had developed a sense of international fashion that most Thai woman envied. While I know that Yii felt no jealousy toward Supattra, I couldn't help but feel a bit sorry for the older sister.

The threesome switched from speaking Thai to Lao, or Isaan, the primary language of Northeast Thailand, leaving me completely in the dark about what was being said. As Supattra caught up on family gossip with her sister, Sakchai and I loaded the bed of the pickup and climbed into the front seats.

Looking at Supattra's sister and her husband, I thought about how their path had led them to meager jobs outside of Bangkok where they labored away six days a week for a paltry hourly pay. Like many Isaan people working in and around Bangkok, they were unable to afford childcare so their two children lived with Sakchai's mother in the city of Phetchabun situated in Northeast Thailand, where they rarely saw them.

While Supattra and I could speak of our struggle and our suffering, this man and woman personified the average Thai toiling away to survive in this developing country. Someone once told me that the average Thai believes that the worst day in their life is when they are born, and the best the day they die, hoping that their next life would be better. There are days, living in this country, that I actually believe that premise.

On the other hand, one of the things I truly love about this country and its people is that you would never guess that was the mindset of the average Thai, for they always smile when prompted and when asked, they are always looking to the future with optimism and hope.

CHAPTER 9

The Emotionless Thug ~ 11 April 2014

It was dark by the time we had loaded all of Supattra's sister and brother-in-law's luggage into the bed of the pickup. With Sakchai sitting next to me, and Supattra and her sister in the rear seat chatting about something in their native language, I put the truck in gear and maneuvered down the narrow street lined with weathered townhouses and pottery bursting with colorful floral plants, now cast into shadows.

As we pulled up to the long road with high shadowy bamboo foliage to one side and three-and four-story buildings on the other, I interrupted their conversation.

"Either we get Bitch'n Betty up and running or I need someone to tell me how to get out of here and onto the highway north."

"Sakchai can help you," Supattra replied from the backseat.

Looking over and smiling at Sakchai, I said, "But he doesn't speak English."

"But you speak Thai."

"I speak *nit noi* Thai." I laughed. "I'm not sure that'll be enough to get us out of Bangkok."

"You speak Thai," she insisted.

"No, I don't," I countered with a chuckle.

"You know how to ask which way. You know left and right. You know stop and go."

"You've nearly listed my entire Thai vocabulary." All humor was gone from my voice.

With clear frustration, she said, "Pat, you know Thai and Sakchai knows the way to Phetchabun."

Looking at him again, I asked, "Okay, Sakchai, which way? *Saai or khwaa*? Left or right?"

Blankly looking back at me, Sakchai smiled.

"Supattra, Sakchai doesn't know the way."

She spoke in brisk Isaan that sounded as if she were reprimanding her brother-in-law. He meekly mumbled a response and she then looked at me. "He didn't know you were talking to him."

"I was looking right at him."

"He didn't know."

Taking a deep breath, I looked at him again and asked, "*Bpai thaang nai?*"

"*Saai*," Supattra answered from the back seat. "Go left."

Dropping my chin onto my chest, I said, "Sakchai didn't answer again."

"I did," she said flatly.

"But Sakchai's the navigator."

"He is."

Realizing that I was not going to make any headway in this discussion and seeing a break in traffic, I stepped on the gas pedal and the truck accelerated out onto road. Looking at Sakchai again, I asked how far, "*Khaae nai?*"

From the back seat, Supattra spoke to her brother-in-law in Isaan again to which Sakchai replied, before she said, "About five kilometers."

Jokingly, I asked Supattra, "Does Sakchai speak Thai?"

To be fair to Sakchai, I know some Thai but my pronunciation is not very good. I can't count the times I've stood at a Seven Eleven counter, asking the attendants for something in their native language, and them giving me the same blank stare that Sakchai did in the truck that evening. Southeast Asian languages are incredibly difficult to speak because the same word, with a slightly distinctive tonal inflection, can mean up to four different things.

A good example is the word *suue* which, with a building inflection, means beautiful. On the other hand *suue,* with a descending inflection, denotes bad luck or ill fated. Imagine trying to tell a woman she's beautiful and mistakenly tell her she is ill-fated, all with an improper tonal inflection. Another example is that mosquito and busy, and dog and horse share the same spelling and elocution but are differentiated with a tonal variance.

Explaining to a friend that you had saddled up your dog and gone for a ride is humorous, but it exemplifies a language that is potentially dangerous for the novice. While Supattra is used to my bad pronunciation of her language, Sakchai is not.

I have no doubt that Sakchai just didn't understand what I was saying. He, in fact, was probably chuckling to himself at my confusing sentence structure and poor tonal inflections.

Supattra broke out into another reprimand in Isaan, to which Sakchai replied, before she told me in English, "He will answer you from now on."

Traveling down the road, he sat silently in the passenger seat while Supattra and her sister continued to chat. Five kilometers later the road emptied onto a six lane highway, heading west, the wrong direction.

"We're headed the wrong direction," I causally commented to whomever would listen to me.

Talking to Sakchai in Isaan once again, Supattra turned to me. "We need to find the exit that takes us to a turnaround."

"Did we make a mistake?"

"No, no, this is how we have to go," she replied. "There is no way to get on the freeway going to Bangkok from their home. You have to use the turnaround."

In the midst of our conversation, Sakchai mumbled something in Thai, and then looked at me and smiled.

Continuing to speak with Supattra, I asked, "Which side of the road do we need to be on? Which side is the turnaround?"

"Let me asked him," Supattra replied, before speaking with Sakchai. After a short discussion with her brother-in-law, she looked at me again. "You just missed the exit. He doesn't know how far the next one is."

"When did we miss it?'

"Just now. He told you to turn, but you just didn't listen."

"He told me?"

"He says he told you."

"He didn't tell me. He mumbled something in Thai but he didn't tell me."

"You need to find a turnaround. We need to go the other direction," Supattra tersely replied, before returning to her conversation with her sister in the back seat.

Having given up on my navigator, I managed to find a second turnaround some twenty kilometers down the highway and got us headed back toward Bangkok. As the lights of downtown skyscrapers began to come into view through a misty haze hanging over the city, about thirty minutes after getting turned around, we finally exited the highway heading into Bangkok and joined a mass of vehicles traveling north on an intersecting freeway.

Looking at Supattra through the rearview mirror, I asked, "Which is the best lane to be in?"

After another short conversation with her brother-in-law, she answered, "He says to get all the way over to the right."

The road was packed with bumper to bumper traffic moving like an accordion and it took me nearly ten minutes to make it across to the far lane. With a small pickup, its bed packed with seven tired and wind-ravaged people, to our left and a black sedan with three bobbing heads in the backseat in front of us, I settled into the rhythm of the traffic. We would surge ahead for two hundred meters, accelerating to forty kilometers an hour, and then screech to a halt for several seconds, before surging ahead again. Within five minutes of cycling through this process, I realized that this was going to be a long night driving to Phetchabun.

"Sweetheart," Supattra sweetly called from the backseat, "I need to *chee chong.*"

Looking at her through the rearview mirror again, I laughed, "You've got to be kidding me. We just got into the far lane."

"Sorry, but I really need to go."

"Why didn't you tell me when we first got on the highway?"

"I need to *chee chong*," she pleaded,

I looked over at Sakchai. He blankly smiled back. Realizing that all the complaints in the world would not change the fact that Supattra needed to visit the bathroom, I silently began the long process of moving back across the freeway, making it to the far lane just in time to exit onto a frontage road with several gas stations.

Supattra looked at me with a concerned expression, as I pulled the pickup into one of the gas stations. "You're not mad at me, are you?"

"No, of course not," I replied, halfheartedly smiling into the rearview mirror at her.

"You looked mad when I told you."

"I was slightly frustrated at first, but it's not worth worrying about." Steering the pickup into a parking spot, I added, "I got over it."

Reaching up and putting a hand on my shoulder from behind, Supattra apologized, "I'm sorry."

"I shouldn't have gotten frustrated. I'm sorry, too," I answered, smiling at my yawning apology.

Sitting in the driver's seat waiting for Supattra to return from the bathroom, I thought about our early dinner discussion and realized that I had begun to change. A year ago that incident would have made me angry and I would have reprimanded Supattra for not telling me earlier. Two years ago, I would have reprimanded her over and over again, and probably complained about it the next day. While I had felt a twinge of frustration when she first announced that she needed to use the restroom, it had quickly faded and had been replaced with the reality of the situation.

After a short break at the gas station outside of Bangkok, we finally headed north again. The traffic was heavy and aggressive as I moved back over to the far right lane. Once there and traveling in it for 30 minutes, I concluded that it really didn't matter which lane we were in, they were all moving at about the same speed. Each time I saw an overhead sign, I would look over at Sakchai, point to the sign above, and shrug my shoulders.

He would either nod or shake his head, indicating whether I should exit or not. To ensure that I understood what he had communicated, I would then ask Supattra about the sign and she, in turn, would ask her brother-in-law in Isaan. He would answer and Supattra would translate, giving me the answer. An obviously inefficient process. I was just happy it worked.

Four hours later, driving along a two-lane road that an aggravated crowd of drivers had turned into a four-lane, we finally headed up a steep incline leading to the Khorat Plateau. With only inches of clearance between our truck and the vehicles surrounding us, I realized just how tired I had become from the hours of driving in the tight horde of stop and go cars, trucks, buses, and giants. Looking through the rearview mirror, I could see that Supattra and her sister were asleep with their heads resting against the doors.

Glancing over at Sakchai, he looked back and blankly smiled. Halfway up the incline, I squeezed between two slow-moving buses and then scooted around a large lumbering giant. Suddenly, the freeway was clear of traffic.

Accelerating to nearly 140 kph, and while not expecting an answer, I asked Sakchai, "What happened?"

He smiled at me.

Stirring in the backseat, likely feeling the truck accelerate, Supattra groggily asked, "What happened? Where's all the traffic?"

Sakchai said something to Supattra and she translated, saying, "He says it will be okay now. There won't be any more traffic."

Puzzled by the sudden disappearance of all the car and trucks, I asked, "Where did they all go?"

"He says it is always this way," Supattra answered. "He says that big giants always break up the traffic going up this hill. They were the reason we were going so slow and now we are ahead of them."

"I guess that makes sense," I yawned, not really understanding at all. "I'm feeling a bit punchy."

"What's punchy?"

"I've been driving for a long time," I replied with another yawn. "And I'm not thinking as clearly as I normally do."

Looking at me with a concerned expression, she asked,

"Are you tired? Do you need me to drive?"

I was exhausted but took a moment to think about the offer, looking at her through the rearview mirror. Realizing that I would recognize the signs of falling asleep at the wheel and she would not, never having been in that situation, I decided to let her sleep. After all, if needed, I could pull over to the side of the road and take a short nap.

Reluctantly I replied, "Not yet, I'll let you know when I need you to drive."

The night was cloaked in darkness and I knew I was missing some spectacular scenery as we sped down a freeway that cut through the rolling hills atop the plateau. As my passengers nodded back to sleep, my thoughts wandered to one my missions during the drive north in Iraq, an event that would confirm my title as "emotionless thug."

❦❦❦

Several days into the drive north, we were directed to land at one of the regimental combat team headquarters for a mission brief, as the marines worked their way through one of the various desert cities on the road to Baghdad. My wingman, a talented young captain, had been badgering me for days, requesting an opportunity to lead our section helicopters into combat. I had reluctantly agreed to let him take the first mission of the day during the morning brief.

Just after the direct aviation support center had transmitted the request for us to land at the headquarters, I heard them contact a section of CH-46 helicopters or troop transports to do the same, telling me we were going to be tasked to provide escort support for either an insertion or extraction mission. Landing in a sea of short brown scrubby plants that populated the desert around the headquarters, south of a city the marines were trying to get through, we shut our two aircraft down and climbed out. With multiple rivulets of smoke rising from the center of the city in the distance and the distinct sound of artillery being fired followed by muted thumps as their shells impacted, we could tell there was a ferocious fight going on. The two CH-46s landed behind our aircraft, creating an enormous cloud of dust as I strode toward a cluster of green canvas tents that made up the headquarters.

Jogging up to my side, my wingman asked, "I get this mission, right? I get to lead?"

"You get it," I hesitatingly replied, concerned that the upcoming mission would occur in the midst of the intense battle we were listening to.

Walking into the headquarters operation center, I found a corner in the musty tent and watched my wingman team up with the CH-46 section leader, another young captain. They shook hands and began talking to one another, likely asking each other if either knew what was in store. Several minutes later, a major called the two section leaders over to a large map on the far side of the tent. Following the captains, I began taking in the surroundings—an enormous map mounted on an equally large wooden easel, six dark-green folding tables topped with color-coordinated radios emitting static and an occasional request by one ground unit or another, and seven desert-camouflage-clad clerks scurrying around in an attempt to keep the standard battle chaos under control. Each salvo from the nearby artillery would shake walls of the tent, raising a thin sheen of dust.

The two young captains were obviously excited about the upcoming mission, trying to keep their giddiness under wraps and appear professional. As we stepped up to the map of the city—filled with red sticky notes at its center, indicating enemy positions, surrounded by green sticky notes on the outskirts, indicating marine positions—I could sense their anxiety begin to grow. The marines certainly hadn't established control over this city, as they were still fighting on its edges.

While the two captains nodded in unison as the major began describing the mission as a troop extract, specifically a medical evacuation, I closely examined the map, noticing one lone green sticky note in the middle of the red cluster. I could have anticipated what happened when the major pointed to that single green sticky note. The two captains simultaneously looked over their shoulders at me standing behind them, to one side of the tent. There was no doubt that these two young marine officers were talented pilots and would go far in the Marine Corps, but even they immediately recognized that this mission was far more difficult than anything they had ever trained for or executed in their relatively short careers. Also knowing that if I had not been at their side, these two well-trained captains would have put their doubts aside and come up with a plan to execute the mission requested by the major, I momentarily pondered what to do.

While they had just begun a career that would require them, from time to time, to make difficult life-and-death decisions, I was a lieutenant colonel who had experienced conflicts around the globe and had been in complex positions similar to this numerous times throughout my career.

Not giving them time or forcing them to ask for help, I stepped up. "I think I'll lead this mission."

Huddling the captains around the map like a quarterback preparing his team for the next play, with the major looking over our shoulders, I quickly came up with a plan. Outlining a path to get into the city, I pointed out a location where the CH-46s would hold until our gunships had established a presences overhead the landing zone and then explained a communications plan to pass word back and forth between the two sections of aircraft.

The ability to create a quick plan to penetrate a threatening situation had not come without practice. I had seen good plans fail and bad plans succeed over the years, and taken each one of those experiences, like every other career marine, and stored them away for days like this one. The trick was to keep it simple, a template of plan that would allow flexibility for the unknown.

Seeing concern in the major's expression as he realized just how difficult of a task he had presented, or maybe he'd cloaked his concern in a veil of professionalism during the brief, I did my best to exude confidence in my plan to the two young pilots standing next to me. Damn Walter Bradford Cannon and his theory of sympathetic nervous system priming an animal for fighting or fleeing. Our adrenal glands could produce all the hormonal cascades they wanted, but we were there to fight.

Giving them each a pat on the back as we sauntered back to the aircraft, I asked if they were sure they understood their part in the mission, each responding with confident a "Yes, sir."

Taking off from the headquarters as a division of four helicopters, we headed west before cutting northeast under the gun line of the firing artillery, flying beneath their overhead arcing rounds. Dropping off the two CH-46s at a bend in the Euphrates River east of our destination, my wingman and I flew over the marine units on the parameter into the city while my co-pilot attempted to contact the unit that had been designated by that lone green sticky note on the map in the regimental combat team headquarters. Circling over a small cluster of buildings on the outskirts of the city, my co-pilot tried time and time again to contact the surrounded unit.

After five minutes of my co-pilot calling over the frequency we had been given for the stranded unit, I said, "Let's go. Let's see if we can find them."

Threatening to knock down television antennas and break windows, we flew across the tops of the buildings, headed for the center of the city. Having studied the map, I knew we were looking for a fairly large bridge that passed over the Euphrates River near the center of the city. With my wingman following in trace, we careened across the building tops and dipped down into wide streets to mask our approach, before finding the bridge and the unit with the wounded marines. Establishing an overhead racetrack pattern, flying 180 degrees out from one another, our door gunners began to carefully target Iraqi soldiers that were shooting up at our overhead helicopters. My co-pilot was finally able to contact the marines below and they relayed where the wounded were located. Flying the helicopter and scanning the surroundings, I immediately realized that the CH-46s had a tough job ahead of them. The wounded marines were located on a wide street outside of the area currently protected on the ground. They would have to land outside the secure parameter.

Shifting our racetrack pattern over the intended landing zone of the CH-46, I knew that there were dozens of Iraqi soldiers hidden amongst the four- and five-story buildings competing to take down our helicopters. With our mini-gun spitting out 3,000 rounds a minute on one side and our fifty caliber machine gun clattering out 700 to 800 rounds a minute on the other, the noise was deafening as the aroma of spent gunpowder swirled through the cockpit.

With the aircraft shuddering from muffled explosions below, shivering from the hundreds of rounds bursting from our door guns, and bouncing in cadence with overhead turning main rotor blades, I directed my co-pilot to call in the CH-46s, but explained I only wanted one. Two more aircraft in the small space we were working would be too much, threatening a midair collision. Several minutes later the lone CH-46 arrived and my co-pilot directed them to land on the street below our overhead track.

While any sane man would have questioned landing in the turmoil west of the marines' secure position in the city, witnessing the two gunships overhead giving and taking fire from the ground, the captain commanding the CH-46 simply replied in a flat, "WilCo," likely realizing he was already dead and there was no reason to draw his death out all the way to Baghdad.

Landing nose into the battle, the CH-46 sat on street in the midst of the fierce firefight, patiently waiting for the wounded Marines to be loaded onboard. With their two fifty caliber machine guns joining the melee, the surrounding windows on the buildings shattered and dust erupted from the brick walls with a bit more intensity. Glancing down at the CH-46 sitting on the road below, I realized that it was one of the bravest acts I had ever witnessed over a career of fighting in every armpit around the world, only rivaled by an event that had happened earlier during the drive north as a convoy of marines stopped in the midst of an equally fierce firefight to pick up dead comrades along a street that would later be coined as Ambush Alley.

Driving down the highway atop the Khorat Plateau, darkness shimmering at its edges, I pondered my emotions as we had circled overhead the CH-46. While we knew our enemy, hidden amongst the buildings below, had but one desire— shoot down any one of the helicopters attempting to rescue the wounded marines, I had felt nothing. Completely devoid of emotion, no sentiment of fear or exhilaration of invulnerability, my only thought outside of trying to protect the CH-46 below was to impassively wonder how many innocent civilians we were inadvertently killing as our door guns blazed away, into the tight web of buildings surrounding the idling CH-46, targeting suspecting pockets of resistance. Watching the shadowy tropical trees on the side of the road pass by the windows of the pickup, as I sped down the highway, I knew it had taken years for me to realize that the numbness I had felt that day had been the result of a professionally cultured shroud designed to mask those regrets. That veil hiding my emotions would eventually falter, forcing me to face every one of my misgivings.

CHAPTER 10

The Three Reeds ~ 11 April 2014

After two hours of driving along the well-maintained four-lane freeway in light traffic, we finally pulled into Phetchabun, a city situated in the foothills near the Laos border.

Everyone seemed to wake as we arrived and the threesome began conversing in Isaan again. Sakchai, with Supattra acting as translator, directed me to a narrow city street, where we parked across from a Seven-Eleven.

Three brown-uniformed policemen sat on the steps in front of the convenience store, eyeing us suspiciously as we stepped from the pickup truck and crossed the street.

Ignoring the police, Sakchai led us to a small parking lot filled with four open kitchens next to the Seven-Eleven.

Surrounded by a surprising number of customers for that time of the morning, the kitchens had bright spotlights mounted on their roofs to illuminate the area, casting shadows across the pavement, and under the tables and chairs.

Sitting down at a wobbly red metal table, on an equally wobbly white plastic chair, I looked at Supattra. "Is this place always open?"

"It opens at eight in the evening and closes around three or four in the morning," she answered.

"Eight o'clock at night seems pretty late to be opening their doors," I remarked, examining the two casually-dressed women and one man in an apron standing near the kitchen we had chosen.

"This is a second job for the people who work here. Many

of the day jobs in Isaan are low-paying and these people are lucky enough to have a second each night."

"Each night?"

"Probably," Supattra replied, as if it wasn't a big deal. "They have a second job and more money. It's worth working every day to them."

Arching my eyebrows in disbelief, I asked, "To work every night of the week?"

"Yes, it is a small thing when it gives them enough money to not worry as much."

"Not to worry as much? What do you mean?"

"They are still poor," she said. "They are just not as poor as they would be if they did not have this job."

One of the casually-dressed women delivered a laminated menu with curling edges to the table, and Supattra and her sister chitchatted, deciding what to order. Pulling a pack of cigarettes from his pocket, Sakchai smiled and held them out to me.

Smiling back, I took a cigarette and handed the pack back. Sitting at the table, I lit up my cigarette, taking in a lungful of smoke while watching the two sisters discuss our early morning meal. Sakchai sat next to me, smoking and smiling.

Looking over, Supattra asked, "What do you want to drink?"

"*Biia Leo, khrap,*" I said, ordering a Leo beer in Thai.

"You are now speaking Thai and claimed you couldn't earlier?"

"*Biia Leo, khrap,*" I repeated, winking at Supattra while hoping I had pronounced my request correctly.

Giving up on making a point about my ability to speak Thai, she asked, "You're now drinking beer?"

"I deserve a few after that drive," I replied, chuckling and yawning simultaneously.

Finishing the first round of beers and nibbling at a plate of *Som Tam* or Spicy Papaya Salad, Sakchai asked Supattra a question in Isaan. I knew it was a question by the expression on her face and her nodding acknowledgement as to whether she understood his inquiry.

Turning to me, Supattra said, "Sakchai wants to know if you were afraid during your war."

While Thailand maintains an army, navy, air force, and, even marine corps—and those services participate in security operations along their own borders—for the most part, real wars are something viewed on the nightly news and the ramifications of such events are unknown to greater population of the country. So presented with his question, I pondered the best way to tell this man—who probably considered combat a glorious affair with the only consequence being the celebrated issuance of medals for bravery after the dust and smoke had cleared from the battleground—the dirty truth.

After a moment, I replied, "No," not really knowing how to explain everything spinning through my mind at that moment.

"Never?" Even Supattra was taken aback by my response. "You were never afraid?"

"No," I repeated, taking a long swig of beer from the bottle even though an iced version was sitting next to my hand in a glass.

After translating to Sakchai, she turned to me again and asked, "Why weren't you afraid."

Watching Sakchai only nod when my answer had been translated, I knew this question was coming from Supattra not her brother-in-law, and shrugging my shoulders, I replied, "I thought I was already dead."

Silent for a moment, she then asked, "If you were not dead, why did you think you were dead?"

Looking back Supattra, I knew she understood my answer and there was no translation issue, so it must have been a legitimate question about the human psyche, and I replied, "Fighting in a war, to do your job correctly, you must believe that you are already dead. You can't think that there is anything you can to do survive. If I had placed my survival over getting the job done, I would have made bad decisions. I wouldn't have been able to do the things necessary to win the fight."

Canting her head to one side, she asked, "Didn't that make you feel sad?"

"No. I'm not sure I felt any emotion during the drive north, all of them were numbed by my situation."

Reaching across the table, Supattra took my hand, and then turned to Sakchai, translating what I had just explained. He, in turn, looked at me with a sorrowful expression.

"Look," I said, sniggering at their moment of sympathetic compassion as I felt a wave of frustration course through my body, "I'm not looking for sympathy. That is just the way it is. War is not about going home to parades or medals for bravery. It's not about survival either. It's really easy. It's simply about doing the job you've been tasked with and supporting those fighting by your side."

Shaking my head, I focused on a plate of food that had just be put in front of me by one of the casually-dressed women, ignoring Supattra's and Sakchai's continued solemn looks of empathy. I have found it impossible to discuss my innermost feelings about the war with people who have never experienced the chaos of combat for two reasons. First, each time I make the mistake of opening up and trying to describe my experience, I become aggravated because I get the impression from those listening that I am trying to solicit sympathy. Second, I have come to realize that those untainted by the experience of combat can never truly understand the needed mindset or the necessity of numbing one's emotions to the turmoil unfolding around them. It inevitably becomes a lesson in beating my head against a wall of misunderstanding. Over the years I have found that I share less and less of my experiences for those two reasons.

Watching me react to her sympathy, Supattra asked, "You supported those around you?"

"Absolutely," I muttered, feeling my frustration beginning to wane.

"And they supported you?"

"Of course," I replied, feeling my former relaxed state take hold and the knot in my stomach loosening.

"You seem upset by something Sakchai and I asked—or something we did," Supattra said. "But we are as much a part of your path as those who fought by your side during your war. Life is not an independent struggle. Everything we do along the path is dependent on many things. During your war you were dependent on the people around you, as much as they were dependent upon you."

"My squadron, my wingman," I acknowledged. "My aircrew."

"Yes, you were dependent on much more, too. Life, our path, is much like your war. The decisions the men above you made, the efforts of those people giving you petrol, food, and the actions of those who were with you when you fought, all supported you in your struggle."

"I get it."

"Your path has brought you to this small parking lot with four small kitchens and poor Isaan people serving you. It has placed Sakchai and myself next to you, presenting our questions," she continued. "We and our curiosity about your past are no less important as those who served next to you in your war."

Nodding my head, I repeated my earlier remark. "I get it. I am sorry."

"We describe this dependence as the three reeds," she continued to explain, ignoring my admission. "Like three reeds holding each other up, everything is dependent, nothing is independent. If you take one away, the rest fall down."

"Like in my war, in the struggle to heal from our past, you and I will stand by each other's side," I said, showing that I understood what she was trying to explain. "Even Sakchai will have a place in that process."

"Yes," Supattra replied, smiling at me.

Two cigarettes; three beers; and a meal of spicy fried pork, chilies, and garlic later, we were ready for the last leg of the day's journey to Sakchai's childhood home. With Supattra now driving, Sakchai directed her down a series of narrow streets and onto a dirt road that led us out of the city.

It is interesting to note that people from Isaan will identify the closest city to their village as their hometown to strangers. I imagine this is because there are so many small rice-farming communities dotting the Khorat Plateau that naming an individual village would not tell anyone anything. By identifying the closest city, they are able to distinguish the region on the plateau from which they hail, and I quickly surmised that Sakchai really wasn't from Phetchabun, but some outlying village.

Once again, the scenery was blanketed by night and I couldn't see the countryside around the road as Sakchai directed us to his home. Eventually, we arrived in a small village, and Sakchai told Supattra to turn down a side road. Talking to Supattra in Isaan, he guided her to a two-story home made of concrete and faded wood, with a short unpainted cinderblock wall separating it from the street.

Jumping from the backseat, Sakchai jogged over to a large piece of bent and rusted corrugated metal that was lying across an opening in the concrete wall and pulled it aside. An older woman in a baggy floral dress stepped from the house, and two girls in colorful pajamas raced around her and up to Sakchai, hugging him. Supattra's sister leapt from the backseat, and jogged over to the two young girls, joining the family reunion.

Looking over to me, Supattra asked, "Pat, can you drive the truck up next to the house?"

Mesmerized by the family reunion, I offhandedly remarked, "It looks easier than the ferry."

"Pat, please," Supattra appealed. "I am too tired."

Stepping from the truck, I walked around the hood and opened the driver's side door for Supattra. She looked at me with red-rimmed eyes and then dropped her head on my shoulder, expressing how tired she was. I helped her from the driver's seat, climbed in, and pulled the truck through the opening, all the while watching Sakchai and Yii's reunion with their children out of the corner of my eye.

Struck by the family scene being played out next to Sakchai's childhood home, I couldn't help but think of and miss my children, and a mixture of guilt and shame washed over me. It had become a common emotion for me since moving to this country, provoked each time I witnessed parents accompanied by their children in a playful or happy setting. Over the years, I had learned to push sentiment to the back of my mind and focus on something else, and I immediately began searching for some other object to captivate my thoughts.

As I stepped from the pickup, I noticed several large piles of empty beer bottles, mixed with an assortment of trash, stacked up next to the cinderblock wall, with more debris scattered across the ground between. I wasn't surprised at the mess. Having lived in this country for several years I could attest to the immaculate hygiene of the Thais. Most Thais shower two and three times a day and are very fastidious about the cleanliness of their attire. On the other hand, the cleanliness of their homes, specifically the areas outside, is less than you would expect, based on their personal hygiene. Once again, I attributed this surprising contradiction to their religion. To the typical Thai, that empty beer bottle has as much right to that piece of ground as that plant or tree, and in the long run it's not a thing to spend too much time concerning oneself over. After all, just as the tree or plant, that bottle or piece of trash would eventually disintegrate, decomposing and returning to the earth, even though there was an exponential difference.

We sat down on a large wooden platform that resembled an oversized table with short legs in front of Sakchai's childhood home. It was a common piece of furniture in Thailand that was usually situated in front of the house and designed for eating and entertaining. Visitors and hosts sit cross-legged on top and share food that is placed in the center. While I have never asked, I assume the elevated nature of the entertaining platform is designed to keep bugs and small reptiles from sharing a celebration or meal.

After Supattra and I were introduced to Sakchai's mother, she disappeared into the house, and quickly returned with a plate of fried bugs, setting them in the center of the platform. While everyone else sat cross-legged on the platform, nibbling at the crispy treat, I sat with my feet dangling over the edge. This was more a function of my flexibility, or lack thereof, than my disrespect for Southeast Asian customs.

Fortunately, having just eaten at the kitchen near Seven-Eleven, I had a reason to turn down the centrally-located snack. Now, I am not opposed to eating bugs and, on occasion, I have tried various types. However, I can't say I have ever craved fried bugs in any form and I didn't feel the least bit hungry, looking at the heaping pile of insects that night.

The two young girls leaned against their parents, eyeing me and whispering secrets to one and other, while slipping bugs into their mouths. There are a lot *farang* tourists in Thailand at any given time, but rarely do they make arrangements to visit poor farming villages, reasonably opting for elephant farms, temples, and waterfalls. So, while these two girls had seen *farangs* on television and maybe one or two local expats while visiting Phetchabun for shopping, they had seldom been within arm's reach of a fair-skinned foreigner. With my blue eyes and brown hair, I became the center of their attention and, by the time the bugs had been consumed and it was time for bed, they had situated themselves on either side of me, examining every detail.

After the girls that been put to bed, Sakchai led us into the house, pointing out a large mat on the floor with a standing fan pointed directly down on it, indicating that was where Supattra and I were to sleep.

Turning to Sakchai, I asked, "*Haawng naam?*"

Politely pointing to the rear of the house, he replied, "*Tee nan.*"

"The bathroom is back there," Supattra said, clarifying her brother-in-law's response.

"He actually speaks Thai." I chuckled, as I began walking toward the rear of the house. Declaring over my shoulder, I said, "For the first time, we communicated and didn't need a translator."

"Now that you and Sakchai have learned to talk, next time I won't help," Supattra replied sarcastically.

The back door led to the kitchen, outfitted with a single counter and gas burner opened to the outside elements. Glancing into a second door leading through a haphazardly built cinderblock wall, I found the bathroom, or *haawng naam*. The unpainted cinderblock and concrete room was obviously an addition to the building and constructed at minimal cost. To one side of the room was a large water-filled, open concrete tank, resembling a square bathtub for storage with a plastic bowl floating on its surface. It was a simple system that did not offer hot water, the plastic bowl used for pouring water over oneself in lieu of a shower. The floor was slightly canted, allowing for spillage to run to one side of the room and out an opening the size of a mouse hole, into the backyard.

Next to the large tank was a Thai style toilet positioned on a step, with a bucket and ladle for cleaning oneself.

Laying in the dark on the floor mat that night, I reached over and took Supattra's hand, remarking, "I have always been amazed, and a little jealous, of how important family is to the Thais. Don't get me wrong, family is important in America, but not nearly to level in Thailand. When our children graduate from high school, they're expected to leave the house. When they start working, all financial ties are cut. And when our parents get old, we send them off to an old folks' home. It's different in Thailand. It's not unusual for children to live in their parents' home after graduating—in fact, it's not even unusual for them to live with one of their parents after they get married. Financial ties are never cut. When young Thais begin working, they support whoever is in need, parents, siblings, and even extended family. And I've never seen an old folks' home in this country. It's traditional in Thailand for the parents, when they get too old to take care of themselves, to move into their children's homes. I look at Sakchai and your sister. They live a hard life but the difficulties of that life are absorbed by the closeness of their family—of your family."

"This is another example of the three reeds. Life is not an independent struggle," Supattra whispered, squeezing my hand. "You, me, our friends, and our families support each other while we travel our path. Like I told you earlier, life is like three reeds holding each other up. If you take one away, they all fall down."

Looking at the stars through a window behind my head on the wall, I absently asked, "And what does each reed represent?"

"Anything and everything. They could be you, me, and

family. It could be our work, our neighbors, and our friends—or even a mix of those things: our work, our neighbors, and our love. The point is that everything is dependent and nothing is independent. Every decision we make affects the strength of those reeds. You knew this truth before I explained it to you at the restaurant in Phetchabun. I heard you talk about this to your friend last year—but in *farang* talk."

"What friend?"

"The man that came to our home who was dying—the American policeman. You talked to him for many hours about his life and about death before he went back to America."

"He was a former state trooper—I remember," I whispered. "He came to Chaloklum on vacation. A week into his visit, he came to me very yellow and feeling very badly. I got him to a hospital on Samui."

"You helped him in many ways," Supattra replied. "You helped him in the physical world but you also helped his spiritual world, too."

"He ended up dying a couple of months after he got back to the states. I'm not sure I qualified as the best death counselor," I mumbled in the darkness. "It's not like I've made great decisions in my life or that my life is the best example."

"The important part is that you have recognized your mistakes," she replied. "After he visited the hospital and found out he was dying, I listened to you talk with him the day before he returned to America. I was sitting on the patio while you two talked on the deck, upstairs. You explained to him how life is a cycle and how our end is as important as our beginning."

"Dying is a part of living," I added. "I always tell my kids that when someone they know has died."

"Yes, and you told him that on his last day here," she continued. "And you told him about the reeds, but in a *farang* way. You told him about how we don't go through life alone and everything around us is important while on the path. You explained how important it was for him to talk with his family in this life before moving on to the next."

"He hadn't talked with his children in years," I said, recalling the man's situation. "I think he was afraid of contacting them. He was embarrassed about his past and the decisions he had made."

"His decisions had become part of the three reeds," she clarified, "even though he had become lost. You explained how his life, regardless of his choices, had been important to the reeds of those around him in ways that he would never know or understand."

Looking at her eyes sparkling in the darkness, I asked, "So where did I learn all that? When did I learn about the three reeds?"

"You saw it while you traveled the path," she quietly replied. "You learned to understand in the last few years."

Lying in the darkness, searching for that necessary tranquil state to doze off while listening to Supattra's breathing slowly change to the rhythmic status of someone deep in sleep, I tried to clear my mind of all the thoughts swirling through my head—wars, regrets, and wondering if I had brought a razor along in order to shave in the morning. Once again, like a translucent spirit, my first wife floated across the room. With her thin blonde hair curling down across her cheeks, she appeared to be wagging a finger at me, as if I was a misbehaving child. Waiting for another ghostly message, I was surprised when it never came. In my semi-comatose state, I found her silence incomprehensible. She had always been able to articulate my failings with a finesse never again replicated by anyone else in my life.

CHAPTER 11

The Christian Buddhist ~ 12 April 2014

Cracking my eyes open, I instinctively blinked at the bright light pouring through the window on the wall just above my head. I could feel the fan, blowing a cool breeze down on me, and hear and smell someone cooking spicy food in the kitchen to the rear of the house, knowing breakfast was going to be a fiery meal, due to the slight burning sensation in my sinuses. Looking over to my right, I saw Supattra leaning against her elbow silently studying me.

"Good morning, beautiful," I mumbled, trying to vanquish the last of my sleepiness.

Ignoring my greeting, she calmly asked, "Did religion help you during your war?"

Mustering my slumbering alertness, I rolled over onto my side so we were face to face. "What?"

"Did religion help you during your war?" she asked again, not in an accusatory tone but as if seeking a vital amplification.

"Why are you asking all these questions about my past lately?"

"You've never talked about your war before," she replied, reaching out and putting her golden hand on my cheek. "When I asked you about Buddhism in Surratthani you started talking about it, and, on the drive to Bangkok, you told me about the airplane that flew into the building where you worked. At lunch yesterday you talked about it and then last night you explained even more."

"You've never asked about it before," I said. "Why now?"

"You've never talked about it. And in two days you've told me more about your war than you have in eight years."

"You never asked me about it before."

"Did religion help you when you during your war?" she asked for the third time

Giving in to her persistence, I sighed and asked, "Why do you ask?"

"In Surratthani, you said that, during your war, you needed to believe in something and you began saying a prayer every day before you flew. You told me that you still weren't sure whether there was a God, but you did it anyway. I just want to know if you think believing in your God during your war, even just a little bit, helped?"

Silently I pondered her query, a question I had never considered before. Had religion or God helped me during the drive north? I had instinctively turned to God when confronted with the chaos, but had that dubious and tentative belief helped me?

Looking into her eyes, I answered, "During the drive north, I was witnessing bad things happen to good people, fueling my doubts about the existence of God. But even with that growing reluctance, I still turned to God because I needed to believe there was something or some plan that would make sense of the turmoil around me."

"But did it help you," she said for the fourth time, "get through your war?"

Running my fingers through her thick black hair, I replied, "My prayers were like smoking a cigarette, only giving me a few minutes of comfort. My hesitant belief in God fell flat each time a firefight began. God or no God, the chaos returned. The only way I was able to continue was by believing the dice had already been rolled and I was already dead. But even given that, I would have to say, yes. I needed something stable to grasp onto and the religion I had learned as a child was only thing available. But that religion, my trust in that source of stability, was cautious at best."

"Maybe it didn't help very much, because you didn't really believe?"

"That could be true. It could very well have helped those who had a stronger faith more, but you'd have to ask them, not me."

"What about now? Do you believe in your God now and has that helped heal you?"

"I believe in a higher power or overriding plan, but I also believe the old adage that 'God helps those that help them-selves.'"

"I don't understand," she said, looking at me quizzically. "Is your religion helping you feel better about what happened during your war now?"

"My religion?" Laughingly, I replied, "My eye for an eye God?"

"What do you mean?"

"That's a lesson in the Christian Old Testament Bible."

"Buddhism has a saying, 'Just as I am so are they, just as they are so am I,'" she replied. "It means you should not kill or cause others to kill."

Jokingly, I said, "I think the Christian version is a little more about vengeance." Then I added, "We have a similar phrase, 'Do unto others as you would have them do unto you,' or something like that. It means basically the same thing."

"So religion has not helped you heal?"

"I didn't say that," I said softly, "and I'm being a bit cyni-cal. I was raised in the Christian church and it will always be a part of who I am throughout the years. I have used religion as a cane, supporting me whenever I have found myself strug-gling. Its teachings, those lessons I learned, during the many hours of Sunday school I attended, have helped support me during difficult times, but like someone who needs to use a cane, it still hurts to walk. It doesn't fix the source of the ail-ment. Fixing the source of the problem is something I've had to figure out for myself. Why do you ask?"

"I believe in Buddhism and I think it has helped me through my hard times, but you are Christian and without the help of your religion you seem to have healed from your past more than me."

Leaning into Supattra, I kissed her on the forehead. "We'll

never be totally healed from our past. Our experiences are as much part of us as our hands or feet. The difference between your experience and mine is bigger than religion. My problems were created in an entirely different environment than yours. What we share is that our pain will diminish with time and our only solace is knowing that we have someone standing by our side while it does, and that should be enough."

Kissing me on the lips, Supattra said, "I love you, Pat."

Making my way to the bathroom, I stripped, hanging my clothes and a towel up on three rusted nails mounted to the back of its flimsy wooden door. Timidly, I walked barefooted across the rough, cool concrete floor to the open square storage tank and examined its shimmering contents. It wasn't crystal clear water but that pumped from an open well, full of particulates and thin bits of floating greenish scum. I poured a plastic bowl of water from the square tank over my head, its coldness sending a shockwave through my limbs. Taking two quick and deep repetitive breaths, I repeated the process four more times to ensure every square inch of my body was wet. Dropping the bowl back into the tank, with the hairs on my body standing rigid, I found a piece of soap and lathered myself. A dousing with more cold water from the tank to rinse the soap from my body and I had successfully completed an Isaan shower.

When I stepped outside that morning, it was cool and the sky was bright blue and clear of clouds. Standing in front of Sakchai's childhood home, next to the wooden platform, I took in the scenery—wide, emerald green tropical plants with bright red and yellow flowers, spindly whitish-barked bushes with more flowering buds, and towering trees with fan and mop-like tops, all surrounded by rolling, jungle-laden hills. A wide range of homes in various stages of repair, indicating differing levels of wealth, lined the road.

Directly across the dirt street stood a beautiful house with fresh paint and wood trimmed windows with a brand new black Isuzu truck in its driveway. Next door was a crumbling, unpainted cinderblock home with a rusted corrugated metal roof. And a home that matched the age and disrepair of Sakchai's stood on the other side. Thick poles ran down one side of the road that held the wires delivering electricity to the homes, looking as if someone was drying twisted black spaghetti overhead. Hens wandered down the road with lines of chicks instinctively following. Brown roosters with bright red caps and jowls cackled and crowed in several yards. Multicolored cats scurried between narrow openings, and dogs, searching out fallen morsels of food, wandered between the homes. As if a scene from Noah's Ark, none of the different species seemed to care that the others were sharing the same space.

Congregating around the wood platform in front of the house, we sat down in anticipation of our pre-drive breakfast. Sakchai's mother appeared in the doorway, carrying two large bowls of food, with his oldest girl directly behind, holding a cylindrical woven-reed basket that I knew held sticky rice. Having observed the oldest daughter the evening before and now that morning, I was struck with her similarity with my middle daughter. Both had darting intelligent eyes as they silently studied the events being played out around them. Once again that familiar guilty feeling that I had failed my children began to wash over me and I turned my attention elsewhere.

Sticky rice, the main product of the northeast Thailand rice farms, is literally sticky and slightly chewy. During my first experience with the fare, I had assumed this version of rice was popular in Isaan because its al dente properties allowed it to swell up in the stomach, filling up the user at low cost. I later realized that it was popular simply because it could be grown in the harsh and seasonally wet fields of the northeast while the more globally popular jasmine rice could not.

The first bowl that Sakchai's mother laid at the center of the table was filled with more fired bugs. When I saw her set down a bowl of what appeared to be light chicken broth filled with bones and other unusual parts next to the bugs, I felt a wave of relief. Pulling out a small clump of sticky rice from the woven basket with my hand, I dipped it into the chicken broth, soaking up the liquid, before tossing into my mouth. Sakchai's mother said something in Isaan to Supattra. She, in turn, glanced at me before replying. His mother then disappeared into the house, reappearing a few minutes later with a lone small tan plastic bowl and an aluminum spoon, placing them in front of me.

"I can eat like you guys," I proclaimed, looking at Supattra.

"You are *farang*," she said. "They just want to make you feel comfortable."

The fact of the matter is that Isaan people will eat many of their meals simply with their hands, sharing the same platters of food and mixing the contents with a pinch of sticky rice and fresh uncooked Chinese cabbage, not to mention the ever-present spicy sauce. While I may have difficulty sitting for long periods in the traditional cross-legged position, I enjoy eating in their customary fashion. On the other hand, I always utilized special utensils when provided because I know it makes my host or hostess feel as if they have met their guest's needs. So, using my newly supplied spoon, I dipped into the chicken broth and began ladling some into the small plastic bowl. On the third ladle I managed to find and scoop out a chicken head, and without a second thought I dropped it into my bowl. Seven years ago, I would have found the sight of a chicken head floating in my soup as somewhat repulsive but, having consumed numerous things most Westerners would consider distasteful, I didn't even flinch. I ate my breakfast, eating bits of chicken mixed with sticky rice, while simply avoiding the face looking up at me.

After breakfast, Sakchai guided me over to several over-sized square crib-like structures wrapped in a cheesecloth fabric. Communicating with his hands and arms, he explained what they were by pointing to the now empty plate of bugs and then to the crib-like structures.

Looking over my shoulder at Supattra, I asked, "Is he trying to tell me that they grow bugs in these boxes?"

Sitting on the wooden platform talking with one of her nieces, she looked over and replied, "Yes."

"Do they have a farm, too?"

"No, Sakchai's mother had to sell their land when his father died. Sakchai was quite young and could not help in the fields," she explained. "So to make money, they began growing bugs to sell at the market. A lot of people in this village grow bugs. It's a village specialty."

"What did Sakchai's father die of?"

"He was cut badly by accident and they could not stop the infection. It took some time for him to die."

Wondering how such an accident could happen, I asked, "How was he cut?"

"He had an argument with a neighbor. They were drunk and the neighbor accidently stabbed him with a knife."

I laughed at her explanation. "The neighbor accidently stabbed him during an argument?"

"Yes."

"And the neighbor? What happened to the neighbor?"

"He lives across the street in the big house."

"He lives across the street in the nice house with the new Isuzu truck?"

"Yes."

"Nothing happened to him?"

"They were drunk. It was an accident."

"The neighbor stabbing Sakchai's father was an accident?"

"Yes."

"And Sakchai's family lost the farm?"

"They sold it."

"To whom?"

"The neighbor."

"The neighbor who stabbed his father and killed him?"

"His father died from an infection. The neighbor didn't kill him."

"Did the neighbor have to pay the police off?"

"Probably."

Shaking my head, I told her, "I'm not sure I will ever understand Thai justice."

"That is because you are still learning to be Buddhist."

"I'm Christian."

"You're Buddhist." She shook her head. "You just don't know it yet."

After a long farewell, we finally got into the truck and backed out onto the road. Sakchai dragged the warped and

rusted corrugated metal back across the opening in the cinderblock wall and hopped into the backseat. With Supattra and
her youngest niece on her lap sitting next to me on the passenger side, Sakchai guided us to a hard surfaced highway. The
emerald green surroundings were spectacular, resembling
scenes from a *King Kong* or *Jurassic Park* movie at times.
With light traffic sharing the route, we drove along a winding
road, in the direction of a large ridgeline jutting up from the
rolling hills. Passing slow-moving law-abiding families and
giants each time we came to a straight section in the road, we
continued toward the looming ridge. The more cars and trucks
I passed, the more aggressive I became. Looking over at Supattra, I jokingly commented that we might want to use seat
belts. She translated what I had said to her sister and Sakchai
in the back seat, and they all laughed. Sakchai then said something serious to Supattra and she told me that we would need
seat belts when we approached the city of Chaiyaphum, as the
police would undoubtedly be out, looking to line their pockets,
at checkpoints.

CHAPTER 12

The Things We Ponder on a Lonely Stretch of Road
~ 12 April 2014

We eventually began climbing the side of the mountain, which Supattra informed me was the Sut Phaen Din ridgeline, twisting back and forth on switchbacks through dense jungle. Coming up behind a slow-moving bus belching black smoke, I quickly became frustrated. When a very short straight section of road presented itself, I didn't hesitate, pulling out in the opposing lane and aggressively stepping on the accelerator. Nearly past the bus, a car going in the opposite direction came around a blind corner. It was the closest I had ever been to having a head on collision. The bus and car slammed on their brakes as I yanked the steering wheel to the left, nearly colliding with both vehicles simultaneously. Somehow, I managed to thread the needle between the two.

The interior of our truck became oddly quiet. Taking a deep breath, I looked over at Supattra and the little girl in her lap, both with wide eyes and pale faces. Glancing into the rearview mirror, I could see the identical expressions on Sakchai, Yii, and their oldest daughter.

Looking back over at Supattra, I said, "May be we should wear our seatbelts before Chaiyaphum."

Without Supattra translating my remark, the sound of seatbelts being pulled across laps and the clicking of their buckles consumed the otherwise silent interior of the pickup.

Continuing up the mountainside—slightly less aggressively—crossing over the top, we passed a lookout busy with other travelers taking in the view. Driving down the far side, we passed the entrance to a temple hidden in the jungle and once again began maneuvering through dense foliage-laden, rolling hills.

Driving through the hills south of the Sut Phaen Din ridgeline, my passengers all falling asleep to the rhythmic vibrations of the speeding pickup truck, I was left alone to find the way to Kalasin. Sitting in silence, navigating along the winding road, I began pondering Supattra's and my conversation that morning. What was the secret to unleashing sufferers from the misery of posttraumatic stress? Coming up behind a slow-moving law-abiding family droning along the road, I began speculating about religion's role in recovering from posttraumatic stress and whether faith in God played a part in the healing process. While it had played a limited role for me during the drive north in Iraq, it had a role nonetheless. Since my move to Thailand, Buddhism had partially replaced my childhood faith, but I still found myself speaking with my God during difficult times. Possibly religion's role, whether Buddhism or Christianity, was not to resolve the ailments plaguing its followers, but to provide support through the relationships created during shared rituals.

Maybe Supattra was right and I had begun to heal. After all, I had stopped my self-destructive spiral and I wasn't overcome with the ever-present feeling of unhappiness and regret. Not to mention, I had begun to talk about my past experiences. Passing the slow-moving law-abiding family on a short straight segment of highway, I considered the implications of healing and wondered how I had begun the process. I wondered what I had done to achieve those ends. I hadn't done anything differently since moving to this country, other than a relatively recent reduction in the amount of alcohol I consumed. But I had posttraumatic stress before I started drinking and turned to alcohol because I felt lost.

As I passed a colorful truck that looked as if it might be a Thai version of a classic farm vehicle, my thoughts turned to an incident that had occurred while we were living in the village of Kitanakagusku on the island of Okinawa.

In my mind it was an event that was more proof behind my recent revelation that posttraumatic stress was not limited to those who experienced the terrors of war...

☙❦❧

Arriving home late one night after returning from a flight to Manila, I stepped through the front door and silently walked passed my wife, who was watching television in our living room, going into the kitchen to see if any dinner had been set aside. Rummaging through the refrigerator, I could hear my oldest daughter walking down the staircase, asking my wife if I had returned home yet.

Stepping into the kitchen, my daughter asked, "Dad, can you take me to the base exchange?"

"It's late," I replied, looking at my watch in the midst of the search for something to eat. "Can't it wait for tomorrow?"

"I need something for school tomorrow."

Giving up my hunt for a meal, I turned and could immediately see that my daughter was upset about something. Closing the refrigerator door, I agreed to drive her, not asking why she seemed distraught. Unusually quiet as we walked out the front door to my silver Toyota sedan, I began examining my daughter's body language, looking for some indicator as to her uncommonly sullen mood.

As I pulled the car out into the narrow alley-like road we lived on, she mumbled, "Dad, I have some really bad news."

Looking over at her as the light from an overhead street light lit the car's interior, I could see tears on her cheeks. "What is it?"

"I was with Kara today and she told me something about her father."

Kara was my oldest daughter's best friend, and her father, Bill, was arguably my closest friend on the island. Peers in the Marine Corps' rank structure, Bill and I were both lieutenant colonels at the time, and we had been sitting side by side when the aircraft had been flown into the Pentagon on September Eleventh.

Our reaction that day differed wildly. While I had attempted to return to our office in order to retrieve my wallet and keys, he had run out of the Pentagon and not stopped until he had flagged down a car on a nearby interstate, somehow convincing the driver to take him all the way home, some ten miles south.

Driving the car through the tight maze of streets of Kitanakagusku and onto a road leading through the cane fields, I asked, "What did Kara tell you?"

"Her father has been assaulting her."

Pulling the car to the side of the road, I looked over at my daughter. "Bill has been hitting Kara?"

With the lights from the dashboard instruments creating a dim greenish glow that illuminated her tear-stained cheeks, my daughter shook her head, softly saying, "No, he hasn't been hitting her."

Scrutinizing my daughter for a moment in the darkened car, what she was trying to tell me slowly sank in and I calmly said, "Tell me everything Kara told you," as I put the car into park and twisted in my seat so we were face to face.

After describing what her friend had told her, my daughter asked, "What are you going to do?"

"I've got no choice," I replied, putting the car into gear and pulling back out onto the road. "Do you really need to go to the exchange?"

"No," she muttered, before asking again, "What are you going to do?"

"I've got no choice," I said again. "I'm going to turn him in."

"When?"

"Tomorrow, after I have had a chance to tell him that I'm going to turn him in."

"You're going to tell him?" She looked at me with a baffled expression, raising her eyebrows in disbelief, as I began to do a U-turn in the middle of an intersection. "Don't you believe me?"

"Of course, I believe you," I replied, glancing over at her, nodding my head.

"Then why are you going to talk to him before calling the police?"

"His life is about to be turned upside down and I'm going to make sure he knows who did it, face to face."

"Why?"

"We have a choice with the penalties we create for ourselves and others. We can either face them directly or hide when things get tough. I've always been of the mind to face them directly."

The next morning in my office, I typed out everything my oldest daughter had told me the night before as we sat in my car parked in the cane fields, before calling Bill on the phone and explaining that he needed to come over and speak with me. In retrospect, by the tone of my voice, he likely knew something was wrong, and I have often wondered if he suspected or knew that I had discovered his incestuous pedophilia.

When he finally arrived, I told him to sit down in a burgundy leather chair that stood to one side of my office while I sat on a matching leather couch directly across from him. Reaching over a low coffee table between us, I handed him the piece of paper with my daughter's allegations.

Reading the piece of paper, shaking his head, he began repeating over and over again, "No, no."

Silently sitting on the couch, watching as Bill's world crumbled around him, when he had finished reading the piece of paper, I asked, "What do you have to say for yourself?"

Looking up at me with tear-filled eyes, he said in a trembling voice, "It's all true," adding, "This will destroy me."

"This will destroy you, but it's a mess of your making and I have no doubt the Marine Corps will give you everything you deserve."

"But, Pat, we're friends," he pleaded, folding up the piece of paper with the allegations.

"We stopped being friends long before I realized it. I'm just not sure how could I have missed it."

"I'm the same person you knew before. I just made some mistakes."

Handing him a second piece of paper, I said in a flat tone, "This is the address of the Base Social Services. You've got twenty minutes. If I don't get a call from them in twenty minutes telling me that you've turned yourself in, I'm calling the Military Police."

With a pale, slack, and confused expression, he asked, "Why? Why are you making me turn myself in?"

"It's not for you. It's because your daughter needs you to turn yourself in and face the consequences of what you've done to her."

Years later, back in the United States, Kara came to visit my oldest daughter. Dressed in black from head to toes, I could see the torment in her eyes and hear the sadness in her voice. Kara and my oldest daughter's lives had led them down entirely different paths and it was heartbreaking as I watched the two once close friends realize that they had no longer had anything in common. I remembered recognizing the traumatic scars that her father had left on his daughter. What I hadn't identified, in the midst of my own denial, was the obvious tell-tale signs of posttraumatic stress.

Driving down the Thai country road, I wondered if she had learned to come to terms with those horrific recollections, or had they plagued her much like Supattra's and my memories?

Surprisingly the naval criminal investigative service (NCIS) decided that my actions had been devised to help the incestuous pedophile who I had once called a friend, and they came after me, investigating my unusual method of making him turn himself into the authorities. They claimed that I should have directly contacted the military police once my daughter had made the allegations that he had been sexually assaulting his daughter. During my first interrogation by the NCIS, it became apparent they wouldn't be happy until I too found myself in the brig, charged with aiding and abetting a criminal. Shortly after my interrogation, they showed up at my office with a search warrant, and took my computer and print-er. It was as if I was being harassed by the Keystone Kops with their child-like lying and badgering. When they demand-ed to interview my daughter, I flatly said "No," but told them they could give their questions to a marine officer of their choosing and I would happily allow that officer to question her. When the Keystone Kops told me that they could obtain an order from the commanding general, allowing them access to my daughter, I laughed. Having served as a legal officer for one year in a light armor battalion, I knew they were trying to intimidate me with more lies. Even the commanding general could not override a decision by a parent when it came to children. Ultimately, one of the general officers, who I knew well and flew quite often, stepped in and told the NCIS to stay away from me. My experience with the NCISs lack of professionalism and their childish tactics had been so distasteful, it took years before I could watch the television series of the same name and based on the organization.

෴

Four hours into our journey from Phetchabun with several more hours contemplating the role of religion in my recovery from posttraumatic stress and wondering about Kara's fate, the rolling hills and thick vegetation lining the sides of road began to abate, replaced with flat wide open fields and grazing black and brown water buffalo. With more traffic sharing the road and small countryside businesses appearing along its sides, I presumed that we were approaching the city of Chaiyaphum. I had driven through Chaiyaphum several years earlier and knew it to be a fairly difficult city to navigate. Looking over at Supattra snoozing in the seat next to me, I considered waking her up to help, just as the Google Maps app warned of an approaching turn. Sakchai groggily stirred in the rear seat, unintentionally knocking his oldest daughter's head from his shoulder, and Supattra reached out, placing her right hand on my thigh.

I decided to let my passengers sleep, figuring that Bitch'n Betty could guide me through the city. Three turns later, as we were exiting a large turning circle in the center of the city, I saw the police checkpoint Sakchai had warned us of and was once again thankful for our truck's tinted windows. Surely, the vision of a *farang* driver would have prompted a search by the brown-uniformed police and a subsequent fine for some minor and creative infraction. As the scene played out, a lone policeman wearing a white helmet and a brown, tight-fitting uniform, standing in the center of the street selecting the vehicles to be searched, scrutinized our truck as I approached the checkpoint. Rotating his head from side to side, trying to see through our tinted windows in the bright sunlight, he finally gave up and waved us through. Driving passed the checkpoint, I wondered if the policeman hadn't been intimidated by the sight of a new Toyota pickup with tinted windows and Surratthani license plates, concerned that its passengers might have some influential standing in the country, having some authority over his future promotions.

Leaving the city and driving north on a four-lane highway, I could feel the rising heat begin radiating through the windshield. Open markets advertising everything from fruits to fireworks dotted the side of the road, selling celebratory gifts and wares to Thais driving home for the festival. I began to feel the fatigue from the two day drive, most of which I had been at the wheel. With heavy eyelids, I considered asking Supattra to take over the driving but once again hesitated.

Another thirty minutes along the highway and the Google Maps app directed me to exit, turning down another two lane country road. I promptly followed its instructions without question. Once again on a narrow road, passing giants and slow-moving law-abiding families, I regretted not waking Supattra. I was too tired to be passing cars on a narrow twisting road, especially one in a country that rated among the top three in traffic fatalities in the world. Supattra stirred again, looking out her window as we approached a large warehouse type building with a faded blue metal roof.

Sleepily she asked, "Where are we?"

"I think we're closing in on the highway that leads to Kohn Kaen."

Sitting up and rubbing her eyes, she asked, "I've been asleep that long?"

"For nearly three hours."

Realizing what the warehouse building was, she said, "Turn in here," just before I passed the entrance to its large parking lot.

Abruptly turning hard to the left, the wheels screeching across the pavement due to the severity of my steering input, I asked, "What is it?"

"We can buy cheap drinks for *Songkran* here."

"We can also give me a break from driving," I muttered, as we careened into the parking lot. "I am bushed and you need to take the wheel."

The sharp turn had awakened everyone in the truck, and as we pulled into the parking lot, Sakchai, Supattra, and Yii broke out in Isaan, presumably talking about what drinks they needed for the three day celebration. The heat was intense as I stepped from the pickup truck, my exhaustion making it more intolerable. Walking toward the building, Supattra silently took my hand, looking up at me with a wide smile. I could see she was excited about visiting with the rest of her family and celebrating the New Year. Smiling back, with my free hand I tossed the keys to the truck up in the air and Supattra easily captured them with her free hand as they dropped toward the pavement between us. I was happy to be at her side and welcomed into her Isaan family as we passed by several stands selling clothes, two colorful coin-operated children's rides resembling a spaceship and a galloping horse and through the warehouse entrance.

The building was broken up into two areas—bulk food and drinks to one side and more shops selling clothes, toys, and trinkets to the other. There was no air conditioning but it wasn't nearly as hot as the parking lot, its roof providing some relief from the blazing sun. With her sister's children following close behind, Supattra released my hand and disappeared into the bulk food and drink area. I wandered amongst the small shops, inspecting the various merchandise. After determining that all the stock in the shops were cheap reproductions, I began hunting for Supattra. I found her with a shopping cart stacked high with cases of beer, soda, and water, and five bottles of Regency Brandy. She waved me over.

"Think that'll be enough?" I said with a laugh, joking about her purchase size.

Looking at me with a perfectly serious expression, Supattra replied, "It should last a day or so, and my sister Aae will bring more." And then after a short hesitation, she added, "I need money."

"How much?"

"Maybe two thousand *baht.*"

Handing her three thousand *baht,* roughly a hundred dollars, I wandered out to the entrance where Sakchai was standing and smoking a cigarette. Seeing me walking toward him, he held out the pack, offering a cigarette. After tapping one from the bundle and lighting it up, I handed the pack back. Taking a deep lung full of smoke, I immediately wondered if smoking a cigarette in intense heat and in an exhausted state was a good or bad idea. Twenty minutes of semi-uncomfortable silence between me and Sakchai later, Supattra appeared with her shopping cart, now topped with new clothes for the two girls. The clothing was testament to the transfer of funds between family members in Thailand, Supattra's big heart, and my generosity when only two thousand *baht* was requested.

Once the drinks had been loaded into the bed of the pickup, I climbed into the passenger side and sank down into the seat, closing my eyes. Feeling the pickup rolling and twisting down the road, I would occasionally open an eye in time to see us speeding down the opposing lane, passing giants and slow-moving law-abiding families. Each awakening ended with the thought that I should have kept my eyes closed. At one point, she pulled out directly in front of an approaching giant just as I opened my eyes and I gave her a thirty second reprimand, telling her that it wouldn't be much of a celebration for her mother if she was called upon to identify the bodies of her children and grandchildren—not to mention one *farang.* Supattra patted me on the thigh and told me to go back to sleep which, against my better judgment, I did.

Waking to a conversation between Supattra and Sakchai sometime later, I saw a Big A shopping center to my left and the Pullman Hotel, the tallest structure in Kohn Kaen, to my right.

"What's going on?" I asked groggily. "What is Sakchai asking?"

"He's not asking me anything. He's telling me which way we need to go," Supattra responded.

Sitting up in the seat, I said, "Why isn't Bitch'n Betty talking? We need to turn right just ahead."

"I turned the lady's voice off," she calmly answered. "Sakchai knows the way."

Watching our turn quickly approach, trying to keep the urgency out of my voice I said, "I'm not so sure about that. We need to make a turn at that next light."

Glancing over at me with a confused expression, she asked, "What turn?"

"The turn to Kalasin," I replied, hearing insistence sneaking into the tone of my voice as we passed under a large overhead green sign indicating Kalasin to the right and Udon Thani straight ahead.

"What turn?"

Realizing that two Thais, who had been through this city a thousand times more than me, had no idea to how to get to Kalasin, I urgently said, "Trust me and turn right at the light," not bothering to point out a second obvious overhead sign indicating a right turn to Kalasin for fear it would distract her.

With Sakchai silent in the backseat, Supattra unhesitatingly pulled into the right lane, before saying, "We thought we needed to stay on this highway."

"No, we need to drive through downtown," I sighed in relief as she made the turn. "Going straight would have taken us Udon Thani."

Glancing over and smiling at me, she said with a giggle, "It's a good thing you woke up."

Running my hand through my hair, I chuckled. "Buddha is with us. We managed to make Kohn Kaen without being involved in a massive head-on collision and found the obvious right hand turn to Kalasin."

"He is." She giggled again, as she maneuvered the truck

past several barricades erected for the upcoming celebration.

As I sat wondering why Sakchai, who had made this trip to Kalasin numerous times before, could not find his way, it dawned on me that he had never been called on to navigate before. Each previous trip to Kalasin he had been sitting in a low cost and cramped public bus.

Driving out of Kohn Kaen, over a wide river, the four-lane highway meandered past large tropical meadows surrounded by tall, silver-barked trees, and shallow freshwater lakes dotted with bamboo huts selling shrimp and other aquatic delicacies. Unmanned police checkpoints with triangular red-and-white placards were set up in each small town along the road, while motorcycles and *Tuk-Tuks*, or three-wheeled taxis, scooted along the shoulders. Supattra finally turned into one of the towns, following a winding road out into the countryside. Passing fields with tufts of last season's rice stalks poking through dry gray-brown soil, the road eventually approached a low, tree-topped hill, where Supattra honked the horn twice and gave her home grounds a traditional *wai* while whispering something indiscernible in her native language.

Chapter 13

A Sea of Regrets ~ 12 April 2014

Turning down a narrow dirt road, we were immediately engulfed into Yaun Kom City. Yaun Kom City was really nothing more than a small rice farming village situated on top of a low, tree-covered knoll. As many times as I have visited Supattra's home, I have never asked why its residents calls it a city. I had assumed the answer would be long and confusing for a *farang* to understand, but as I type this story, I wonder if calling it city wasn't a village joke that stuck, perpetuated by years of repartee.

Driving into the village, we passed two-story concrete-and-wood houses with garage-like first floors, either outfitted as small businesses or sparsely furnished into common living areas. Each with the traditional platform in front, every building's wooden shutters stood open on the second floor to allow any possible breeze to whisk away the intense spring heat. We passed two tall temples on our left. The first was painted white with colorful blue-and-gold decorative trim and embellishments on a steep red roof. The second was a skeleton of construction with its gray supporting concrete columns revealed. The road, only wide enough to handle one vehicle at a time, came to an intersection where roads thrust out from the center of the village like the spokes on a wagon wheel amid the tight web of buildings. Carefully driving through the intersection, Supattra steered the truck down a slightly sloping dirt road, stopping in front of a white house with a wide double wooden door entrance that was masked by several tall and slender mango and papaya trees.

The truck doors popped open in unison and its occupants sprang from their seats like Jack-in-the-Boxes whose tune had just reached their climax. Supattra's pudgy middle sister Aae, dressed in a gray oversized T-shirt and black spandex pants, carrying a glass with brown whiskey sloshing over its edges, hugged her younger and then older sister, welcoming them in slurred Isaan. The sight of an intoxicated family member was not unusual for this time of day during the celebration, and Supattra and Yii returned her greeting as if nothing was wrong. Moving past her drunken sister, we were then greeted by Supattra's father and mother—who were keeping a good distance from one another—Aae's young daughter, an uncle, and five nameless neighbors. Beyond the greeting crowd, plates of food were spread out on a shaded royal blue tiled front patio with squadrons of flies circling overhead like vultures waiting for the more intimidating carnivores to finish their meal.

After unloading the pickup, Supattra handed me the keys and I drove to the end of the street, parking in a small grass-covered field between a dirty white Ford pickup and an open sided thatch-roofed hut that looked as if it had been constructed with abandoned wood and fallen tree limbs. Sitting on the hut's platform was a group of four shirtless old men with tan lean bodies and bloodshot eyes. Passing a brown bottle between them, the men smiled at me as I climbed from the pickup, raising their glasses in a silent invitation for me to share their drinks. Walking around the truck and over to the hut, I took the glass from the closest old man and sipped the shimmering clear liquid. The taste buds on my tongue exploded as if someone had doused them with sulfuric acid and when I swallowed my throat felt as if it burst into flames. With sweat suddenly sprouting on my brow, when the intense heat finally reached my belly, it took three vicious rolls. Taken back by the predictable and somewhat uncomfortable sensations, I had to take several deep breaths to keep myself from immediately vomiting. I had known prior to drinking the liquid that it was Thai whiskey, or *lao kow*, a drink more akin to grain alcohol than any other beverage I can think of, but the offer was a sign of respect and turning it down was not an option in this traditional village.

Dust plumed from the road with each step as I walked back to Supattra's home. The heat was stifling and most of the village residents sat in front of their homes, drinking one iced beverage or another. Many of the people along this street knew me from previous visits and waved or nodded their heads as I passed by. It dawned on me as I moved up the dirt road that, unlike the United States, Thailand still had a front porch culture. People would still sit out in front of their homes, watching their neighborhood and greeting pedestrians walking down the street, while Americans had moved to the privacy of their backyards.

As I stepped up to Supattra's home, a mixture of family members and neighbors sat on the patio around a white plastic mat with black and red numbers printed on top. The plates of food that had once been center stage had now been pushed to one side, shifting the battalion of flies. Sitting cross-legged at the top of the mat, Supattra's uncle carefully arranged three dice on a plate before placing a small wicker bowl over the top. The crowd around the mat began jabbering in Isaan and laying down money on one number or another. When the betting and talk died down, the uncle carefully picked up the bowl covered plate with his calloused and deeply tanned hands, giving it a quick sideways jerk. He then placed the bowl back down and the betting began heating up again. Once the bidding had subsided for a second time, he slowly lifted the wicker bowl, revealing the dice underneath.

Screeching with a wide smiling face, Supattra sat to the right side of the mat and raised her hands in victory, having obviously just won. Her sister Aae cackled a loud drunken piercing laugh, and Yii silently scrutinized the results. Turning, I saw Supattra's father sitting at a concrete picnic table next to the patio, smiling at me. Stepping over to the table, giving him a traditional *wai*, I sat down.

At sixty-five years old Supattra's father was lofty for a Thai. Standing six feet tall, he had large ears under a tight military style haircut. His body lean and muscular from working in the fields, the man had become an alcoholic in recent years but it didn't seem to affect his strength or the brightness of his dark brown eyes. Supattra once told me that in his younger years her father had been the manservant for a wealthy Bangkok Chinese businessman while her mother worked a small open-air kitchen in the city, not unlike the one we ate at in Phetchabun the night before. He had stayed with the Chinese businessman for many years and, as the man grew older, her father's role had slowly changed from manservant to caregiver, cleaning and feeding him. The Chinese man eventually passed away but his son had been so taken with her father's loyalty that he gave him a job at the family factory. The Chinese man's son had returned his faithfulness, ensuring Supattra's father had steady income in a country where nothing was taken for granted. Some ten years ago, her father had decided it was time, moving back to his home and the family rice farm in Isaan.

Beyond his drunkenness, it had been easy to see the good-hearted nature of her father the first time I met him. It was easy to imagine this tall Thai man carrying his master to the bathroom and cleaning him off. It was easy to see her lean muscular father feeding a man incapable of the task. I had given Supattra's father an expensive Seiko watch on my second visit to her home and it would have been logical for him to sell it in order to buy food or needed essentials when things got tough. But to this day the poor man sitting next to me on the concrete picnic bench wore it with pride.

He handed me his glass of shimmering white liquid. I smiled back at her father and took a sip. Once again my taste buds exploded into a tingling sensation, my throat burned, and my stomach took a violent turn as I consumed his respectful offer. And once again I took several deep breaths in order to fight off the urge to throw it back up. Grabbing a brown bottle from a box at my feet, I quickly filled another glass with ice and beer, pouring the cool liquid down my throat to smother the smoldering fire and settle my turning stomach.

To the far side of the house, across the patio, piles of empty bottles and trash, not unlike those at Sakchai's childhood home, stood next to a low cinderblock wall that separated their home from the one next door. An enormous five-foot-tall and wide clay pot with a tin lid, that I knew held water for the daily tasks in the absence of a functioning village plumbing system, separated the picnic table from an open kitchen that ran along the other side of the house.

Supattra's mother, busy in the kitchen, squatted over a small charcoal cooker, preparing a late afternoon meal. I observed her mother's movements as she flicked something inside a wok back and forth with a large bamboo spoon. The woman had obviously been as beautiful as Supattra in her youth, with large dark eyes, a round face, and full lips. I also knew that she was an astute businesswoman, who had managed to quadruple their rice field holdings in the eight years I had known the family. Even with all her rice farming achievements, life in this village was tough and I could count the number of times on one hand that I had seen Supattra's mother smile during all the years I had known her.

Normally keeping their distance from one another, over the eight years I had known Supattra, only once I had witnessed a loving interaction between her mother and father. It was an obscure moment when Supattra translated a statement her father had made about his wife, saying that she was the most beautiful woman he had ever known. And while it might seem a contradiction to what you've read in this story, there have been times I have wondered if Thai women weren't culturally taught to treat their partners as if they were a bad family pet— as if all men were dogs and only worth the value of their monetary prowess or their ability to sow and reap rice from the fields.

After a meal of rice noodles and fresh water clams doused in hot sauce and wrapped in cabbage, I stood over the small group of people playing dice and drinking whiskey and coke. Watching the boisterous crowd that had been at the game for nearly four hours swiftly exchange money on the white mat, I decided I needed a break. The long drive and lack of sleep the night before was weighing heavily on me. Grabbing a bottle of water I walked down the dirt road, passing a hen with six chicks picking amongst the grass, to the thatched hut next to the truck. Another shirtless older man, short with faded Buddhist tattoos festooned across his chest and back and a distended stomach, who I knew to be Supattra's uncle, and two other obviously drunken men were sitting on the hut's platform, swaying back and forth, talking, and drinking more clear liquid from small glasses. Silently, I hoped they wouldn't offer me a courteous sip of their drinks.

Seeing me approach Supattra's uncle waved me over, saying something in Isaan. As I stepped up to the hut, he offered me his drink and, preparing myself for the oral misery that was to follow, I unhesitatingly took a swallow. After a short discussion with Supattra's uncle, limited by my Thai vocabulary, I said, "*Mai Sa Baai Dee, ngunaang*," explaining I wasn't feeling well and was tired. Jumping up, Supattra's uncle moved to the back of the platform and laid out a woven mat. Once he'd flattened the mat out, he turned and gestured for me to lie down. Without hesitation, I removed my flip-flops, hopped onto the platform, and patted the old man's bare brown shoulder before lying down.

A rooster crowed behind me and a wide black water buffalo pulled grass from around the edges of the hut as I placed my hands behind my head and tried to relax. Another rooster crowed from overhead that I assumed was sitting at the top of the hut's thatched roof. Causally inspecting the structure holding the hut's roof up—long smooth white branches hand cut with mortise and tenon joints binding them to together—I felt my eyelids become heavy. Listening to the old men mumbling on the far side of the platform with a background of Isaan music coming from the various parties around the village occasionally interrupted by a high-pitched crow from one of the two roosters surrounding me, I noticed a short wooden staff wedged between the overhead rafters that had been carved with refined detail. One end was crafted into the shape of a penis and fashioned near the other was the figure of woman wrapping her naked body around the staff. I chuckled at the sight, knowing that a wooden penis displayed in Thai homes was not uncommon and was considered a sign of household strength and virility. The sight of such a decorative touch in a thatched hut seemed amusing in my exhausted state. Ten minutes later, the three old men grunted something in Isaan to me and stumbled off to join one of the village New Year's celebrations. Lying on the woven reed mat, under the thatched roof, I closed my eyes and began thinking about a famous mountain climber and his words after a tragic accident that one of my brothers had told me of years before.

My father, who at the time was struggling with prostate cancer, and my oldest brother had flown over to Okinawa for my change of command, and we had a late night discussion about what I was going to say during the ceremony in two days.

Looking at me, my brother asked, "Have you ever heard of guy named Edward Whymper?"

When I said no, he explained that Edward Whymper had been a nineteenth-century mountain climber who tried seven times to ascend the Matterhorn, failing at each attempt. On his eighth try, he finally succeeded with a party of seven, being the first to do so. When the team of seven began the precarious descent, one of the climbers slipped and fell, pulling three others over the edge of the north face. All linked together by a common rope, Whymper and two other climbers found themselves being pulled over the edge from the weight of their four teammates dangling below. The four were lost and a controversy ensued as to whether the rope had been cut, but a formal investigation couldn't find any proof. Whymper later wrote a book called *Scrambles Amongst the Alps*, where he talked about the experience.

The next morning, the day before my change of command, my brother handed me a slip of paper scribed with the most famous of Edward Whymper's quotes: *Still, the last sad memory hovers round, and sometimes drifts across like floating mist, cutting off sunshine and chilling the remembrance of happier times. There have been joys too great to be described in words, and there have been griefs upon which I have not dared to dwell; and with these in mind I say: Climb if you will, but remember that courage and strength are naught without prudence, and that a momentary negligence may destroy the happiness of a lifetime. Do nothing in haste; look well to each step; and from the beginning think what may be the end.* Looking the quote up on the internet, I found Whymper went on and advocated that each step we take is a reflection of our last.

Having survived two wars and numerous conflicts around the globe, I was fascinated by the notion that each step we take is a reflection of our last and ended up using Edward Whymper's words during the change of command ceremony. During my short speech, I equated Whymper's reflection idea to every decision we make in life, our past decisions influencing our future choices.

As I began to understand that I was suffering from posttraumatic stress, my fascination turned to his most celebrated quote, perceiving the pain that was written between the lines in his words. As I explored Edward Whymper even more, I found that the accident haunted him, another quote from his book revealing that pain: *Every night, do you understand, I see my comrades of the Matterhorn slipping on their backs, their arms outstretched, one after the other, in perfect order at equal distances—Croz the guide, first, then Hadow, then Hudson, and lastly Douglas. Yes, I shall always see them.*

Lying on my back, looking up at the thatched roof above, it dawned on me that Edward Whymper, whether he had cut the rope or not, had been plagued by posttraumatic stress. Like Supattra and my former friend's daughter Kara, he struggled with posttraumatic stress brought on by something other than war.

The rooster a shrieked another high-pitched crow behind me as I watched a woman herd two water buffalos down the road, swatting them on the shoulders with a thin section of bamboo. A brown male buffalo, ignoring the woman's swats, pushed his way over to the hut and joined the one pulling grass from its edges. Jabbering something in Isaan, the woman looked at me with a wide smile, revealing bright white teeth, and shook her head, pointing at the buffalo with her bamboo stick. Looking back at her dark, weathered face, yellow-tinted eyes, and deep lines, I nodded, silently agreeing that her buffalo was being difficult. Shouting at the stubborn animal, the woman slapped the bamboo across the buffalo's back. The buffalo, with wide brown eyes, turned and looked at the woman before letting out a loud bellow. This was followed by each of the two roosters sounding off with another shriek. The old woman calmly walked behind the stubborn water buffalo, first kicking the animal in its haunches and then slapping its rear with the stick. Turning its wide head again, the water buffalo seemed to glare at the old woman before begrudgingly moving back to the road.

About the time the weathered woman had successfully moved her buffalos down the road to their pen, hidden someplace in the village, Sakchai walked up to the hut with two bottles of beer and cups of ice. Shaking my head, I wondered if I shouldn't have selected a less conspicuous place to take a break. I moved to the side of the platform, dropping my legs over the edge, and smiled at Supattra's approaching brother-in-law. Handing me a bottle of beer and one of the ice-filled cups, he sat down next to me. Filling our cups, we silently toasted each other. I tried to explain in a mix of English and Thai that I wasn't feeling well and needed a break from the festivities, and he responded with a smile. Our silence became slightly uncomfortable as we sat next to each other swinging our legs over the edge of the platform and sipping at the beer. The sun had dropped below the horizon, and the village cast a dim light across the hut as I looked up and scrutinized the overhead moon, its details standing out in the clear night.

"We call that the moon," I said to Sakchai, pointing upward, once again trying to communicate to the man next to me. "What do you call it in Thai?"

Looking over at me, Sakchai smiled and nodded his head.

Again gesturing overhead to the moon, I asked, "How do you say that in Thai?"

Still smiling, Sakchai looked at me with a puzzled expression and shrugged his shoulders.

Brushing off my limited Thai, I asked, "*Kham nee waa?*"

Still smiling, he shook his head.

Laughing, I raised my glass for another silent toast.

Eventually, Sakchai said something to me in Thai and walked back up the road. I hoped he hadn't left to replenish our dwindling supply of beer—I needed a break. Scooting back to the mat, I lay down again and closed my eyes. Drifting off, I was awakened by someone sitting down next to me. All I wanted to do was sleep and I kept my eyes closed, hoping the newest offender would change his mind at the sight of my slumbering prone body and go away. I didn't want to entertain anyone, especially someone who required me to speak in a language that I barely had a handle on. I was exhausted.

"What do you regret the most?"

Hearing Supattra's soft voice and realizing that she had just sat down next to me, I cracked my eyes open and groggily asked, "What?"

"About your war," she clarified, her big brown eyes sparkling under the moonlight. "What is your biggest regret?"

I sighed and asked, "Do we need to talk about it right now?"

"I just want to know."

Pondering her question, I thought about the sea of regret that I created during a career in the Marine Corps. I considered all the things I had done during the drive north that weren't pleasant and wouldn't be understood by someone who had never experienced combat. "Do we really need to talk about it right now?"

"Please," she said, looking down at me and gently cupping her hand over my cheek. "I want to know why you are the way you are. I want to know what you are learning to let go."

Again, thinking of all the things I had done during the drive north that I regretted, a vision of Edward Whymper cutting the rope pulling him over the edge, letting his comrades fall to their death, flashed in my mind.

"I was leading a section of helicopters, reconnoitering ahead of the main column of marines driving north. We ran into a small group of Iraqis at a pumping station and, after a short skirmish, they jumped into two cars and began driving north along a narrow dirt road. Knowing they were likely forward observers, reporting on our movements, I began chasing them down the road." Taking a moment to think about that day, clearly visualizing the incident in my mind, I continued, "I could see their heads bobbing inside the cars through the rear windows, turning and looking back at me bearing down on them. I had never trained at shooting rockets at a moving target before and so it took several before I got one close enough to do any damage. The third or fourth hit right next to the passenger door of one of the cars. I could see all their heads jerk to one side when the rocket exploded. The car abruptly turned to the right and rolled out onto the desert floor in torrent of billowing dust."

"And that's what you regret the most? Shooting at the cars?"

"No," I continued. "There was a lot of dust and smoke in the air. I turned to the left and flew out a ways. I then told the gunner to open up with our 50 caliber machinegun. As he pulled the trigger, the dust and smoke began to settle and two shadows appeared."

"What were they doing?"

"They were standing on the road with their hands high in the air."

"What did you do?"

"I told the gunner to stop but it was too late. I could see the ground around the two shadows erupt as the bullets found their mark. It was a mistake. It was one of those things that happen in war. I didn't set out to kill unarmed or innocent people. I had never intended on killing men trying to surrender but it happens. It's unavoidable. I think the thing that really bothered me later, after I had left Iraq and had time to think about it, was that I had already defeated them. The rocket had already forced the car off the road and had likely killed several of the occupants. Later, I asked myself why I felt it was necessary to kill them again—or kill men who had no real means of defending themselves after such a bad crash."

"Why did you?"

"In a situation like that, with people constantly shooting at you and, in the midst of all that turmoil, there is no measured violence. The winner comes down to who can dole out the most brutality in the quickest amount of time."

"There were two cars," Supattra asked, "What about the other car?"

"I let it go." I sighed. "Even in the madness of the moment, I was shocked at the destruction I had just orchestrated. I let it go."

With the roosters suddenly quiet, I could see Supattra's eyes in the glow of the moon looking down at me with a deeply sorrowful expression.

"The funny thing is." I chuckled. "Twenty minutes later, as we flew back toward the advancing columns of marines, we came upon twenty or thirty unarmed Iraqis in a wadi in the middle of the desert."

Interrupting, Supattra asked, "What is a wadi?"

"A depression or low area in the desert. These Iraqi soldiers were obviously hiding from the advancing marines. They were unarmed and held their hands up as we flew over them."

With a concerned tone in her whispering voice, Supattra asked, "What did you do?"

"I had the crew chiefs on both aircraft drop out all our water and food. They had to be thirsty and hungry. It was a blazing hot day and they had probably been out there for hours. I wasn't being shot at and I could make decisions based logic and compassion—not on some primitive response to my life being threatened."

Scratching my head, I looked over my shoulder at one of the roosters that had been keeping me company and hesitantly added, "I've often wondered what it must have felt like to be in that car, watching two helicopters chasing you down with rockets exploding, each one a bit closer. They must have realized that those were to be the last few moments of their life. The terror inside that car must have been overwhelming."

CHAPTER 14

Forgiveness, Ignorance, or Just Not Worth the Effort
~ 13 April 2014

The next morning, I woke stretched out on top of a wide bed covered in a colorful floral quilt with a standup fan blowing semi-cool air down on me. Finding myself lying across a seam between two hard mattresses under the quilt, I shifted to reduce the discomfort of their cutting edges as the distinctive stale smell of a closed tropical room wafted through the air around me. The small room looked as if it doubled for a storage space with boxes and folded stacks of clothes lining flat white walls. A wide aluminum window was mounted above me that I knew looked into the living room. I had decided long ago that the window had been placed there to allow air to flow from the living room into the small space in an effort to keep it cool and free of the muggy aroma, neither of which had been accomplished while the window had been shut all night. The desire for privacy or drunkenness had impelled Supattra to leave the window closed when she put me to bed.

Recalling Supattra leading me home the night before from the thatch-roofed hut and tucking me into bed before returning to the party outside, I rubbed my eyes and yawned. I remembered falling asleep within minutes after she had guided me to the bedroom, even with the loud family celebration taking place on the front patio. Rolling over on my side, I could see from the disheveled sheets that Supattra had slept next to me even though I didn't recall her coming to bed. I had been exhausted and wondered if it was yet another sign of the aging process combined with the long drive, or whether I was simply sick. Her suitcase was lying on the floor next to the door with its top propped open and several changes of clothes placed to one side, as if she had been searching for a specific outfit. I could hear people talking and laughing outside the door, and through the closed window above me.

Climbing from the bed, I grabbed a towel, wrapping it around my waist, and selected a change of clothes from my suitcase before stepping from the room. The girls were watching a Thai comedy on television in the living room and the adults were out on the patio, once again laughing, drinking, and playing dice. Walking into the bathroom, I prepared myself for another cold Isaan shower.

A showerhead was mounted on the wall of the bathroom but the village lacked adequate water pressure for it to function. As a result, in the corner of the bathroom, next to a Western-style toilet, stood a tall black plastic garbage can filled with murky water and a plastic bowl floating on top. The bathroom's single sink attached to the wall below the dormant shower head was filled with toothbrushes, toothpaste, and other hygiene tools and creams, turned into its next best function due to the lack of water pressure: a storage shelf. Stepping over to the black garage can, I dipped the plastic bowl into the murky water. Dousing myself eight times with cold cloudy water, a lathering someplace in-between, and my Isaan shower was complete. Dressing, I wandered out onto the patio.

Squatting around the white mat on the covered patio, I saw Supattra and her two sisters with their backs to me, her uncle and mother orchestrating the game, and four strangers that I had never seen before. Two of the strangers, a slender old man with skinny arms and legs, and crooked teeth, and a small rotund woman in tattered but clean clothes, looked up, grinned, nodding their heads in a silent greeting as I walked past. Turning their heads to see who the couple had welcomed, the three sisters smiled up at me.

"You're up," Supattra greeted me, as she turned back to the game and began placing money on one of the black numbers printed on top of the white mat.

I yawned, sitting down at the concrete picnic table. "What time is it?"

Looking down at her watch, Supattra said, "Nearly one o'clock. You were tired."

"Or sick," I added.

Squatting next to Supattra, Aae glanced over and asked, "Do you want a drink?"

"No, too early for me," I replied, instinctively knowing she was offering an alcoholic beverage.

After babbling something to Supattra, Aae also began placing money on the white mat.

Knowing she had been talking about me, I calmly asked, "Aae, what'd you say?"

"Nothing," Aae answered, examining the other bets on the white mat.

"She says you used to be a lot more fun," Supattra offhandedly translated, as she pushed one of Aae's bets to another number.

"What'd you mean?" I already knew the answer.

"Since you quit drinking," Aae piped up as she pushed her bet back over to the number she had originally selected, glaring at Supattra.

"I didn't quit drinking. I simply slowed down."

"You slowed down too much," Aae said flatly, before saying something to their uncle in Isaan.

"Leave him alone," Supattra snapped, flashing her dark brown eyes at her sister. "I like it better when he doesn't drink as much."

"I don't," Aae said. "He was more fun when he drank more."

Their uncle raised the small basket, revealing the dice, and the crowd of people around the white mat erupted in laughs and cries as they tallied their wins and losses. Standing from the crowd, Supattra walked over to the picnic table and filled a glass with ice, before pouring in beer.

Handing me the glass, she said, "It will make you feel better."

"I don't want it." I laughed. "If I drink this earlier, I'll be a mess by dinner."

"It's *Songkran*," she persisted. "Drink it."

Taking the glass from her hand, I asked, "What's the plan for the day?"

"We have to go to the temple soon."

"Why?"

Turning and moving back to the dice game, she said over her shoulder, "To give them our offerings for *Songkran* and the new temple."

Thirty minutes later, we moved to our small bedroom with the window looking into the living room. Closing the door, Supattra slipped out of her shorts and T-shirt and began rummaging through her suitcase. I fell back on the bed, placing my hands behind my head.

Looking at her standing next to her suitcase in her underwear, I asked, "Why are you changing?"

"There will be a lot of villagers at the temple that I haven't seen in many years."

"So this is like a reunion?"

"No, it's a celebration for *Songkran* and to give money to the temple," she answered. "The new temple is not yet finished and they need more money." Then after a short hesitation, she causally stated, "You don't drink as much anymore."

"I've been listening to you commenting on my slowed alcohol consumption for nearly two years."

Ignoring my remark, Supattra said again, "You don't drink as much as you used to."

Shaking my head at her stubbornness, I replied, "And according to Aae I'm not as much fun."

"I like it better when you don't drink as much."

"You keep telling me I don't drink much, as if you don't remember why," I responded in a serious tone. "I know you remember why I quit drinking."

"Yes, you hit me."

"I got drunk and slapped you." I examined the white ceiling tiles overhead as I lay on my back. "And you left me. I didn't think you were ever coming back."

"I have never had a man hit me."

"I had never slapped a woman before. I am sorry." I sighed, remembering how drunk I had been. "I was drunk but I have been taught differently."

"But you kept drinking, even after that."

"I felt like I couldn't stop," I admitted. "It got me through the day."

"What do you mean?"

"I was good in the mornings when I felt fresh and rested. But in the evenings, when I began to get tired, I started thinking about everything that had happened to me—everything I had done and regretted."

"So you drank to forget?"

"It numbed me," I explained. "When I was drunk, I didn't think about my guilt, my shame. Without a belly full of alcohol, I couldn't sleep. I was relaxed when I was drunk. I didn't think about my regrets and I could sleep."

"It made you mean."

"Not often but sometimes." I shrugged my shoulders. "It took something to set me off and make me mean."

"And you drank to forge." She pulled a dress from her suitcase and held it up as if inspecting its suitability. "And if you don't forget, you can't sleep?"

"Something like that," I mumbled, wishing I could somehow make that day go away. "I certainly don't sleep since I quit drinking as much."

"But you kept drinking even after you hit me," she said again, thrashing the dress in a whipping motion, presumably trying to remove some of the wrinkles. "Why did you quit drinking after that?"

"You know why."

"Because you got very drunk with your Russian friend and then said some bad things to me."

"Yeah, we drank several bottles of tequila that night." I sighed again. I'd recalled very little about that night the next morning and had to piece together what I had done over several days. "And you left me again."

"I spent the next three days with my friend Pun—and you stopped drinking."

"I stopped the day after I called you names, but I still drink a little."

"Yes, but many nights you don't drink at all," she calmly replied, flipping the dress over in her hands. "Why did you stop after that? Why did you stop after calling me names?"

"It was the final straw," I said, watching her slip the dress over her sleek golden body. "I never thought my drinking was causing problems. I thought of it as helping me get through another day, but in reality it was keeping me from confronting what was really bothering me. I stopped drinking the next day and, after a week of sobriety, I realized that alcohol was tainting everything I did. My reality was viewed through a drunken stupor or the haze of a hangover, depending on the time of day. When you finally came back, I had been sober for nearly three days. That was two years ago, and you have been commenting on how I don't drink as much since then, as if it happened yesterday."

Slipping a beautiful dark blue silk knee length dress over her head, she asked, "Do you like being sober?"

"I see life in an entirely different light." I sat up on the bed and slipped my legs over the edge. "I spent years getting drunk each night and every morning struggling through a hangover, but that first painful morning, trying to remember what I had done to drive you away for a second time in as many months made me worry about who I had become and where my life had taken me."

"You mean thinking about the war?"

"Far more than the war," I explained, thinking that her dress seemed a bit too elegant for the dusty streets of Yaun Kom City. "The choices I had made during and after the war. I realized that, in many ways, what I needed all along was to see it all with a clear vision and come to terms with it."

"Drinking helped you sleep, too," Supattra said, sitting down next to me on the hard mattress. "You don't sleep anymore."

Laughing again, I said, "I sleep—sort of."

"No you don't," she countered my claim, tilting her head to one side.

"I sleep in one hour increments," I responded, running my fingers through her thick black hair.

Looking confused, she asked, "Increments?"

"I sleep an hour here and an hour there. By the end of the night I've got three or four good hours of sleep."

"Why don't you sleep unless you drink?" she asked. "Do you think about your past?"

Answering her with a question of my own, I asked, "Do you think about your past before you fall asleep?"

"I am Thai," she replied in a perfectly serious tone. "I sleep anywhere and anytime I want. I think about my past but it doesn't keep me from sleeping. Do you think about your past and does that keep you from sleeping?"

"Sometimes, but not always. I just don't sleep," I answered. "I really don't know why I don't sleep if I don't drink, but I prefer not sleeping to getting drunk each night and risking the chance of running you off again."

"You will never lose me."

"You might have left me had I continued drinking as much as I used to."

"I was worried about you. I didn't like seeing you get drunk each night and I was worried about your health. I do not want to lose you. You must live to be a very old man."

"And you told me."

"For years." She sighed. "It took me leaving before you understood how tired I was of you being drunk each night. I will always remember those two nights—the two nights I left you."

Soliciting the obvious question, I asked, "Why did you come back?"

"I have spent many lives with you," she whispered, looking into my eyes. "I knew that the hand that struck me and the tongue that yelled at me was not yours. It was your body but not your spirit. You were inside trying to come out and I knew what was holding you back."

After a moment she added, "I know you have seen the

same with me, at times, when I get crazy and do bad things."

"You never do crazy things like that."

"Do you remember the night I held a knife to your throat?"

"Well, there was that."

"I had too much to drink and was mad at my life," she whispered. "I was mad at the decisions I had made."

"I knew you were angry with your choices, but also I knew I was the only person you could show your frustration to."

"But it has been more than that time. It has been many times." A tear broke from the corner of her eye. "Yes, you are the only one I can show my anger to. It is the same for you. I am the only one you can show your anger to."

"That all seems like such a long time ago." I sighed again. "We haven't been like that since I quit drinking so much." Then, after a moment of silence, I asked, "Why do you keep commenting on my drinking, or lack thereof, as if I quit drinking last week?"

Looking me in the eye, Supattra matter-of-factly stated, "I want you to remember why I left you so you never drink that much again, and when you tell me, I remember all the times that I have hurt you and it helps me remember that I should never harm you again."

Leaning down, I kissed her on the lips.

Smiling at me, she stood and took my hand, saying, "It's time to go."

Stepping from the room, we joined the rest of the family on the front porch. Most of the family members wore colorful shirts with bright floral designs, another *Songkran* tradition. Supattra's mother was holding a vase overflowing with paper money mounted on slender bamboo sticks, a temple offering. I knew that Supattra had probably donated one of the larger bills protruding from the top of the money tree, but I also knew not to ask. After the family chattered in Isaan for several minutes we began the short walk up the dirt road toward the temple in the center of the village.

Numerous families began appearing on the street, each carrying a similar money tree bursting with various amounts of flopping, colorful bills. It quickly became apparent that the amount of money topping each vase was a testament as to a family's *naam jai* or water from the heart and—undoubtedly—the depth of their pockets. The hordes of families joined together into one long parade that made its way to the temple grounds. Three or four bald and eyebrow-less orange-robed monks stood inside the unfinished concrete skeleton of a building as several village officials organized the arriving families.

The family members carrying the money trees were directed up the steps leading up to the unfinished temple.

Standing in the crowd, watching the money trees being paraded up the steps to the awaiting monks, I scrutinized the scene around me. There were at least two hundred people dressed in a montage of the bright flowery shirts, talking and drinking. Some watched the ceremony, but most were socializing with their family and neighbors.

Placing a hand on my forearm, Supattra asked, "Do you see that woman?"

Looking around the crowd, I asked, "Which woman?"

Gesturing to a woman with heavy makeup and dressed in a red silk blouse, black miniskirt, and tall patent leather boots, an outfit that was more suited for a bar in Pattaya than a village *Songkran* celebration, she said, "There—that one," just as the woman turned and, recognizing Supattra, waved.

Glancing at the woman, I offhandedly commented, "She looks like a bargirl."

Waving and smiling back at the woman, Supattra explained, "There are some women in this village who chose to become bargirls. When they find someone they love who will take care of them, they leave that life behind. That woman and I were friends when in school and she too became a bargirl but she was there much longer than me before meeting someone."

"She has a *farang* boyfriend?"

"Yes," Supattra replied. "But we must stay away from her."

Looking down at Supattra in the knee-length, tasteful, dark-blue silk dress, I asked, "Because she still dresses like a bargirl?"

Turning her attention back to the ceremony, Supattra answered with a flat, "No."

"But you were once friends," I continued. "And, like you, she went to Pattaya. You have more in common than just friendship or the fact that you were classmates. You both have experienced the same difficult times and made the same decisions."

Still watching the ceremony, she repeated her earlier declaration, saying, "We must stay away from her."

I'm sure you immediately picked up on the hypocrisy of Supattra's statement about the other woman, one former bargirl exiling another. I've seen this tendency several times during our relationship, the most recent occurring on Koh PhaNgan at a temple festival. Visiting one of the many festivals that occur on the island throughout the year, with two unattached male friends, we wandered through the small stands selling trinkets and played several gallery games before deciding to finish up the evening by listening to live music. As we walked into an area surrounding by tall palm trees, designated for live entertainment, my eardrums immediately began painfully convulsing from relentless shock waves of loud rock and roll music emanating from six large speakers positioned to either side of an elevated stage. The chairs were filled with people drinking and eating, and free tables were nowhere to be seen. The brightly dressed vocalist, with sweat-soaked hair and a damp face, screamed into a microphone as the guitarists and drummer punished their instruments behind him. Scores of drunken people danced, and swayed back and forth to the music in an open area between the stage and the tables. Spotlights illuminated the band and the dancers, casting shadows across the people sitting around the tables.

While we stood at the entrance, gawking at the gyrating crowd, three attractive young women gestured at us, offering seats at their table. I nudged Supattra, pointing at the offered chairs, and without hesitation, she surprisingly shook her head, looking away as if the mere contemplation of accepting the proposal was out of the question. I looked back to the three women, shaking my head and shrugging my shoulders. Eventually, not too far from the three young women, we finally found an empty table and sat down, ordering a round of beer.

Turning to Supattra, I asked over the deafeningly music, "Why didn't you want to sit with the three women?"

Looking at me, she simply stated, "They are bargirls."

One of our friends looked at me and asked over the loud music, "What did she say? Why didn't she want to sit there?"

I simply responded, "They're bargirls," once again shaking my head and shrugging my shoulders.

Asking the obvious question, he queried, "So what?"

For a third time, I shook my head and shrugged my shoulders. The friend next to me then leaned over and mumbled something to our other friend before both stood up and left our table. I knew where they were headed and a part of me wished to join them, leaving my seemingly stuck-up girlfriend sitting at the table alone.

Leaning back in my chair next to Supattra, listening to a Thai rock and roll tune whose lyrics I couldn't understand while sipping beer from a flimsy, clear plastic cup, I began wondering why my former bargirl girlfriend would not want to sit with the three alleged bargirls who had graciously offered seats at their table. Sitting there I recalled an incident several years earlier where we had been invited to a posh party on the mainland put on by a former publishing house CEO until the host had discovered Supattra's former profession during one of my drunken confessions. The next day we had been unceremoniously disinvited. After discussing the incident with Supattra, we had decided to keep her past a secret as best we could; making up some stupidly transparent story about how we had met. However, as Supattra had once explained to me, there is a good chance that a Thai woman attached to a *farang* man meant that they had met in a bar—and not many *farang* men work in bars.

Our concocted story merely became a method of saving our friends and customers the trouble of pitying or despising Supattra for her past choice of professions. It also lent an air of respectability to the relationship of an older man with a younger woman, removing any doubt as to the question of our relationship being about love and not about a financial transaction.

Suddenly, sitting next to Supattra at that temple festival on Koh PhaNgan, the difference dawned on me. The lovely woman sitting next to me had worked hard to erase her past and, by sitting with the three bargirls, she would have lowered herself back down to that place. The Samui Archipelago was a relatively wealthy region by Thailand standards. Her island friends had never had to wonder where their next meal was coming from and they certainly didn't understand the level of despair that would drive a woman to sell her body. Bargirls on these islands were all transplants, brought here because the local crop of women never needed to consider such a low lifestyle. Our friends would never understand her sitting at a table populated by women who sold their bodies for a living and, Koh PhaNgan being a small island where both Supattra and I were well known, someone in the crowd would undoubtedly see us and spread the word. That simple act would link her to her past. Sitting at that table that night on Koh PhaNgan I was suddenly impressed by Supattra's ability to understand the infinitesimal fundamentals of island—and human—politics.

While the dynamics of the village were a bit different, the same basic premise held true—Supattra had worked hard to put her past behind her and was proud of her standing in this village. She didn't want to tarnish her reputation by associating with another former bargirl who still dressed the part and had not managed to rise above her sordid past. Because of her history, Supattra was under constant surveillance by the villagers, scrutinizing her daily conduct in order determine her overall standing in the village. By dressing respectfully and treating the woman standing across the yard with a level of disdain, someone who had yet to banish every element of a lifestyle considered low, she was showing the villagers that she had risen above her past and could stand toe to toe with the best the village had to offer.

Standing in the brightly clad crowd at Yaun Kom City's temple on that hot day, I suddenly wondered if I, too, had been avoiding my past in a similar fashion. I certainly didn't socialize with military retirees on the island, I didn't keep up with my past professional friends in any way, and I had even let my ties with my sister and brothers languish. Had it been an unconscious reaction similar to Supattra's? Had detaching myself from everything I had known been a response to my posttraumatic stress? Had I disassociated myself from nearly every element of my past in a failed effort to rid myself from the sensation of hollowness? Had that reaction been partially responsible for the demise of my marriage? Standing in that crowd of strangers in a foreign land, I promptly came to the conclusion that I had reacted the same way the beautiful woman standing next to me had to her time in Pattaya, but in even a more extreme form. I had left everything I had known behind. Pondering my revelation, I causally scanned the crowds around us. I saw a teenage boy wearing a blue and white plaid sundress, looking angry and defiant, shifting my thoughts from leaving lives behind to the tolerance of this wonderfully forgiving and accepting country.

While most people think of prostitution and sexual deviancy when Thailand comes up in a conversation, in reality, promiscuity is looked down upon in the country, especially in the poor northeastern areas, from which most of the bargirls hail. While this may seem unbelievable, it is another aspect of their culture that I attribute to their Buddhist roots, turning their eye to other people's decisions along their path. This is somewhat affirmed by the fact that prostitution per capita in Thailand is well below many of its neighbors and Western countries. I have been told that Thailand's soiled reputation is largely due to the country ignoring the prostitution trade and, as a result, the flesh business being out in the open. Pictures of old, pot-bellied men slobbering over sparingly-attired young dancing women on Soi Cowboy in Bangkok and on Walking Street in Pattaya flood across the television and Internet, while a much larger demographic of girls selling themselves in Venezuela or China are never seen.

But there is another element of Thailand we Westerners culturally and mistakenly align with the sex trade, and it is likely one more reason that we associate this country as a leader in the global sex market. That element is Thailand's robust *katoy* population.

In its most basic form, a *katoy* is a male who prefers to act and dress as a female. Based on Western culture, this behavior would be classified as that of a transvestite—cross-dressing males with a heterosexual identity. However, this Western classification would be misleading, because *katoys* are not restricted to heterosexual identities. *Katoys* can have a heterosexual, homosexual, bisexual, or asexual orientation. The interesting element of trying to define a *katoy* is their standing among their fellow countrymen and women. When asked to explain *katoys*, I often start by telling people that Thailand has three sexes: male, female, and *katoy*. While looked down on in Thailand, even lower than prostitutes, *katoys* are a tolerated and accepted demographic amongst their citizens.

A good example of the complex *katoy* standing in Thailand occurred in our village on Koh PhaNgan not too long ago. The village had one of our Seven-Eleven clerks called to duty with the Thai military. This in itself is not unusual, except for the fact that this clerk also happened to be a *katoy* with either implants or estrogen created female breasts. When I asked Supattra about a makeup wearing, female-dressing, big-bosomed male showing up for military duty, she shrugged her shoulders and said it wouldn't be problem. The military had many *katoys* in their ranks.

Nudging Supattra on the shoulder amidst all the families on the Yaun Kom City temple grounds, I asked, "Who's the *katoy*? He seems a bit young to be flaunting his sexual preference in a rice-farming village."

Looking across the crowd to the boy wearing a blue plaid dress with disinterest, Supattra offered, "One of my classmates in school was a *katoy*."

"How old was your classmate?"

"Twelve or thirteen," she replied, looking back at the ceremony occurring on the unfinished temple. "Boys can choose early what they want to be."

"Your school in this village?"

"Yes."

"And the villagers didn't mind?"

"Why would they?" she asked. "He wanted to act like a girl. It was not their business."

"What about his parents?" I chuckled at the vision of a young Thai boy showing up for school wearing his hair in ponytails, and dressed in the traditional white blouse and blue pleated skirt. "They must have been disappointed."

"Do you remember the man that found the snake in his bed last year?"

"Yeah." I laughed. "He gave the local temple a dowry and married it, claiming the snake was a wife in a past life."

"And you found it unbelievable that he would marry a snake."

"I did think it was a little outlandish," I admitted.

"Why?"

"What does this have to do with your *katoy* classmate's parents?"

"Because Buddha works in mysterious ways and we shouldn't judge what other people believe or do in this life. It might be an important part of their path."

Once again, this woman half my age pointed out the flaws in my Western-developed judgments. Each of us were on a unique path in life and who was I to judge what was right or wrong when it came to the decisions made along someone else's path? This world and our lives were far more complex than the dubious manmade line between right and wrong.

Mark Twain once wrote: *Laws are coldly reasoned out and established on what lawmakers believe to be the basis of right. But customs are not. Customs are not enacted. They grow gradually up, imperceptibly and unconsciously, like an oak from its seed. In the fullness of their strength, they can stand up straight in front of a world of argument and reasoning, and yield not an inch. Customs do not concern themselves with right or wrong or reason.*

My time in Thailand has taught me that a nation's culture and customs taint the already obscure process of man's ability to establish a just boundary between right and wrong. I'm not writing of murder or other obvious heinous acts men and woman commit, but the intangible or minuscule things we do on a daily basis that others judge us by, one way or another. Whether we live in the United States or Thailand, the difference between right and wrong is affected by culture, a guideline that Mark Twain rightly points out does not concern itself "with right or wrong or reason."

I think the most interesting element of the *katoy* at the temple during *Songkran* was that if a teenage boy had showed up at a Fourth of July celebration wearing a dress in America, he would have been unmercifully ridiculed by other boys his age. But in this nation of tolerance, none of the other teenage boys in Supattra's village gave the plaid-skirted boy a second look.

As I stood examining the un-harassed teenage boy in the blue plaid dress—with visions of Supattra's *katoy* classmate's parents welcoming him home every afternoon in his pleated skirt and white blouse—witnessing exceedingly poor families giving away their hard earned cash to bald eyebrow-less monks dressed in orange robes, and pondering why Supattra reacted to her past differently than the re- bloused and patent-leather-shod woman in the crowd, I wondered if there could be a better place to find oneself while struggling with the loneliness and emptiness of posttraumatic stress. Those strangers standing around me on the Yaun Kom City temple grounds were culturally inclined to turn their heads to the decisions and actions of others, good or bad. Unlike their Western counterparts, these strangers standing around me were culturally disposed to judge a book by its contents—not its cover.

CHAPTER 15

The Fine Line between Courage and a Sense of Duty
~ 14 April 2014

On our second day in Yaun Kom City, with my morning routine beginning to congeal, after a chilly Isaan shower, I slipped on a pair of tan cargo shorts and a gray T-shirt advertising my alma mater. Moving from the bathroom to the patio, passing the small crowd playing dice on the blue tiles, I turned down an offered alcoholic beverage from Aae, before taking a seat at the picnic table. Our banter matched that of the day before, punctuated by Aae telling me I wasn't any fun. Standing up from the dice game, Supattra walked over to the picnic table and informed me that she was going to a high school reunion, of sorts, delivering donations she had collected on Koh PhaNgan for the construction of a new school building here in Isaan. I asked if I was expected to attend. She indicated that it was for former students and I would be bored if I accompanied her, not to mention no one there would speak English. The news brought with it an immediate wave of relief.

"But Aae has a good friend coming to visit and she is with her husband. He an Englishman," Supattra added, taking my hand in hers.

"English?"

"Yes, from Liverpool."

"Wherever that is."

"It is a big city and has a famous football club," she said curtly, eyeing me suspiciously as if I knew something about the English city that she did not.

Looking at her expression, wondering if she thought I was building up to a sarcastic crescendo, I tried to defuse her growing irritation and responded, "I know, but I have no idea where on the island of Britannia Liverpool is located."

When she brusquely asked, "Does it matter?" I realized she must be nervous about her reunion and likely concerned that her former classmates would know that she worked the bars in Pattaya and look down on her past.

Changing the subject, I replied, "Well, if you're off to your reunion, I'm headed out for a walk."

The agitated tone in her voice all but vanished when she asked, "Where will you walk to?"

"Just around the village. Out into the rice fields."

"Why?"

"I could use the exercise."

Nodding her head, indicating she understood, she gave me a *hom noi* on the cheek, before returning to the dice game.

Slipping on the first shoes and socks I had worn in over a year, I left the small horde of dice players, jabbering and laughing, and stepped out on the road in front of the house, walking toward our pickup parked next to the thatched roof hut. At the bottom of the hill, I turned right and walked along a paved road, filled with potholes and cracks as evidence of its age, and passed a raised barrier made of a single long tubular steel pole, marking the village boundary. Turning down an intersecting narrow dirt road, I wandered out into the rice fields with small tufts from last season's harvest poking through dry gray-brown dirt. Each quadrant of paddies seemed to have an associated thatched roofed wooden hut. Rice paddies stretched as far as I could see—each partitioned from its neighbors by low-mounded dirt walkways and tall, willowy silver-barked trees. Yaun Kom City seemed to be an island floating amidst a sea of dry rice fields. With the sun beating down on my head and shoulders, and dust pluming from each of my steps, I took in a deep breath, smelling the earthy aroma. I could feel every fiber of my body relax as I sauntered down the narrow dirt road, taking in the countryside sights.

The road twisted and turned between more willowy trees,

passing several more huts. I finally came upon a familiar-looking hut I knew belonged to Supattra's family. The hut's wooden supports were faded, its thatched roof nearly white, and its platform planking warped from years of standing in the hot Isaan sun. Examining the structure, I wondered how many generations of rice farmers that single hut had served. A threadbare hammock hung precariously under the thatched roof and trash had been heaped next to a rusted barbed wire fence. A hen with a line of chicks following close behind wandered around the edges of the hut and a water buffalo grazed on the dry tufts of rice in one of the nearby fields.

I recalled that during one of my first visits to Supattra's family farm when I had come out to the hut to read a book, to pass the time. I remembered, as the sun began to set, Supattra's father had come out and beckoned me to return to the village.

He was adamant when I first refused his advice. I found out later, having reluctantly followed him back to the village that night, Thais did not stay in the rice fields after sundown because of all the ghosts and spirits that roamed the countryside when it was dark.

Just beyond the hut, I walked past the small pond partially filled with muddy water that her father had dug several years ago, hoping to raise fish in order to feed his family during the off season. It had been a gallant effort but a failed venture, as the small population of fish had fed off each other when the natural food supply dwindled. The pond looked sad in the dry weather currently consuming Isaan and I wondered what it would be like when the rains came.

The narrow dirt road coiled through countryside and I began taking pictures of the huts I passed, each handcrafted and unique, as if abandoned watchtowers from past crops. An hour into my stroll, I came upon a man in a plaid, short-sleeved shirt, with a machete in one hand and a slender bamboo stick in his other.

Smiling, I asked what he was doing in Thai, "*Tham a rai?*"

With the slender bamboo stick, he pointed to three water buffalo munching on dry rice stalks in the field next to us.

Gesturing toward the machete, I then asked what it was for, "*A rai?*"

Realizing that my Thai was limited, he responded with a simple, "*Nguu,*" or "snake."

Thirty minutes later, I could make out the north end of the village in the distance and spied the slopes leading up to Yaun Kom city filled with fruit trees and tall grass. Wandering down flowery paths shielded from the sun by tall trees bristling with foliage, I climbed the hillside to the edge of the village and stood looking into the grounds of the school Supattra had attended as a young girl. Standing at the top of the incline with the school to one side and the fertile rice fields to the other, I scrutinized my surroundings and wondered how such a beautiful place could be filled with so much struggling and sorrow. I pondered how poverty and hunger had changed this picturesque village into a living hell for the woman I loved. I realized, standing at the edge of Yaun Kom City, that I would never understand the level of despair that she had endured in her youth or the depth of the scars that existence had created. All I could do was to stand by her side and show her that she was not alone.

Wandering back through the village streets, spiraling through the maze of buildings, I finally found the dirt road that Supattra's family home was on and stopped. Without her company, I knew the next few hours, waiting for her to return, would be long and tedious, with no one to chat with in my native language, even if it had only been in spurts during pauses of a crazy game of dice. Taking a deep breath to bolster my courage, I started walking toward the house.

Within earshot of the house, I heard a familiar language, although with an unusual accent. Stepping up to the covered patio, I saw a *farang* sitting at the picnic table and remembered Supattra's claim that an Englishman from Liverpool would be at the house sometime during the day.

Walking over to the picnic table, I introduced myself to a burly man about my age. He introduced himself as Sam, and he was indeed from the City of Liverpool, located on the River Mersey, northwest of London. Sitting down across from Sam, with the endless game of dice going on next to us, we spent the next hour talking about Thailand and the trials of living in this country as a foreigner. A former business owner, Sam was very intelligent and well read about current events, which I have discovered over the years is unusual for an expatriate.

On our fourth beer, Sam looked at me across the picnic table and said, "My wife tells me that you were a marine and served in Iraq."

Feeling my heart sink at the predictable subject, I said, "Yeah, I was there."

Seeing my distress at his comment, he apologetically said, "We don't need to talk about it."

Thinking the guy must be have owned a used car lot back in the United Kingdom because he had just indirectly challenged me by implying that I might not be able to talk about my experiences, I replied, "No, it's okay," while giving him a confident smile.

To be honest, of late I hadn't minded talking about Iraq, but I *had* grown tired of the topic. Since opening up about the war with Supattra in Surratthani, in the midst of an enormous increase in recollections of my military exploits, the subject had come up at least once a day. Sitting at that picnic table with Sam, I suddenly wondered if I hadn't been instigating the daily questions, subconsciously prompting those around me to ask about my experiences with the equally subconscious goal of ridding myself of all my locked up and untold baggage.

Looking quizzically at me, Sam asked, "Did you find it unsettling to be shot at?"

"Unless the aircraft was hit, it was difficult to know you if you were even being shot at."

"What do you mean?"

"With a bright desert sun, lots of dust relentlessly blowing around, and loud engines spinning directly behind me, it was hard to tell if someone was shooting at me unless I heard a round hit the helicopter. It wasn't until I spent the night in the old Iraqi secret police compound in Baghdad, surrounded by tall concrete walls, that I found out how much we were being shot at."

"What did you see that night?"

"Sitting on the top of my helicopter in the compound, I watched the helicopters flying across the city, all illuminated by the city lights and a big fat moon, and each one of them had a constant stream of tracer rounds following them from the ground. Likely unbeknownst to the pilots, hundreds of bullets were being fired up at each of the aircraft at any given moment," I said, adding, "Fortunately, the Iraqis had never been taught to lead a moving target—all verified by both my witnessing the helicopters being shot at over Baghdad that night and the fact that the bulk of the battle damage our squadron took was in the tail sections."

He nodded. "What was the most daring thing you witnessed while in Iraq?"

Thinking about his question, two different occasions immediately came to mind. One occurred during a medical evacuation mission for a unit stranded in the middle of a city and the other while the marines below me fought their way through the streets of An Nasiriyah. "I saw a lot people do a lot courageous things."

"Just tell me one—the most daring."

Flipping a coin in my mind, I selected the An Nasiriyah story, and began, "We had a tough time fighting our way through the first city we came to in southern Iraq. The preferred route north required us to push through the center of a fairly large city called An Nasiriyah, and we were hit hard by the Iraqis along a wide north-south bisecting road. I was flying cover for four or five helicopters picking up causalities from a large group of marines that had traversed the road under heavy fire when I got a call about a small group of marines trapped halfway up the bisecting road. After a few minutes of talking to these guys on the radio, we finally found them holed up behind a small cluster of buildings. The marines who had made it to the north end of the city had been traveling in armored vehicles and these guys had nothing more than thin skinned Humvees and trucks."

"I would imagine that they were pleased to see you arrive overhead," Sam commented.

"Yeah, the guy I was talking to on the radio said the minute we showed up the Iraqis quit shooting at them." I laughed. "I explained to him that they had quit shooting at him because they were now shooting at me."

"How did you extract them from the city?"

"One side of the bisecting road was lined with two- and three-story buildings and the other was a wide open field of dirt and short scrub brush, dotted with smaller buildings. The road itself was littered with our burning armored personnel carriers left behind by the first unit that pushed through the city. So we arranged for the artillery to drop a barrage of smoke rounds into the open field and then we flew cover above them as they sped up the road."

"And what occurred that was so daring?"

"As planned, when the smoke rounds were dropped into the open field, the small column of thin skinned vehicles began racing up the road. We circled about fifty to one hundred feet overhead the small column. Our door gunners were firing at the bad guys and the bad guys were firing at the column—and probably us. I'm sure it was sheer pandemonium on the ground. At least it looked that way from my perspective. At one point, I jokingly turned to my co-pilot and told him that I was glad he was in the left seat."

"Why did you tell him that?"

"Circling overhead, we were doing right turns, and he was in the outside seat when we were closest to the enemy. A bullet would have to get past him before it hit me. Well, anyway, in the midst of all the chaos, these Humvees and trucks that we were protecting began stopping at each burning armored vehicle they came upon, the remnants of the vehicles left behind by the first group that had made its way through the city."

"What?" he exclaimed, raising his eyebrows. "What in the world for?"

"They stopped in the midst of all the turmoil to pull the dead marines from the armored vehicles that had been knocked out and left behind by the first guys that traversed the road. These marines in thin skinned vehicles stopped to pick up what the guys in armored vehicles had left behind because they had been trained to never leave a marine behind. It was one of the most courageous things I had ever seen. It made me proud to be a marine."

"Wow."

"Yeah, wow," I chuckled again, before adding, "But I'm not sure the marines below me would characterize their actions as courageous."

"Why on Earth not?"

"They probably felt like they were just doing their job. They were doing what any marine would have done, given the same circumstances."

Silently looking at me for moment, Sam asked, "A sense of duty?"

I nodded. "A sense of duty."

Another hour of conversation with Sam and two more beers, his wife told him it was time to leave and visit more friends in the area. Sam begrudgingly complied and stood from the picnic table.

"I can't tell you how enjoyable it was to speak with another *farang*," he said, as he shook my hand.

Laughing, I replied, "Dually noted. Spending a week in Isaan with my poor Thai language skills is a test in patience. Although it doesn't really seem to matter how good my Thai is because they're all speaking Isaan."

After saying our farewells, Sam climbed into his car and drove off with his wife, leaving me to myself. Glancing over at the crowd playing dice, I walked into the small bedroom with the wide bed covered in a colorful quilt, and lay down, quickly falling asleep.

Around six p.m. Supattra stepped into the bedroom and lay down next to me.

"How was it?" I mumbled, slowing waking from my slumber.

"I saw my English teacher," she replied with a wide smile. "I told her I have been with an American for many years and have learned a lot of English."

"What did she say?"

"She was very happy for me. She said I was the best pupil

she had in her English class. She never had worry about me passing a test. I always did very good."

"Did you have a nice time?"

"Yes, it was nice to see all my old friends." After a moment she added, "We are invited to a party at one of my friend's house tonight."

"Where?"

"In a village not too far from here."

Lying on the bed, looking up at the white tiled ceiling, I thought to myself that getting away from the endless dice game out front and Aae's persistent push for me to drink would be nice. Wrapping my arm around Supattra, I rolled onto my side and nestled up to her, slipping my hand under her shirt. Her skin felt warm and trembled slightly at my touch.

"No way." She giggled, looking up at the window above. "The window has no curtains. The girls might peek inside."

"We could take a chance, or we could pretend we were taking part in their ongoing sex education program."

"No." She giggled again, removing my hand from under her shirt.

Rolling over onto my back, I let out a deep sigh.

After a moment of silence, she quietly said, "You have changed over the last two years, especially this last year."

I sighed again. "Do we have to talk about this again?"

"You almost seem happy at times."

"That would imply I was never happy in the past."

"You never seemed happy before. You always seemed preoccupied and hardly ever smiled. What has changed? Why have you begun to change?"

Looking over at her watching me, I asked, "Didn't we have this conversation the other day?"

"You never answered me," she replied in a serious tone.

"Yes I did."

"No you didn't."

Looking back up to the ceiling, in a moment of frustration, I sarcastically announced, "Buddhism has taught me that a single life doesn't damn us for an eternity. I've quit trying to figure out the difference between good and bad because the line between being moral and wicked is thin, and defined by man, which makes it innately inaccurate. Life is unfair and bad things happen to good people." Lying on the bed, staring past the white ceiling tiles, thinking about everything I had just spouted off in that moment of frustration, I chuckled and looked back over at Supattra. "Really, I think all those statements are true and the reason I've begun to change. In my opinion, we can't change any of those truths. We can't spend our lives fretting over the things we've done or what's been done to us. We can't be defined by man's view of what's right and wrong. Life is unfair and we can't expect anything but a struggle. So what are we left to do? We just need to get on with living and make the best it."

"Yes," she whispered, as she lay next to me. "Someone else's definition of what is right and what is wrong might not be correct because we each walk a private path. That path could be very different than that traveled by those judging us. And even though this is but one single life, we must still try to do the best we can, hoping for something better in our next. You are learning to put your past behind you. I wish I could do the same."

Reaching out and taking her hand, I said, "You will, and I will be by your side when you do."

Leaving Supattra to touch up her makeup, happily walking past the dice game on the front patio, I felt sorry for the three young girls trapped watching their parents get drunk and lose money at the hands of their uncle and grandmother. Sauntering down the road to the pickup, I saw Supattra's tattooed uncle sitting with three of his friends on the platform and made my way directly over to the thatch-covered hut as he predictably offered his glass full of clear liquid. Tossing the *lao kow* into my mouth, I grimaced as the painful oral experience took its course, ending when my stomach took four long nauseating rolls. Handing the glass back to her uncle, I thanked him in Thai and walked over to the truck, starting it and driving it up the hill to Supattra's family house.

Dressed in a long black dress, Supattra climbed into the

passenger side and looked over at me. "You look nice, sweet-heart."

"Wow," I commented, examining her outfit, brown eyes, and long dark hair that seemed to disappear in the blackness of her dress. "You look absolutely stunning."

"I feel sorry for the children," she said. "They are so bored."

Shrugging my shoulders, I replied, "We could take them with us to the party."

"If it is fun, I will come back and get them."

With that, I put the truck in gear and stepped on the accelerator, once again happy to be free of the dice-crazed horde. Supattra guided me to a neighboring village and down a road filled with more two-story houses. With excitement in her voice she pointed out a home next to a house with its garage-like first floor converted into a small convenience store.

We parked the truck on the far side of the road and, as we walked across to the house, I could see six men and two women sitting around a small table with a yellow tiled top on an unfinished concrete patio and hear Isaan music blaring from two oversized speakers. Supattra greeted the eight with a *wai*, and began chattering in Isaan. I found my way over to the table, taking a seat next to one of the women. It quickly became evident that most of the men were drunk with the women quietly tolerating them. Someone handed me an ice-and-beer-filled glass, and I took a long swallow, hoping that this party would be something slightly more exciting than the dice game back in Yaun Kom City.

Looking at the woman sitting next to me, I noted her wide shoulders and large hands. I examined her throat and spotted the telltale sign, an Adam's apple protruding just below her chin. Taking another long swallow of beer, as Supattra sat down next to me, I began watching four of the men, who had now moved out to the road and were splashing people passing by on foot and scooters with water. The best descriptive phrase as to their activities would be "gaily frolicking." I immediately began scrutinizing the two men seated directly across from me. Smiling at me, they both were talking in slurred Isaan, swaying back and forth in their chairs to the music, clearly in a drunken stupor.

Leaning towards Supattra, I whispered in her ear, "You do realize that all these guys are *katoys*, don't you?"

"They are not all *katoys*." She giggled. "Most of them are gay. Only the one sitting next to you is a *katoy*."

"What about the two drunks sitting across from me?"

"They are not gay or *katoy*, but both their wives have recently left them. Although the wife of the one in the blue shirt just came back because she is pregnant with their second child."

I sarcastically said, "I wonder why?"

Watching the four men, merrily flirting with one another, I asked, "Does your friend only know gays and *katoys*?"

Giggling again, Supattra explained, "Everyone in Kalasin knows that there are many gays and *katoys* in this village. No one knows why, but it is unlike any other village. Nearly all of the boys born here turn out to be *katoys*—or gay."

"What about the girls?"

"Not so much," she explained. "Most of the girls are normal. They leave the village to marry other men."

"Do most of the women who leave the village have children who end up being gay or *katoys*?"

"I don't think so," she replied, looking at me quizzically. "Why do you ask?"

"If the girls who married outside the village had a lot of gay and *katoy* children, it would mean there was a genetic reason behind the high preponderance of gays and *katoys* in this village. But if not, it means that it's something in the water."

"It's in the water?"

"There is something about the village that makes them a *katoy* or gay."

Spending the next few hours drinking and listening to the partygoers talking in Isaan, I actually had a good time. Several of the men tried speaking with to me in English and, at one point, I joined them on the street, throwing water at each other. I returned to Supattra's home a little later, picking up the three young girls and bringing them back to the party. Eventually, I safely drove both the two drunken men home—one to an empty house and the other to an angry pregnant wife. The evening was far more fun than watching the nonstop dice game.

That night, I was visited by my first wife's spirit again, her translucent figure drifting across the dark room's ceiling. With an expression that only a former husband knows, her ghostly green eyes seemed to glare down at me from above. Her wispy golden hair billowed around her head as if she were submerged in a tank of water. In my semi-conscious state, I suddenly wondered if she hadn't placed a mystical curse on me during her final hours, causing my life to somehow spin out of control. On the precipice of sleep, it all seemed so clear. My first wife was the source of all this misery. Then, as quickly as that thought had come to me, I drowsily grasped that our failed relationship had simply been one of the many obvious markers that indicated I had begun to walk the wrong path. This life was wrought by me alone.

CHAPTER 16

Waking early in the morning on the oversized bed with the colorful bedspread, I turned and looked at Supattra sleeping next to me. She was tucked under the vibrant bedcover as the standing fan blew a semi-cool breeze down on us. Examining her slumbering beauty, I contemplated how much my life had changed over the last eight years. For those who didn't know me or care to delve into the details of my life, I had evolved from the respectful position of Marine Corps squadron commanding officer to an expatriate living in what many would categorize as a third world country and shacked up with a former prostitute. However, if someone took the time to probe deeper into my psyche, they would have discovered an entirely different story—a different evolution. They would have seen a story about a man lost to his world and to himself, saved by a woman who carried as many scars as himself. They would have realized that only such a woman would have been capable of the feat. It took someone who had experienced the same brand of torment to see passed my careless actions and bad decisions, knowing that while the exterior might be rotten, the core remained true. Pulling myself up so that my back was leaning against the headboard, I continued to study Supattra, reminiscing how we had come to know one another, and how that seemingly innocent meeting had grown into a love.

Coincidently, I met Supattra during a *Songkran* celebration. After flying into Utapoa, a former US Vietnam-era airbase that is now a combined Thai military and civilian airport south of Pattaya, earlier in the day, my co-pilot and I stepped out of our hotel for a beer in one of the many bars that populate the city. Within a block of our hotel, we were soaked from the celebratory water fight. Turning down Soi Yamato, a short street named after a Japanese restaurant at one end, I reached into my pocket, extracting my cell phone, a critical tool when commanding a squadron. It too was soaked and water had seeped behind its screen. I quickly turned the phone off and began looking for refuge from the water tossing celebration.

Soi Yamato is narrow and filled with five or six bars, two hotels that could only be described as flop houses, and several small restaurants, all situated along two equally narrow cracked and crumbling sidewalks that stood three steep concrete steps above the street. A rat running along the edges of street or a drunk passed out in the gutter would not have been a surprising sight.

I quickly dismissed a bar to my right with a red velvet drape hanging over its entrance and two *katoys* in heavy makeup, dressed in tight-fitting dresses and spiked high heels, attempting to lure people passing by to enter. Looking to my left, as someone tossed a bucket of ice water across my shoulders, I spotted a small bar with a garage-sized entrance. Gesturing toward the bar to my co-pilot, I climbed up the steps to the cracked sidewalk, glancing at a small sign mounted above the entrance that advertised *The George and Dragon*, before entering. The George and Dragon, obviously owned by an Englishman, had several tables and chairs situated around a small pool table with a short bar to one side. Three bargirls sat on a long neon yellow vinyl couch at the rear of the room chatting with one and other and one stood behind the bar, smiling at what was presumably their first customers of the day.

Stepping over to the bar, I set my cell phone on the top of the counter and dug into my back pocket for my wallet while ordering two Singha beers. The woman behind the bar was tall for a Thai, standing at five feet, four inches, with golden skin, a round face, large half-cloaked dark brown eyes, full lips, and a rounded Thai nose. Wearing a short jeans skirt and a white blouse, her thick black hair dropped below her shoulder blades and she had an athletically toned body. She appeared to be in her early twenties and was exotically beautiful. Without a word, the exotic bartender pulled two ice-cold beers from a cooler behind the bar and placed them on the counter before picking up my cell phone, removing the back, and taking out the battery.

I silently watched as she pulled a jar full of dry rice out from under the counter and shoved my cell inside, flashing her large brown eyes at me.

I was completely mesmerized. Before even asking her name, I blurted out, "What's your bar fine?"

Smiling, she responded, "300 *baht*."

Not taking my eyes off of her, I reached into my wallet and placed three hundred *baht* on the countertop. At this point, I should probably explain the term "bar fine," the cost of buying a bargirl from her place of business for the evening. The price varies from bar to bar, depending the establishment's location and the quality of its women. The bulk of this payment goes into the bar's coffers and the subject bargirl or boy receives only a fraction. His or her pay is received when their services are completed, and is solely based on the size of the client's wallet and his or her satisfaction.

Two women who had been sitting on the couch at the end of room wandered over and began asking my friend and me our names. I ignored them as the exotic woman picked up my money and placed it in a small box behind the bar before holding up one finger, wordlessly telling me to wait.

As she began walking around the bar, I asked, "What's your name?"

"Aom," she replied with another smile, as she continued walking toward the rear of the room.

My co-pilot laughed as she disappeared through a door in the back. "You were about five seconds quicker than me."

Taking a long swig of beer from the bottle, I turned and asked, "What do you mean?"

"Those eyes are unbelievable." He laughed again. "If you hadn't paid her bar fine, I would have."

Although things were not good at home, I was still married. From my perspective, my wife was constantly angry, scrutinizing and criticizing everything I did. I couldn't remember the last time I had come home to normality or a loving relationship. In my view, her anger had driven a wedge between us and, as a result, we had quit sleeping with each other a year earlier. In retrospect, I was as much at fault for the division as she. Neither of us expected a friendly face when I walked through our home's door at night. I was as convinced that she had become a controlling wench, as she was confident that I was a self-absorbed bastard. We became the poster children for Robert Merton's concept of a self-fulfilling prophecy. We had become incompatible, driven apart by our incorrect definition of what we thought the other had become, elicited by our differing reaction to posttraumatic stress. Our mistaken classification of each other provoked us to act in a way that made our false concepts about the other to come true, giving us further proof that each of us was right and the other was responsible for our marital demise. I had not yet cheated on my wife, but I could see that day approaching as I was losing my desire to stay married.

Ten minutes later Aom reappeared dressed in blue jeans, black flats, and a red silk shirt, sitting down next me on a barstool. I asked her what she wanted to drink and she said something in Isaan to a new woman tending bar. The new barmaid placed a can of Sprite on the countertop, which Aom opened and began to sip. After two more beers, Aom, my co-pilot, and I stepped out of The George and Dragon and spent the afternoon bouncing from bar to bar, while partaking in the water fight on the streets in between. Even though Aom's English was limited, we seemed to communicate just fine. Eventually, my friend wandered off on his own, and Aom and I continued barhopping by ourselves.

At some point in the evening, we ended up at a massage parlor, sitting down on two side-by-side chairs to have our legs and feet rubbed down. By the expression on her face as she chatted with the masseuse, once again in Isaan, I quickly surmised that she had never had a massage before. At the end of the evening I walked her back to The George and Dragon, ordering a final beer.

The other bargirls crowded around Aom, chatting with her in Isaan. With her dark brown eyes flashing, she talked with the other girls, glancing at me every few seconds. I assumed they were asking her about our night and wondering why we had returned to The George and Dragon.

"Aom," I said, after draining the last of my beer from the bottle. "I'd like to see you again tomorrow."

Looking at me with a confused expression, she shook her head before saying something to one of the women standing next to her.

"She does not understand," the woman interpreted for Aom.

"I'd like to see her again tomorrow," I repeated my request for a second date. "I had a lot of fun and would like to take her out again tomorrow night."

"But she is yours for the night," the woman replied, her expression now matching Aom's confused look.

"I don't need to sleep with her. I just enjoy her company."

The woman interpreted what I had said to Aom. She said something in response before our ad hoc interrupter, in turn, said to me, "But she wants to go with you."

"Look," I said, reaching into my back pocket and pulling out my wallet, "I'll pay her for the night, but she doesn't need to sleep with me."

After another short conversation with Aom, the woman turned to me and said, "She doesn't want your money. She just wants to go with you. You don't need to pay her anything. You don't need to sleep with her. She just wants to go with you."

At this point, I hadn't known that Aom believed that we had already met, even before I stepped into The George and Dragon that afternoon. The last thing she wanted see happen was that I would walked out of the bar, with the possibly that I never came back, before I had time to come to the same conclusion that she and I had spent many former lives together and been searching for one another for years. Shrugging my shoulders, I nodded to Aom and her smile quickly reappeared. Before leaving the bar, she stepped behind the counter, retrieving the jar full of rice and extracted my cell phone, inserting the battery and turning it on. It worked perfectly.

As a serviceman working overseas, I was required to stay at a US Embassy approved hotel, for which the Marine Corps reimbursed me. In Pattaya, the Marriott was on the list of approved lodgings, and I gladly stayed there every visit. It was arguably the nicest hotel in Pattaya, with its U-shaped building wrapped around a lush tropical oasis of wide ferns, multicolored blooms bristling from the bushes, and tall palm trees. Situated in the midst of the striking courtyard was an enormous crystal clear swimming pool, with a slide at one end sculpted into the form of an elephant. Lines of heavily padded wood lounges surrounded the pool on elevated decks, and a bar hugged one side of the clear sparkling water. The rooms were impressive as well, with polished wooden floors, oversized bathrooms, balconies overlooking the courtyard, and queen sized beds with soft, comfortable mattresses.

Holding her hand as we entered the grand lobby, I guided her through the courtyard and up a single flight of stairs to the door of my room. I could tell she was shocked at the level opulence of hidden behind the walls of a hotel she had likely walked by numerous times, never having seen such luxury in her life. As we stepped into the room, her eyes nearly popped from her head. At that moment, I could feel innocence radiating from her like rays of sun light as she examined a height of comfort that she had never experienced.

After catching her breath she turned to me and said, "*Aap Naam,*" wiggling her fingers above her head.

"You need to shower?"

"Yes, shower."

Opening the bathroom door, I showed her the soap and shampoo. She shook her head at the shampoo, so I handed her a small disposable shower cap that was lying next to the sink. A quizzical expression indicated to me that she didn't know what it was for, so I opened the plastic bag and placed the shower cap on my head. She broke out into a giggle at the sight of me wearing the shower cap, before pulling it from my head. She then pushed me out of the bathroom and locked the door.

Listening to the water running in the bathroom, I lay back on the bed and turned on the television, watching the BBC news. After her shower, she stepped from the bathroom wrapped in a white towel, and walked over to the bed. Pulling the covers aside she climbed into the bed and pulled them back over herself, keeping the towel in place. Laying under the covers she silently watched me. Smiling at the beautiful woman next to me, I turned out the lights and quickly fell asleep, fully clothed on top of the covers.

Over the next four days, as my co-pilot and I flew missions across Thailand, I learned that Aom's beauty was matched by her intellect. I learned that she had come to Pattaya three months earlier after being laid off from a factory job in Bangkok. I learned that she had a big heart, giving what little she had to her less fortunate friends. I learned she was twenty years old. I learned that poverty had kept her from experiencing any form of luxury. And I also learned that she was stubborn and angered quickly. I found her stubbornness amusing and it was easy to ignore her quick temper. She returned my patience by ignoring my heavy drinking and occasional outburst. I was just happy to be around this bright beautiful woman and found myself feeding off her innocence. With each of her new experiences, I felt a small bit of my former self return. I felt a level of happiness that I hadn't for years.

One night, sitting in The George and Dragon drinking beer, I turned to Aom and asked her what her name meant. With her limited vocabulary, she told me that Aom meant nothing, it was her nickname.

"What's your real name?" Then in an attempt to find a phrase that she would understand, I asked, "What's your given name?"

"Supattra," she shyly responded, gently placing her hand on my thigh.

"Supattra?"

"*Khaa*, Supattra."

"That's a beautiful name," I replied. "Why don't you go by your real name?"

"*Than niiam*—custom," she explained in broken English. "All Thais—*mee* nicknames."

From that moment, I have always called her by her given name and, over time, all of her friends and family began too as well.

On my third or fourth visit to Pattaya, I explained that I didn't want her working as a bargirl anymore, and asked how much it would cost me. She gave me the price that would allow her to move out of the bar and rent an apartment, as well as take care of her living expenses. She also explained that another man from England wanted to do the same for her, but he had yet to send the money. While she did not really care for this man, she was desperate to leave this life and he was due back in several weeks. Without hesitation, I readily agreed to the price. I learned on my next visit that the other man was in town, and she and a friend had gone to see him. With her friend interpreting, Supattra had informed the Englishman that she did not want to be with him anymore. She told me that he was devastated at the news and couldn't look her in the eyes after learning she only wanted to be with an American she had met. I understood his grief and actually felt sorry for him.

I continued to see her each time I visited Thailand on business. Normally, when I was in town we stayed together in my hotel room. When I asked about staying in her apartment, she explained that there was no air conditioning or hot water, two essentials to living comfortably in Pattaya, and she shared it with a girlfriend from her home town and they only had one bed.

It was quite some time into our friendship before I realized just how serious she was about our relationship. We had known each other for nearly a year when we met up during one of my many visits and she asked me to stay at her apartment. I asked her where her girlfriend was and Supattra informed me that she had gone back to Kalasin to see her parents. After dinner we walked to a large four-story apartment building on the outskirts of the city. Climbing three levels of stairs, I could see concern on her face as she inserted her key and began opening the door. A blast of muggy air erupted from the apartment as she swung the door open. The apartment was tiny with a bathroom the size of a closet. After she was sure I wasn't appalled at her living conditions, she pushed me back on the bed before disappearing into the bathroom. A few minutes later, she reappeared, wearing a blue and red sarong, and walked over to the bed.

Smiling at her standing above me, I asked, "What's going on?"

Silently, she slipped onto the bed next to me and gave me passionate kiss on the lips.

After the kiss, I asked again, "What's going on."

Without a word, she began unbuttoning my shirt.

I pulled at the sarong. It easily came off, revealing her slender naked body, and we made love. This was not the first time we had made love, but this night obviously had special significant to Supattra. Lying on the bed afterward, I realized why the act of making love in her apartment was momentous to the beautiful woman next to me. It was the first time we hadn't made love in a hotel room. It was the first time the act of making love was not in the venue of her former profession. It was her way of telling me that I was different. While she had whispered that she loved me many times, this was her way of showing it to me.

I will never forget that she gave her heart to me in that tiny, muggy apartment, one year after I had first stepped into The George and Dragon.

Back on the bed in Yaun Kom City, Supattra rolled over on her side and opened her eyes, looking up at me leaning against the headboard.

Reaching out and placing her golden hand on my bare chest, she yawned and smiled at the same time. "Good morning, sweetheart," she muttered.

"Good morning, beautiful," I replied, "What time did you make it to bed?"

"I'm not sure," she groggily explained. "Aae pleaded for me to stay up and play dice with her."

Knowing that there was no possible way, I asked, "Did you win anything?"

"No." She giggled. "I think I lost nearly a thousand *baht*."

"You do realize that the odds are so stacked against the players in that game that it would take a miracle for someone to walk away a winner?"

Yawning again, she said, "I am just trying to support the family business."

Laughing, I asked, "The family business?"

"Yes, it's my mother and uncle's business. A lot of villagers like coming over and playing dice."

Knowing I was treading on thin ice, I said, "I think your mother and uncle are taking advantage of their kin. They've been taking everyone's money, pocketing it, all as we shell out money for food and drinks."

"They are poor." Supattra sighed, as if I could never possibly understand. "They need the money. We can lose some to help them."

"What about their poor neighbors?"

After a brief hesitation, she proclaimed, "They eat and drink for free."

Shaking my head, I said, "With food and drink that you and I bought," and then changing the subject before she became angry, I asked, "What's planned for today?"

Slipping her legs over the edge of the bed and sitting up, she replied, "Today is the final day and we are taking the family to Lam Pao Reservoir."

Having been to Kalasin's Lam Pao Reservoir several times over the years, I figured a day on the water might be another refreshing break from the endless dice game on the front patio—and I would undoubtedly save some money, even if I footed the trip's entire bill.

After another cold Isaan shower, I wandered out to the patio to find Aae and Yii drinking what was probably their third whiskey and coke of the day. With a big grin, Aae pointed to her drink, silently offering me an early morning cocktail. Shaking my head, I walked past Supattra's two sisters and down the road to the truck parked next to the thatched-roof hut. Sitting in the hut, drinking *loa kow*, Supattra's tattooed uncle raised his glass in a respectful offer to share. Taking a sip of the old man's *loa kow*, my taste buds screamed in agony. When I swallowed, my throat felt like it had erupted into a fiery inferno, and beads of sweat immediately broke out on my forehead. When the searing sensation finally reached my belly, my stomach took two violent rolls. Stunned by the predictable nausea, I took two deep breaths to keep myself from immediately tossing it back up.

Silently thanking the old man with a *wai*, I climbed into the truck and drove back up to the house. The family had assembled on the patio, outfitted with sunhats, a case of beer, two bottles of Jack Daniels, and several bottles of Coke. Sakchai swung a large plastic trashcan into the bed of the pickup, as Supattra dropped the tail gate and helped the children into the back. I grabbed the garden hose from the side of the house, and dragged it over to the plastic trashcan, dropping the spout inside. Sakchai jogged back over to the side of the house and turned the water on. I couldn't help but laugh at the sight of water trickling out from the end of the hose.

Looking over at Sakchai standing at the side of the house, I shook my head and said "*Naam leerk*," telling him to stop the water in Thai.

Sakchai looked at me and smiled.

"*Naam Yoot*," I tried a different Thai phrase to tell him to stop the flow of water.

Shrugging his shoulders, Sakchai remained standing immobile next to the side of the house.

Realizing that he was incapable of comprehending my bad Thai, I pulled the end of the hose from the trashcan, and began coiling while it still was trickling water from its end. Realizing that Sakchai and I were having difficulty communicating again, Supattra began analyzing what was happening from the far side of the pickup. Her mother, watching me coil up the dribbling hose, called out to Sakchai in Isaan and he promptly turned the valve off.

"Thank you," I mumbled to Supattra's mother, even though I knew she wouldn't understand my English.

"What's happening?" Supattra called out.

"It'll take two hours to fill the trashcan at the rate the water is coming out of the hose," I explained.

"Didn't you tell Sakchai to shut it off?"

"He didn't understand my Thai."

After a brief conversation with Sakchai, Supattra said, "He didn't understand what you wanted."

"*Yoot* is not a difficult Thai word for me to pronounce."

"You should have said *leerk*," Supattra replied.

"I did."

After loading the last of the gear into the pickup, Aae, Yii, and Sakchai jumped into the back, and Supattra and her mother climbed into the cab. I slipped into the driver's seat and looked over at Supattra, cocking my head to the side and raising my eyebrows, silently asking her if everyone was ready. She nodded to me, then began chatting with her mother.

Driving from the village we made our way through the dry rice fields back to the freeway that connected Kohn Kaen and Kalasin, turning east. Having traveled this route a dozen times, I always found it to be a relaxing drive. Passing wide open meadows and large shallow lakes, I could have been traveling through the countryside in Kansas or Oklahoma if it were not for the bamboo thatched-roof huts dotting the roadside that sold shrimp harvested, from the shallow lakes, and fat water buffalos grazing in the tall dry grass—not to mention the tropical plants and trees.

The traffic picked up when we turned down an intersecting highway that the led into Kalasin. Most were trucks with their beds loaded with people and large cylindrical containers that I knew were filled with water. The turn onto the road that led to the reservoir, marked with orange traffic cones, was clobbered with a small traffic jam of vehicles attempting to make the same journey. As Supattra and her mother continued their conversation, I maneuvered the truck into the line of cars. Just as we turned the corner of the intersection, I pulled over to the side of the road, behind four other pickup trucks, and a man carrying a fire hose with water gushing from the end tossed it into our plastic trashcan, quickly filling the container. Supattra rolled down her window and handed a young girl, who could have not have been more than twelve years old, twenty *baht*, paying for the water.

Pulling from the roadside water point, we were immediately engulfed in a massive water fight, as passengers in the beds of all the trucks fought with their liquid ammunition. It was one of my favorite events during *Songkran*, the forty-five minute drive from the freeway to the reservoir, watching a massive water fight between dueling vehicles inside the comfortably dry cab of a pickup truck. Each time Sakchai would tap on the rear window, indicating that they were out of water, I would pull over to another water point for a refill and Supattra would roll her window down to pay the 20 *baht*, more times than not to a child under the age of twelve.

With a clear blue sky overhead, the jungle closed in as the narrow road wended its way through the Isaan countryside. The windshield wipers thrashing back and forth, the truck was drenched from bumper to bumper with the passing of each vehicle. Completely soaked, Sakchai, Yii, Aae, and the children sitting the truck's bed, were laughing and tossing water at any target they could find. People, and even animals, loitering on the side of the road became targets of opportunity. No mammal, no matter how many legs they stood on, was safe. Occasionally we would come upon a small gathering at the side of the road and I would slow down, allowing the roadside crowd to toss water and talcum powder across the truck and Supattra's extended family. It was a hilarious sight and everyone, whether in the bed or the cab, sported wide grins.

The water fight continued as the road twisted its way up a low hillside in a tunnel-like vegetative cocoon, with long and thick tree branches bursting with bright green foliage hovering overhead, and willowy flower-topped, white-barked bushes surrounding us. Suddenly the water battle came to an end when we passed along the base of a tall and wide concrete dam. Dipping down onto a dry waterway, we began driving up one last tree-topped hill and the reservoir's awaiting parking lot.

CHAPTER 17

Little Things Don't Matter ~ 15 April 2014

Seven hundred yards wide, Lam Pao is a gravity-supported dam with two waterways situated along its base—one concrete runoff for the sluiceway that is normally bone dry, and the other a ravine cut out of the terrain allowing overflow to escape downstream from the spillway. After we drove through the dry sluiceway and up the hill that separated the two waterways, a man dressed in blue jeans, a long-sleeved white shirt, and a floppy wide-brimmed camouflage hat guided us to a parking spot under the dense trees that populated the top of the knoll.

I could feel the excitement in the air as the family climbed from the bed and cab of the pickup. The three girls slipped off their clothes, revealing swimsuits underneath, while their parents babbled to them in Isaan. Leaving the rest of the family standing next to the pickup, Supattra and I walked hand in hand between several open-sided buildings filled with women dressed in white aprons cooking behind gas burners or chopping vegetables on wooden tables. Boxes of food supplies and enormous red-and-blue coolers took up the space in the corners. Entering into large seating area covered with an enormous thatched roof with faded blue tarps covering worn areas, Supattra led me over to a rickety wooden platform with a low table on top that was on the edge of the steep slope looking down into the wide ravine that the spillway runoff trickled through. Inspecting the aged platform teetering on the edge, it looked as if it could fall down the steep incline into the ravine at any moment, to which Supattra seemed oblivious. Ladder-like stairs built from thick bamboo stalks reached down into the gorge, allowing access to the brown waters below. Looking across to the wide gully, I saw an identical restaurant setup on the other side, extending as far as I could see along the crest of the ravine. At the bottom of the ravine, hundreds of people frolicked in the muddy waters, splashing and playing.

As Supattra slipped onto the platform and behind the low table, her youngest niece appeared next to me, peering down into the gorge, then looked up with the obvious expression of needing help. I slipped off my flip-flops, picked her up, and began the hazardous journey to the bottom of the ravine. With the bamboo steps of the ladder leading downward agonizingly digging into the arches of my feet, I descended. At the bottom, I negotiated across large, jagged boulders that had obviously been put in place to reduce erosion at the base of the ravine, creating an entirely new sensation of pain on the pads of my feet. Finally I stepped into ankle-deep brown water, its coolness almost making up for the painful passage, and set the young girl down.

Looking up at me again, Supattra's young niece pointed toward a small, lopsided, faded wood hut displaying inflated car inner-tubes, and I promptly rented three. As she swam off, mixing with the other children swimming in the muddy brown waters, the other two nieces appeared by my side to whom I handed each one of the rented inner-tubes. Not long after that, Sakchai walked passed and joined his children, playfully splashing and pushing them about in the inner-tubes.

It was moments like that where I couldn't help but think about my own children, as the familiar mixture of disappointment and guilt washed over me. Sadly, it was a feeling that I had become accustomed to while living halfway across the world from my three children. Watching Sakchai merrily playing with his two girls, I would have given anything to have my children there with me. I had asked my ex-wife numerous times to allow me to bring my youngest son and daughter to Thailand for the summers. Surrounded by an international crowd of children their age and living on a beach, it would have created a memory where they would never question my love for them. She flatly denied each request, going as far as hiding their passports at her place of work during my visits.

Enjoying the coolness of the waters in the ravine that easily fought off the heat above, I looked up at Supattra, now sitting with her sisters and mother on the rickety platform, gazing down at me from a hundred feet above. Waving, I gestured for her to join me. I was so comfortable that I briefly considered sitting down in the murky water before realizing that I had no change of clothes for the ride back to Yaun Kom City. Turning, I again watched Sakchai playing with his daughters, secretly wanting to join them in the waist deep water. A few moments later, Supattra stepped up next to me and took my hand. We stood in silence watching the families and children around us playing in the dam's runoff. At its deepest point, the water at the base of the ravine could not have been more than four feet with a very slight downstream current, an obviously safe and exciting place for the children.

Having spent years advising Supattra to move on and find someone her own age, I have never had the guts or self-discipline to make the move myself. This lack of courage, when it came to making the wise decision to leave the woman of my dreams, has given me the motivation to ponder the aging process quite a bit over the years. In the midst of all this thoughtful contemplation, I have decided that most people remain young at heart, and the only difference between the old and young is simply the number of experiences that have tainted and colored their lives. Older people had more events that either contaminated their view on life or highlighted the allure of getting up each day.

Beneath slack or firm skin, depending on our age, we all have the same spirit that was genetically conveyed upon us at birth. Our souls never changed—whether optimists, pragmatists, or pessimists we were the same people who traveled through the birth canal on our very first day in this world. Whether outfitted in a nineteen, thirty-nine, or a fifty-nine-year-old body, we were the same person we were while learning to walk, making our first joke, or having sex for the very first time. Stripped of all the preconceived notions of the elderly, there was no difference between me and my children, other than a few wrinkles, a belated smile, and a plethora of experiences that had slightly tarnished my otherwise happy-go-lucky spirit. As time went on, I began viewing people as cars—the person behind the steering wheel a timeless spirit trapped in an aging vehicle.

My first car had been a used 1964 Volvo 544. The Volvo 544 happened to be considered an incredible automobile in its day, winning numerous awards. But in 2014, anyone looking back would laugh at that acclaim—its body style, achievements, and safety features lacking in every respect to today's vehicles. My next car had been a Triumph TR250 which, after driving along a mountain highway at 140 mph, I promptly told my father, in a moment of uncommon common sense, I needed to sell—which we did. The next was a mellow yellow AMC Gremlin, a hand-me-down from one of my older brothers and absolutely the ugliest car ever created. The Gremlin would not go into second gear, forcing me to shift from first to third in order to accelerate to a proper cruising speed, all the while listening to Willie Nelson or Jerry Jeff Walker, two popular country singers in my day, on a bulky eight track player.

My point is that our bodies are like cars. While our spirit may remain young, we will always be trapped in that old car of our youth. When we were twenty, driving that brand new sports car, we not only felt young but we appeared youthful. As that car aged we are still trapped in the front seat behind the steering wheel as our coolness began to ebb. We may feel young, but those watching us drive down the street recognized our car as out of date. Our ability to keep that automobile looking good is important. A well-maintained 1964 Ford Thunderbird is far more impressive than a beat up one, attracting a second look, even as an old car.

I see my oldest daughter as a Porsche 911, my middle daughter as a safe Volvo XC90, and my son in an age appropriate marine light armored vehicle with an unreliable 30 mm Bush gun bristling from its turret. I see Supattra driving a Land Rover. And while I may have transitioned into a pickup truck over the years, it is still a vintage 1958, and my soul is every bit as young as my children and the lovely woman I hang out with.

The reason I have taken the time to explain this unusual view of ageless spirits trapped in aging vehicles is that while standing ankle deep in the brown water next to me, Supattra asked, "Will you hold me when I die?"

Laughing, I replied, "There's a better than even chance that you'll be holding me. If you're looking for someone to hold you when you die, you had better find someone else to spend your time with—someone a little closer to your own age."

Arching her eyebrows and flashing her dark eyes at me, she replied, "I hate it when you say that."

"What?"

"You spent our first three years together telling me that I should find someone younger."

"Well it was true—and still is. I'm twenty-six years older than you." I laughed again. "When you're thirty-eight, I'll be sixty-four. When you're forty-eight, I'll be seventy-four. You'll be hanging out with an old guy during the best years of your life."

"We don't know what the future holds," she snapped in response, ignoring the implications of my statement. "I could die before you."

We have had this conversation at least a hundred times over the course of our relationship, most prompted by her telling me that she wanted to die in my arms. Looking down at her standing next to me, I knew she understood the repercussions of our age difference but chose to ignore them, as she had since the first day I recommended she find someone closer to her own age. It was terrifying to me, imagining this beautiful woman helping me walk down a street or watching me as I withered away in bed. I truly wished I could have suddenly become twenty years younger to save her the anguish of caring for an old man—not to mention the prospect of spending an extra twenty years with her would have pleased me. To this day, she will occasionally claim to new people we meet that she is in her late thirties, not because of our age difference or that she was embarrassed to be with an older man, but because she really wants to be older. She is concerned about her next life. She is concerned about me not waiting for her again.

"You know that I will die before you," I said flatly. "It is a foregone conclusion."

"Then you need to take care of yourself," she snapped again. "You need to live to be a hundred years old."

"You'll be seventy-four."

"I will be an old woman."

"And I'll be in a wheelchair."

"Not if you take care of yourself." Then visibly loosening up, she said, "Thais do not look at age the same way as *farangs*. In this life, you are older than me, but who's to say what the next life will bring. I could be older than you."

"I don't date older women," I teased.

Releasing my hand and slapping me on the shoulder, she giggled. "I am serious."

"This is one of those Thai qualities that I don't believe in," I jokingly said. "There are way too many old Thai guys hanging out with young *miia nois*."

"Yes, it is true," she admitted, taking my hand again, "many Thai men have young shadow wives, but those women do not mind the wrinkles on their husband's faces. They see what is in their hearts and whether those men love them or not. Age is a little thing to Thais."

When I added, "And don't forget the thickness of their wallets," she released my hand and slapped my shoulder again.

"You are thinking like a *farang* again."

Thailand is a wonderful place that is consumed in Buddhism, which professes looking beyond a person's physical state. But I also know that, no matter the color of one's skin or nationality, people are genetically designed to be attracted to strength and virility.

While Thailand is remarkable and its people have numerous outstanding traits, after several years of living in the country, I take talk about their exceptional qualities with a grain of salt. Thais are an incredibly nationalistic people and trying to convince them that people are people, no matter their nationality or religion, is nearly impossible. It is a point I have endeavored to make numerous times over the years and failed at each attempt. It is now a discussion I have learned to steer clear of.

"You're right, I am sorry." I waited for her yawning response.

"I am sorry, too. I did not mean that all *farangs* are bad people."

Studying Sakchai playing with his children in the muddy waters twenty feet away, I asked, "What does Sakchai do for a living?"

"He is an electrician," Supattra responded, joining my gaze on Sakchai while reaching up and pushing back a strand of hair from her face.

Keeping my eyes on Sakchai, I offhandedly said, "I'm surprised he hasn't electrocuted himself."

Looking at me quizzically, she asked, "What do you mean?"

"He doesn't seem like the sharpest tool in the shed," I replied, using a fairly common American expression I doubted Supattra would understand. "He can't understand a thing I say, whether in English or Thai."

Slapping my shoulder for a third time, she said, "That is not nice."

Laughing, I asked, "You understood what the sharpest tool in the shed meant?"

"I am not dumb—and neither is Sakchai," she snapped. "He works with very powerful electricity engines in Bangkok."

"He works in a power plant?"

"He is the youngest nighttime manager they have ever had."

"He's a shift manager at a power plant? Then why can't he understand anything I say?"

"Because, like you, he cannot hear well. The engines are very loud and have hurt his hearing. He asked me to tell you that after he went down to the hut and drank with you on our first night in Yaun Kom City. He could not hear anything you said to him. You did not speak loud enough."

Laughing again, I asked, "Why didn't you tell me that? Why didn't you tell me that during the drive north from Bangkok?"

Taking my hand again, she asked, "Would it have made a difference whether you knew he couldn't hear or not? It would not have made a difference. He is the same person."

"Knowing he was deaf would have made all the difference in the world," I said, trying to comprehend the logic in what she was trying to explain. "We can't communicate because we're both deaf. I could have used hand and arm signals; I could have gestured."

"Why?" Looking at me with a serious expression, Supattra said, "Gesturing would not have made you better friends. Neither of you can hear well. You still would not be able to talk to each other. It would not have made a difference."

"I would have understood the problem."

"It is a little thing that does not matter. It does not matter whether you knew he cannot hear or not. He is the same person, whether he can hear well or not. You are the same person whether you can hear well or not. It has nothing to do with who you are or the friendship you share."

Muttering, I replied, "There seem to be a lot of little things that don't matter in Thailand."

"No, there are not a lot of little things in Thailand," she calmly stated, "but there are a lot of things that do not matter that are important to *farangs*."

Pulling me from the murky waters, Supattra led me across the painful, jagged rocks and up the excruciating bamboo stairs, to the rickety platform overlooking the ravine. A soft warm breeze blew across the platform, carrying with it a smell of the musty water below and of fried chilies and garlic from the nearby restaurant, as she joined in the discussion between her sisters and mother. Their Isaan conversation became a relaxing background harmony as I sat silently watching the playful activity below, wishing my feet were still planted in the cool brown waters of the ravine.

Plates upon plates of spicy food showed up, and we all dug in using our hands. I filled my belly with a mixture of shrimp, noodles, and *Som Tam*, while avoiding the tasteless white rice. Dousing my spice burning mouth with beer every few minutes, I waited patiently for Sakchai and the children to finish swimming and then eat, knowing that the alternative was watching a dice game on the front patio.

Sitting next to the four women on the wobbly platform as they chattered in a language I couldn't comprehend, peering down into the deep ravine, I began reminiscing about a flight in Iraq during which I had no idea how I survived.

෴

It was a hot day as we flew out of Baghdad and north towards Saddam's hometown of Tikrit. Leading a section of Huey gunships, two helicopters with a rocket pod mounted next to one of the skids and door guns, my co-pilot was on the radio scribbling down a mission from the direct air support center onto a piece of paper that was mounted on his kneeboard.

"We need to pick up the division commanding general from a building in Tikrit and bring him back to Baghdad," my co-pilot explained to me over the inter-cockpit communication system.

The young marine next to me was not my usual co-pilot, nor was the helicopter following us filled my usual wingman or his aircrew, but the remnants of another section that had raised questions about the ferocity of their usual section leader.

Rather than confronting the section leader with allegations that his aircrew and wingman felt he lacked an appropriate level of aggressiveness in carrying out his duties, I decided to let the disgruntled marines fly with me so they could use my leadership as a measurement of his audacity.

Believing there is a fine line between level-headed leadership and a perceived lack of aggressiveness, I had learned over the years that in the heat of battle everyone wants to charge in and kick ass, but good leaders tend to use more methodical and efficient techniques.

Glancing over at my co-pilot, I asked, "How many strap-hangers does he have?"

"They didn't say," he replied. "They just told me that we're to pick up the division commanding general."

"It's a hot day. Let's drop the rocket pod in case he has an entourage. It's pretty obvious with the lack of power available in this helicopter that our bleed air valves are starting to go and, in this heat, we'll have a hard time picking up anything."

Some sixty miles out of Baghdad, we landed at a forward refueling point and filled up with fuel while an ordnance crew took off our single rocket pod, dropping some four hundred pounds from our overall weight. Even having dropped the weight of the rockets and pod, our helicopter struggled to pull up into a hover, providing confirmation that the dry and dusty desert air had indeed began to savage aircraft's engine mounted rubber bleed air valves.

Following the Tigris River north, we flew over the wide shallow river for thirty minutes before Tikrit appeared along its banks on the horizon. Having been given grid coordinates, we followed the aircraft's GPS as it directed us to a high bluff surrounded by a deep ravine next to the river. An enormous building with a small courtyard took up the entire top of the bluff.

As I flew around the building, I causally commented, "Looks like the courtyard is the only option."

"It's pretty small."

"Big enough for two Hueys," I countered.

Looking down at the building, as we circled overhead, for some indication of which way the wind was blowing, I decided it was coming out the north and lined the helicopter for an approach from the south. It was an uneventful landing, and I shifted the helicopter to one side, giving my wingman room to land behind me. Choosing a different approach, he came in from the west and once he was on the ground, we both rolled our throttles down to idle.

The cockpit quickly heated up under the slow spinning

main rotor blades as I took in the sights around me. With a marble façade, the front of the building was carved with elaborate insets and the front doors appeared to be solid copper or maybe even gold. Several long narrow windows stood to either side of the entrance. The courtyard itself was covered in manicured grass and was encircled by a low marble wall, separating it from the deep ravine that surrounded the bluff.

Several minutes later the large metallic doors opened and a slender man dressed in marine fatigues stepped from the entrance of the building. Saying something over his shoulder to whomever he had been talking with, he trotted down the steps to the courtyard, walked under the turning rotor blades, and hopped into our helicopter. The crew chief directed him to a jump seat situated between the pilot and co-pilot seats, and he slipped on a helmet that was attached to the inter-cockpit communication system. Looking over my shoulder, I saw General Mattis, the Marine Division Commanding General, smiling at me.

"Where you headed, sir," I asked, smiling back at him.

"Baghdad," he replied in his usual happy tone.

I rolled up the throttles on the collective and the overhead blades began speeding up, as my co-pilot read through the pre-takeoff checklist. Checklist complete, I slowly raised the collective, paying close attention to the aircraft's power available. In a four-inch hover, the instrument gauge power needles had pegged on 100%, telling me that we weren't getting off the bluff with our failing bleed air values in the heat currently consuming Tikrit.

Suddenly, with no control inputs, the tail boom began rising up as our helicopter was seemingly pushed toward the marble wall separating us from the ravine surrounding the bluff. When it became evident that the nose of the helicopter was going to strike the marble wall, I pulled up on the collective, placing more pitch in the main rotor blades that requested additional power from the struggling engines. With the low RPM horn now going off in my helmet telling me that there was not enough power to accomplish what I had just requested, that small control input momentarily raised the helicopter eight feet off the ground before dropping us down onto the marble wall with an aircraft shivering impact as the skids struck the top. There was complete silence in the aircraft as we bounced off the marble wall and fell into the ravine.

My first concern, other than the fact we were dropping into a ravine with no power, was that the tail boom might impact the marble wall or the side of the ravine. Slamming the cyclic against the forward stop, the nose pitched down into arguably the steepest dive I had ever been in while flying a helicopter. Watching the base of the ravine race toward us, I felt a sudden calmness wash over me. While my life did not pass before my eyes, I had no doubt we were going to die in that ravine, as years of training kicked in, and my hands and feet began to methodically make control inputs.

With the accelerating wind whistling across the open window next to me, as a vision of our unavoidable fiery crash flashed into my mind, I glanced up to ensure there were no power lines or other obstacles in our path before yanking the cyclic back into my lap, trying to abate our steep dive. The hydraulic servos began loudly pounding beneath my feet and behind the rear bulkhead, adding more confusion to the cockpit, as once again my control inputs demanded too much from the aircraft. The second the servos started their hammering complaints. My new co-pilot began screaming over the inter-cockpit communication system, "The transmission! The transmission!"

As if God had reached down into the ravine, the helicopter's nose began to rise. Once again overwhelmed with a level calmness that only a dying man must know, I heard myself casually reply, "It's the servos. I've pulled too hard on the controls. It's not the transmission."

Miraculously, the helicopter leveled off, and I flew out of the ravine and over the Tigris River. The inter-cockpit communication system was silent, as I turned south and headed toward Baghdad. My former calmness was replaced with immediate giddiness, a feeling I had become familiar with during my years with the Marine Corps, as the danger had passed but adrenalin continued to course through my veins. Realizing that my control inputs seemed a bit erratic, I looked down at the console and saw that our violent bounce off the marble wall, or maybe my aggressive pull on the cyclic, had knocked the computerized stabilization system off line.

"Turn the SCAS back on," I evenly said to my co-pilot, breaking our silence.

General Mattis, just as evenly, then asked, "What happened back there?"

Not really knowing what had happened, my mind raced for an explanation. The uncontrolled rising of the tail boom and aircraft's forward movement exhibited classic properties of strong tailwind. While there might have been a small breeze on the bluff swirling through the courtyard, it certainly wasn't the level that would cause the aircraft to become uncontrollable. Then, while looking down onto the Tigris River searching for an answer to the General's question, I realized what had likely happened. My wingman must have waited to pull up his collective, increasing the pitch in the main rotor blades, until he saw me taking off from the courtyard. As I hovered several inches above the courtyard, trying figure out how to get off the bluff, the increased breeze created from his aircraft's rotor downwash must have gotten under my blades and forced my aircraft forward.

Not wanting to blame the incident on my wingman on a hunch to I explained the commanding general, "It was trick we learn while flying off ships, sir. When we don't have enough power to take off, we jump over the edge of the flight deck to get the speed required to fly."

While I had told a true story about flying off ships in the underpowered UH-1N, it was not what had happened on that bluff. I had provided the General with a plausible explanation to something we might never know the answer to. Flying over the Tigris River, we were all still recovering from as close a call with death that many on board would ever have, until their final day on earth, that is.

Landing that evening, my wingman explained that watching us bounce off the top of the low marble wall and falling over the edge, everyone thought we were dead, expecting to see a crumpled and burning Huey at the bottom of the ravine. Shocked at the spectacle of our aircraft falling into the ravine, even the members of the media, who had been filming the general climb onboard the helicopter and fly off, had dropped their cameras and raced over to the low marble wall, peering over its edge. The sight of our helicopter pulling out of a steep dive in the narrow canyon was the last thing anyone had expected. Presenting me with a piece of marble that we had broken off the wall, my wingman shook his head and claimed I was the luckiest man he had ever met. Taking the marble from his outstretched hand, I chuckled and told him that our survival had simply been an example fine airmanship, knowing that neither of us believed that bullshit.

❧❧❧

Watching the families frolic in the waters below, I wondered how I had survived that day. Surely that tail boom could not have missed the marble wall or the wall of the ravine. Then I wondered why I had looked down at that the instrument panel on the stormy night with Mike Lueck of the coast of Southern California, pulling back on the cyclic and up on the collective at the last moment. I wondered how I had been able to pull my aircraft out of Vortex Ring State during the First Gulf War, while absolutely knowing that my flight was about to end in a violent and fiery crash on the desert floor. I wondered how Jeff Couch had known he was going to die in a helicopter accident and I was not. I wondered why one of the squadron pilots who had perished during the drive north in Iraq had been the only one in the unit to leave a video message to his unborn daughter, and I wondered why the other pilot in the aircraft who had died along with him had canceled his life insurance policy prior to leaving the states. Was the video message one's acceptance of his future and the canceled life insurance policy a rebellion by the other?

I wondered why I had survived and so many of my peers had not. Was this the real basis of posttraumatic stress, the guilt of survival? Or was it the trauma of countless adrenaline surging episodes during a career of violence? My thoughts were interrupted when Supattra poked me in the shoulder and said, "You're doing it again."

"What?"

"Going someplace else in your mind."

"I was just thinking," I replied with a smile.

Shaking her head, she said, "You think too much."

"I've been thinking too much for as long as you've known me."

Leaning over and giving me a *hom noi* on the cheek, she whispered, "Yes, you have."

It was late afternoon when the family began making moves to gather themselves together, packing their reservoir version of beach bags, and leaving the wobbly platform that threatened to fall into the ravine at any moment.

Retracing our route along the jungle road towards Kalasin, we once again joined the roadway water fights, washing the reservoir mud from our pickup and the family members sitting in its bed. The youngest girl, having opted to ride in the comfort of the cab for our return trip, quickly fell asleep in Supattra's lap, as her mother dosed off in the back seat.

Leaving the water fights behind, we turned onto the freeway that connected Kalasin to Kohn Kaen and, Supattra said, "We need to go to the jungle market before going home. My mother wants to pick out some food for dinner."

I had been to the jungle market numerous times during previous visits to Kalasin, a popular outdoor bazaar that serves up items not found in the standard city markets: bugs, raw honey, frogs, and other items scavenged from the surrounding countryside. Thankfully, cold beer was also readily available at this market.

Easily locating the turn to the jungle market, we once again found ourselves on a narrow two-lane road, twisting through the countryside. As the road turned upward, we drove through dense thickets of aspen-like trees, passing several giants and law-abiding families along the way.

Suddenly the dense foliage opened up on one side, revealing a large roadside dirt parking lot that was packed with other cars and trucks. Pulling in, I found a spot to park on the far end.

Moving her sleeping niece to one side, Supattra asked, "Do you want to come along?"

Knowing from experience that a shopping trip at the jungle market could take a considerable amount of time, I nodded and stepped from the pickup. With her mother following close behind, we left her niece under the care of her father as she slept in the cab, and walked toward swarms of people milling around rows of wooden thatch-covered stalls lining the far side of the parking lot. Stopping at the first booth to purchase a can of beer, I quickly lost sight of Supattra and her mother in the crowd.

Walking down the single aisle that separated the two rows of booths selling bright-colored fruit and vegetables, glistening black bugs, dusty brown frogs, gray and tan mushrooms, and small featherless birds I sipped on my can of beer while perusing the merchandise with interest. The market seemed to go on forever, the merchants of each stall beckoning me with smiles and waves of their hands. Midway down the aisle, I found a stall selling asparagus, an unusual find in any market or store in Thailand. Knowing that Supattra loved the vegetable as much as I, the planned purchase of a single kilo quickly turned into two. The merchant, beaming from my large purchase, slipped the asparagus into a white plastic shopping bag that was bore the imprint of some high-end store in Kohn Kaen or Kalasin. Near the far end of the market, I finally caught up with Supattra and her mother, loaded down with food in more reused white shopping bags, and saw that she, too, had found the asparagus stand and made a similar purchase.

Laughing at what should have been unsurprising sight we turned around and backtracked through the wooden booths, once again perusing the merchandise to make sure we hadn't missed anything. As I passed the beer stand at the end, on the way to the pickup, I purchased another can of beer, dropping my empty in a nearby bucket that I knew would be recycled by these fastidious people.

Choosing to ride in the bed of the pickup with her sisters, Supattra directed Sakchai to ride up front with me. Looking at her brother-in-law in a new light, I happily patted him on the shoulder as he climbed into the cab and sat down next to me. Knowing what I had learned about his hearing impairment, I could now see an intelligent sparkle in his eyes as he smiled.

Driving down the aspen-like tree-covered hillside, I could see a dark, ominous-looking storm brewing on the horizon, speeding toward us as quickly as we were speeding toward its leading edge. Glancing into rearview mirror at the laughing cargo of people in the pickup's bed, I silently shook my head, knowing that we would not make Yaun Kom City before the inevitable collision with the storm. Pointing out the window to Sakchai, I gestured toward the approaching storm.

"*Chai*," Sakchai chuckled, "*Jat*," which I found out later meant bad weather.

Chuckling to myself, in a loud voice I asked, "Should we warn them? *Dteuuan mai*?" knowing he wouldn't understand a word I said.

Looking over at me with a devious expression, Sakchai replied, "*Mai*," or no.

Giving him a double take, I asked, "Did you just understand me? *Khao Jai mai*?"

With a playful expression he answered, "*Khrap*," indicating yes.

Having left the protection of the aspen-like trees, we smashed into the leading edge of the storm in a relatively open area. Torrents of rain and wind slammed into the pickup, soaking the passengers in the back in a matter of seconds. The wind seemed to get under the truck, pushing it around on the road and blowing anything loose from the bed. Looking through the rearview mirror, I expected to see frantic and troubled faces peering at me through the rear window. What I saw shocked me. Supattra, her sisters, and the young girls were laughing and playfully flailing their arms in the air, as if tempting the gods to give them more.

I looked over at Sakchai. He smiled and, speaking in his own pidgin version of Thai, said, "*Fohn dtonhk, mai mee bpan haa,*" a term I immediately translated as "falling rain is not really a problem."

Chuckling again, I asked in broken Thai, "*Bpan haa, lek mai?*" asking if it was just a small thing.

"*Khrap.*"

After an evening playing dice, eating lots of asparagus and other spicy food picked up from the jungle market, and drinking beer, I collapsed onto the wide bed with the colorful bedspread in the small bedroom with the standup fan blowing semi-cool air. Supattra jumped on top of me, giving me ten sloppy *hom nois* in a row on my face while giggling before rolling off to the side and passing out. Looking over at the beautiful woman lying next to me, I wondered where I would be had I never met her.

CHAPTER 18

The Reeds Revisited ~ 16 April 2014

Sometime before dawn I was visited by my first wife's spirit for the last time, her filmy figure roaming across my drowsy awareness. Her somber expression and waging finger had been replaced by the woman I remembered in happier days, sparkling green eyes and a crooked grin. I tried to ask her why she was there and what had made her suddenly content, but she only nodded before vanishing into the recesses of my mind. I knew my subconscious thoughts must be playing tricks, and it was only wishful thinking that I had somehow obtained her approval, but I was lost as to what imaginary approval she might be giving me.

Waking and showering that morning, unable to shake the apparition of my first wife's approving green eyes, I loaded our luggage into the pickup truck, and we said our farewells to Supattra's mother, father, uncle, and sister Aae, along with several neighbors looking for an early morning game of dice. With Supattra sitting next to me, and Yii, Sakchai, and the two girls in the backseat, we began to backtrack the same roads we had driven six days earlier, heading for Phetchabun. Leaving Yaun Kom City, I watched from the corner of my eyes as Supattra *wia'ed*, whispering some indiscernibly Buddhist maxim. Glancing over at her, I could see her eyes had filled with tears. Pondering her sadness, I wondered if she was emotional about leaving her village or about my inevitable departure in two days.

Three hours later, having just passed through the city of Chaiyaphum, the roadside businesses and wide-open fields with grazing black water buffalos vanished into rolling hills filled with thick vegetation. My passengers all asleep, lulled by the sound of the truck's engine and it tires spinning across the pavement, I once again found myself in deep thought about posttraumatic stress and the path that I had travelled over the last eight years.

Traveling down that country road, I thought about my downward spiral, recalling the hollow feeling and my tainted decisions. I reflected on Supattra's notion that we had been together for many lifetimes, suffering collectively over the centuries. Passing a lumbering giant, I contemplated my sudden ability to open up and speak of things I had hidden behind an emotion dulling shroud. I wondered about God and religion's place in my life, and whether it had been partially responsible for my healing. Coming to a halt at a crossroad stop light, I considered the ghosts that lived in our home and the challenges of living in Thailand.

I then began wondering how I could have missed the fact that the woman I had been living with for eight years also suffered from posttraumatic stress. I thought about the three reeds that Supattra had described to me and how she told me I had already known about them, speculating on where I had learned about the Buddhist words of wisdom enough to speak of them to the dying man at our home. I considered all the regrets I had collected over the years, and wondered if I could ever come to terms with them all.

I deliberated my use of alcohol, and how it had nearly destroyed me and driven off the woman I loved. I reflected on all the courageous acts I had seen during my years fighting in the different conflicts in which I had participated, contemplating the minuscule difference between bravery and cowardice. And I thought about the woman asleep next to me and how she had saved my life, wondering why she was uncharacteristically concerned about my departure in two days.

As I pondered the last six days, I realized just how important it would be to remember every aspect of this weeklong experience. Having never kept a journal, I wondered if I shouldn't write it down, passing what I had learned during this trip to my children—and possibly providing the account to others suffering from the same ailment.

Sitting behind the wheel of our truck with the lush jungle bracketing the road we were driving down, I began pondering another Mark Twain passage that had recently caught my eye: *Through want of reflection, we associate repentance exclusively with sin. We get the notion early and keep it always that we repent bad deeds only; whereas we do a formidably large business in repenting good deeds which we have done.* After reading his words, I wondered if I had been repenting sins or good deeds that went bad. Had my intentions of an honorable career and following the family tradition of military service been authentic, or had they simply been a façade?

Mark Twain went on to write: *Often when we repent a sin, we do it perfunctorily, from principle, coldly and from the head; but when we repent a good deed, the repentance comes hot and bitter and straight from the heart. Often when we repent a sin, we can forgive ourselves and drop the matter out of mind; but when we repent a good deed, we seldom get peace – we go on repenting to the end.* As I drove down that road surrounded by thick green vegetation, I decided the intentions that had led me to posttraumatic stress had been principled, evident by the soul searching I found myself undergoing at the end of my career.

Leaving the fertile rolling hills south of the Sut Phaen Din ridgeline, we began twisting back and forth on switchbacks through the dense jungle up the side of the mountain. Through breaks in the thick vegetation, I could see beautiful vistas of the surrounding countryside, dark rivers cutting through emerald green tropical forests, and gray rocky formations jutting upward toward the clear blue sky. The beauty of this country was astounding and so different from America—the splendor of its culture and generosity of its people eclipsing it all.

Stirring in the seat next to me, Supattra groggily asked, "Where are we?"

"Just climbing up the south side of Sut Phaen Din," I replied, looking over at her.

"We need to go to the temple in the jungle here."

"We can stop by if you like," I said, "and take a break from driving."

"I would like to see it," she sleepily requested. "Sakchai says it is a nice temple."

Having lived in Thailand for nearly eight years, I have been to a lot of temples and, quite frankly, they all seem a bit alike after a while—large buildings with steep red roofs trimmed in gold, filled with equally sized statues of Buddha, normally painted gold as well. The ritual had been deeply worn into my memory—kneeling on the floor in front of the Buddha, sticks of burning incense wedged between clapped hands, bowing three times before adding the smoldering tribute to those left by previous visitors. Dressed in orange robes, monks wander the grounds and nod knowingly at visitors, providing a calming and serene atmosphere, as well as giving whispering cryptic advice when requested.

Seeing the temple entrance, I turned onto a winding forest road which, several kilometers later, delivered us to a large covered parking lot that would have been more appropriate next to a city shopping mall. Above us, I could see three different small shrines situated on the steep lush mountainside, each containing a Buddha statue. Parking, we left the two girls in the pickup truck and followed a staircase leading up the side of the mountain to the shrines, where Yii and Sakchai split off and went their separate way. Silently, I watched as Supattra entered the first shrine and knelt in front of the Buddha, bowing three times while *wiaing* with her incense and whispering something in Isaan. In sequence, we visited the other two shrines where I silently watched as Supattra repeated her whispering *wai* and kneeling bows.

When she had completed the ritual at the third shrine, I asked, "Why three shrines?"

"This temple is famous in Thailand for their three shrines. Each represents something different," she explained. "The first is to strengthen your love, the second is to make your marriage last many years—"

"To give it longevity," I quietly interrupted.

"Longevity," she repeated the word, before continuing,

"And the last is for bringing you back together in the next life."

"They're for marriages—for married couples?"

She smiled. "For people who love each other."

"Is that why you wanted to visit this temple?"

"You are leaving me to go back and see your children, and I wanted Buddha to strengthen us before our separation."

Listening to her tell me what the shrines were for, I decided that the tearful departure from Yaun Kom City was indeed because she was worried about my trip back to the United States. Taking her in my arms, I said, "We been apart before. This time will be no different. I will return and we'll pick up where we left off."

"This time is different," she replied, looking up into my eyes.

"Why?"

Before she could answer Yii and Sakchai walked up and began discussing something with Supattra in Isaan. Picking up the girls at the truck, we wandered along a cracked sidewalk that twisted it way up the hillside past the three shrines, spending another hour touring the grounds and visiting the main temple situated near the top of the ridgeline. Under construction, the temple stood eight stories high and was easily the largest I had ever seen in Isaan. The girls played on three gongs out front of the unfinished temple, one an enormous disc that rang a deep thunderous bellow that carried across the grounds when they struck it with a wooden mallet. The other two gongs, each slightly smaller, rang out tones commensurate with their size.

Watching the children play on the gongs with several monks standing nearby, I wonder if this deafening scene could ever be played out in the Western Hemisphere without the predictable complaints from other visitors.

Leaving the temple, we dropped the two girls off with Sakchai's mother an hour later. The farewell was tearful and sad as their parents reluctantly climbed back into the pickup truck. Our departure was followed by phone call after phone call from the girls, prolonging the final farewell well into the trip back to Bangkok. The phone calls only ended when Sakchai's cell battery finally died.

The traffic was heavy but the trip to Bangkok seemed to be vastly quicker than the journey to Phetchabun six days before. Another tearful farewell occurred in front of the weathered pink townhouse, as Yii and Supattra said their goodbyes.

Shaking my hand and then *Waiing*, Sakchai smiled and said, "Goodbye," in near perfect English.

Yii hesitantly and uncharacteristically hugged me, before Supattra and I climbed back into the pickup truck and drove down the narrow street filled with pots overflowing with colorful flowering plants and spindly Doctor Seuss-looking trees, all seemingly designed to hide the harshness of tightly packed concrete homes. Finally alone after a week, I reached across the cab and took her hand, and she leaned over and gave me a *hom noi* on the cheek, silently communicating to one and other that we were glad it was over. Back tracking our path to the freeway, we found the correct turnaround and headed toward Bangkok.

Speeding along the highway, Supattra seemed unusually quiet as I began passing law-abiding families and giants, Bangkok's tall high-rises bristling and twinkling in the moonlight ahead of us. Glancing over, it seemed as if she was contemplating something important while staring out the side window at the passing suburbia scenery.

"What are you thinking about?"

"Nothing," she muttered, just loud enough for me to hear.

"Nothing?"

She continued to stare out the window. "I don't think you will want to talk about it."

Splitting my attention between the highway and her, glancing back and forth, I said, "Try me."

Looking over to me, she asked, "How did you feel when you left your army?"

"The Marine Corps," I corrected.

"Yes, your army."

"The Marine Corps," I corrected again before asking, "Why do you want to know?"

She sighed, once again turning her attention to the passing scenery. "I knew you wouldn't want to talk about it."

"No, no, I'll talk about it. I felt lost. The only stability I had known for years was wrapped up in climbing into a uniform each day, and yet I chose to leave it all behind."

"Why?"

"While I didn't understand what was happening to me, I wasn't blind to it. I could feel it each morning when I woke up. I could see it in every decision I made. I could taste it in every bottle of beer that I drank, and I could feel it again each night as I lay in bed trying to find an elusive sleep. For reasons I was unable to comprehend, I was subconsciously committing simultaneous personal and professional suicide. I began grasping at straws. In the midst of all the self-made turmoil swirling around me, I got it my head that there were two things in my life that seemed to be at the heart of all my problems. One of those of was the Marine Corps and I suddenly decided it was the most important thing to be done with. I decided that I had mistakenly thought it was a crucial element in my life, supporting me through difficult times, when it had been one of the sources of my problems all along."

"You chose to take away an important reed in your life but the others did not fall down."

"We are dependent creatures." I began, knowing she already knew what I was about to say. "You and I both know there are more than three reeds supporting us at any given time, but I had been dropping reeds aside for years before I decided to leave the military; some purposely but most unintentionally. I was down to the last few. It was a difficult decision to leave the marines. On one hand, it was a major source of my support. On the other, in my mind at the time, it was one of the primary catalysts behind my self-destruction."

"Did your army have someone that could have helped you?"

Answering her question with one of my own, I asked, "Doesn't Thailand have doctors that could help you?"

"I don't think they could help me."

"And that was the way I felt at the time."

"But you also took away the most important reed a person has on their path—your family."

"You have to understand, at the time I didn't think my problems were due to my experience in Iraq. I wasn't seeing anything around me clearly. In the midst of all this uncertainty, I decided that there were two elements in my life that were completely out of whack: my profession and my relationship with my wife. And I saw no future in either. And the funny thing is that, in the end, I think I was right. I was working in an organization that had slowly transformed me into an emotionless thug and I was living with a woman who had transformed into someone I didn't know. I knew if I stayed in the military and didn't leave my wife, I would end up being a bitter old man with a slew of regrets."

"Why did you feel that you needed to take away those two reeds?"

"Do you remember not wanting to sit with the bargirls at the temple fair on Koh PhaNgan and wanting to stay away from the woman wearing high boots and a short skirt at the temple celebration in Yaun Kom City a couple of days ago? You felt that way because they are a part of a past that you are trying to escape from. I felt the same way. I felt as if I needed to expel everything that reminded me of my past while I dealt with what was destroying me."

"But you changed your life so much in such a short time. Why?"

"Because we have a choice," I replied. "Presented with the overwhelming need to change our lives, we can choose a route in which we make small changes that might take years, a lifetime, or eternity to reach our goal, all the while suffering from a slow mild despair, or we can we choose a different method that significantly alters our life all at once and limits the damage to those around us. Our despair might spike and hurt like hell, but the overall pain will come to an end much quicker. You were presented with the same choice and chose the same path as me, leave your life behind and directly confront what was slowly destroying your soul—toiling away in poverty and living a life that held no hope for opportunities. You think of your choice to work in Pattaya as a mistake but I think of it as a direct challenge to what was destroying you and a bold move. In reality, it was no different than me leaving my wife while I pursued a business in a place she could never hope to visit. We choose to leave our lives as we had known them, breaking every moral or ethical rule in the book, to minimize the suffering to ourselves and those around us. Most would call it a selfish decision and, based on manmade definitions of right and wrong, they would be correct. But what if we take a moment to consider the teaching of Buddha, a religion that that you have shared with me over the course of our relationship? It might not be as selfish as most would like to claim.

"Why?"

"Buddha teaches his followers to not admonish the decisions of others because an individual path is a personal journey. No one knows that path better than the person traveling along it."

After a moment contemplating what I had just explained, she said, "And without those two reeds you still survived."

"It was important for me to leave the marines and to get away from my wife, but those two decisions threw me into an abyss unlike any I had ever known before. I was lost before those decisions and exponentially more so afterward. And piling on to this overwhelming emotion of being rudderless and lost, I was consumed with guilt over leaving my children behind. However, that disorientation and those shameful feelings were the short term consequences to good decisions."

"How long did you suffer when you threw those reeds aside?"

"I had to find new reeds to support me. As soon as I found those new reeds, I was better."

"But you still miss your children. I can see it in your eyes when we are around other families. You must regret giving that reed up."

"Sadly, when I gave up my wife, my children became collateral damage and that is one regret I will never come to terms with," I confessed, grimacing at her correct observation while nodding my head.

"We all must suffer," she whispered, reaching out and touching my shoulder. "You chose one path and the suffering that goes along with it. If you had chosen another path, it would have still involved suffering, and it might have been worse for you and your children, but you can never be certain what the truth would have been."

"I once had a man tell me that we always make the right decision."

"Why?"

"Because we have nothing to compare the outcome to. We can theorize about good and bad decisions, but we only know the outcome of the decisions we make."

"Yes, but we can still feel bad about our decisions."

"Yeah, I try and justify my decisions in my mind but the guilt is evidence that I will never know whether I was right or wrong," I said, looking over with a half-hearted smile. "But at the time it seemed like the only logical decision."

Letting her hand slip off my shoulder, she smiled. "How did you replace your reeds?"

"You know how." I chuckled, glancing over at her again and seeing the mischief in her smile.

Giggling, she asked again, "How did you replace them?"

"With our business on Koh PhaNgan and you."

Once again looking out the side window, in a sober tone she said, "I know our business and I can never fill the hole your children have left and I am sorry. I wish things had been different for you—for both of us."

Interrupting our conversation, Bitch'n Betty directed me to exit the freeway and we found ourselves driving along a city street in downtown Bangkok. The Google navigation app then guided us to another highway, telling us to exit an entrance along a side street before getting onto the freeway. With Supattra trying to help me navigate and Bitch'n Betty calling out instructions, we seemed to be doing circles in the city.

And, in fact, we were. When I recognized passing a building we had seen five minutes earlier along the street, I said, "I think Bitch'n Betty has lost it."

"The lady's voice has gone crazy," Supattra affirmed.

"What's wrong with her?"

"I think my battery is almost gone. Maybe the lady's voice has no power."

"That shouldn't make her quit working and we're going to need her when we get close to the airport. Our hotel is hard to find," I replied, stopping under a red light. "Turn your cell off and let's see if we can find the way to the airport without her. We can turn her on when we get close to find our hotel."

Finding the freeway entrance that the Google app had steered us away from earlier, we accelerated through its entrance and found ourselves traveling in the wrong direction. Chatting back and forth, trying to figure out where the airport was located, we exited off that freeway and onto one headed in the general direction of Suvarnabhumi International. Scanning each of the green overhead and roadside signs, we looked for some indication where the highway was taking us. With cars and trucks speeding past, we both sighed in relief when we finally spied a large overhead sign that revealed the freeway we were on would take us all the way to the airport. Several kilometers later, seeing familiar buildings I recognized from previous trips, I realized we were getting close. Sensing our proximity to the airport as well, Supattra pulled her cell from her imitation Gucci purse and turned it on.

"I think it's time to turn on Bitch'n Betty," I said, glancing over to Supattra. "Let's see if she got enough power to tell us how to get to the hotel."

Supattra giggled, happy at the prospect that our drive might be coming to an end. "The lady's voice might tell us to go back to Isaan."

Bitch'n Betty came to life and immediately said, "Exit the highway left in 800 meters."

"Turn left in 800 meters," Supattra repeated, looking over at me with raised eyebrows, as if silently asking whether we should trust the Google Maps app.

Finding the exit Bitch'n Betty was talking about, I continued following her instructions through a succession of several quick turns, with an intimidating sense that the Google Maps app had gone haywire again. Suddenly we found ourselves on a street thick with three- and four-story buildings paralleling the freeway. Several blocks along the street, Bitch'n Betty sputtered a half sentence of instructions before Supattra's cell finally died. About the same time, I saw a convenience store that I knew was near the hotel and let out a long exhale of relief. I was tired of driving and looked forward to a hot shower and sleep. Recognizing and turning down the street where the hotel was located, we found the entrance and parked across from the lobby.

The hotel consisted of three four-story structures, with the lobby located in the center building. Pulling our luggage from the bed of the pickup truck, I followed Supattra into the lobby and, after a quick discussion with the clerk, she paid 2000 *baht* for two nights. Handed a key card, we walked up the stairs and found our room at the end of short hallway.

We had a large, ivory-colored room with a small balcony overlooking the road out front. A television sat on a table at the foot of a queen size bed covered with a red spread. Dropping the suitcases near the wall and stepping into the bathroom, I stripped off my shirt and turned the shower on, hoping it would provide hot water. Listening to me checking out the bathroom, Supattra collapsed onto the bed, slipping a gold fabric pillow under her head.

Calling out from the bathroom I asked, "Are you hungry?"

Over the sound of hot water spraying from the shower head, I heard her reply yes and say she didn't want to go out. She was too tired.

Stripping the rest of my clothes off and happily climbing into the hot shower, I then asked, "Do they have room service?"

After a quick shower, I stepped from the bathroom with a towel wrapped around my waist, and asked again, "Do they have room service?"

"I've already ordered food," she replied, sitting up and slipping her legs over the edge of the bed.

"What'd you order?"

Pulling her shirt over her head, she said, "Soup and spaghetti for you and *gaaeng khiaao waan gai* for me."

"I like green curry. You should have ordered *gaaeng khi-aao waan* for me."

Wrapping a white towel around herself, she stripped her shorts, underwear, and bra off underneath, saying, "You were in the shower. You like spaghetti, so I ordered you that."

Stepping up next to her, I kissed her on the lips and began to pull the towel from her.

Stubbornly holding the towel in place, she pushed me away. "I need a shower and some food."

"We could make it a quickie."

She giggled. "Maybe I don't want a quickie."

"Okay, then let's make it a longie."

"Yes, but later. I need to shower and eat."

CHAPTER 19

A Distant Island ~ 17 April 2014

The next day Supattra told me she wanted to go to one of the nearby malls to look for a Fuji restaurant, a popular Japanese chain in Thailand and one of her favorites. I also knew from experience, that she appreciated the fact that the limited fashion selections of Koh PhaNgan was in her immediate future and wanted to stock up. Without the aid of Bitch'n Betty, we drove along one of the freeways back toward Bangkok, taking an exit that emptied into a large business district on the edge of the city. Driving through streets that were thick with late morning traffic, we passed over two of the many rivers that coiled through the city, their waters brown and murky, and found the shopping center she had wanted to visit. It was actually two malls on opposite sides of a busy city street that were connected by a several pedestrian bridges.

Because it was relatively early, we easily located a parking spot in a small lot directly in front of one of the shopping centers. Her favorite eatery was nearly empty and we were obviously some of the first customers of the day. The fresh waitress delivered menus as quickly as we ordered our meal.

Sitting across the table from one and other, Supattra reached out and took my hands into hers. "You have healed and I have not."

"Neither of us will ever entirely heal." I squeezed her hands. "We will simply learn to manage our regrets and experiences."

Looking me in the eyes, she said what had been hanging

uncomfortably between us all week. "You have healed and do not need me anymore. I am worried you will not come back from America this time."

As I began to understand that I was coming to terms with my posttraumatic stress over the course of the last week, that possibility had dawned on me as well, and I was deeply divided as to how to proceed. On one hand, with my drinking well under control and the hollowness that had plagued me somewhat filled, I realized it was time for me to return to America to try to repair the damage I inflicted to those around me over the last ten years. I had neglected my parental duties for long enough. It was time for me to become a father to my daughters and son. I had broken my marital vows and rebuffed my responsibilities as a husband. It was time to attempt to make it up in some small way and show that I was sorry. I had abandoned my brothers and sister. It was time to return and rejoin my family. I had rejected my friends. It was time to re-establish those ties. It was time for me to go home.

On the other hand, I loved the woman sitting across from me and could not imagine a life without her. She had been instrumental in my coming to terms with my past. She had forgiven me for my countless failures and faults during the healing process and had stood by my side through the difficult times. More importantly, she still needed my support to heal from her wounds. The easy choice would have been to cut all my ties with those who had once been important and live this life in Thailand with this wonderful woman, leaving my past in the past.

I had considered taking her with me, but knew that bringing a woman half my age back from a country considered the hub of the global sex trade would undermine the perception of my efforts. Her presence would taint any and all efforts to repair my misdeeds. While there might be a time in the future when she could join me, I needed to make this initial trip alone. I needed to show those in my past that I had healed and returned to take up those responsibilities that I had once abandoned.

"Supattra," I said firmly. "You are right. I have begun to

come to terms with my past but I will never be healed. I will never forget who was by my side during that journey. I will never leave you but we both know that I hurt a lot of people back in America and I need to make up for what I have done. This is a trip that I must make alone, and it will take some time to repair the damage I have inflicted."

A tear broke from the corner of her left eye and rolled down her cheek, hanging at the edge of her jaw, as she quietly pleaded, "Please don't leave me. Please come back."

"I owe you so much." I squeezed her hands again. "I love you even more and can't imagine a life without you. I'm not sure how our past lives came to a conclusion, whether we were together at the end or not, but I know in my heart that we belong together—forever and ever."

"I think in our past lives one of us always died in the other's arms," she whispered, taking her right hand out of my left and wiping the tears from her cheek and jaw. "I think that our love has always been spicy and we argued, but I also think it is eternal. Whether you come back or not from America, we will meet up in the next life."

After our meal, Supattra visited a hair salon before roaming the retail stores, looking for something while looking for nothing at all. I realized after the third store that her shopping was an attempt to relieve her stress over my imminent departure. We eventually ended up at the shopping center movie theater, scanning the various choices before deciding that we should just head back to the hotel room.

Returning our room, I turned on the television and fell back on the bed. Her silence and fidgeting were good indicators that my departure was weighing heavily on her mind. She went into the bathroom and inspected her hair, combing out the curls the hairdresser had created several hours earlier.

Stepping from the bathroom, she walked over to the bed and stated, "I need to go someplace by myself."

Looking up at the disquieting mood that consumed her, I asked, "Where?"

"I just need to go someplace."

Though she would not tell me, I knew exactly where my

beautiful girlfriend was going and nodded. "How long will you be gone?"

"I'm not sure."

"Fair enough. I'll wait for you here. Maybe I'll take a nap."

"Thank you, sweetheart." She picked up her imitation Gucci handbag and turned to walk out the door.

After her departure, I lay on the bed while listening to one of the NCIS series programs on a Western station and began reminiscing about an incident that took place a year before my retirement from the Marine Corps.

ℭℑℭℑ

Having just flown across the South China Sea between Vietnam and the Philippines, I was at the controls of a Cessna Citation Encore cruising at 39,000 feet. As my co-pilot began switching our radio over to a frequency to contact the appropriate air traffic controller as we crossed into Philippine airspace, I glanced over my shoulder, through a small passageway, at our three passengers relaxing in the plush leather seats behind me.

With the new frequency dialed in, we heard the aircrew of a jumbo airliner talking to the controller. As I listened to the conversation over the radio, I realized that the larger jet was someplace below us, headed for the same destination, Manila. Searching the skies, I saw a glint from their white fuselage six or eight thousand feet below, flying the same airway.

Looking over at me, my co-pilot asked, "You see them?"

"Yeah, passing us directly below," I responded, knowing that a jet that size had a considerable speed advantage compared to the small aircraft we were flying.

My co-pilot then contacted the air traffic controller and in fairly good English we were directed to descend to 25,000 feet, preparing us to be handed off to Manila approach control. I dialed in the new altitude into the aircraft's autopilot and pulled back on the throttles. The jet began to descend. While many people might think that a pilot always has his hands on the yoke of an aircraft, the truth is that the air is so thin at the fuel preserving altitudes that long range jets fly, the human touch is not nearly delicate enough to make the necessary minuscule inputs to keep the aircraft straight and level. As a result, unless there is an unforeseen in-flight event requiring a pilot's input, the aircraft is normally controlled by a computer, except during takeoff and landings.

Searching the airspace below again, I began looking for the jumbo jet again, asking, "Where's the Malaysian jet?"

"He's about five miles ahead of us," my co-pilot responded, pointing out the windscreen.

Stretching in my seat, I raised my arms and twisted my head trying to get a kink out of my neck. "Well, at least the weather is good today. Last time I flew the general in the back into Manila, it was a nightmare. We had to weave around these towering thunder bumpers filled with tons of lightning. We were slammed with rain and knocked all over the place by wind. As the general climbed off the aircraft, he commented it was the worst weather he had ever flown in."

Laughing, my co-pilot asked, "Was it the worst weather you had ever flown in?"

"No way." I chuckled. "It was child's play compared to some storms I've found myself flying through."

The aircraft shuddered before suddenly being snapped to the left and dropping several hundred feet. The harnesses of the seatbelt dug into my shoulders as I was lifted out of my seat. I reached out and grabbed the yoke with my right hand and the throttles with my left when the jet was then violently tossed upward and yanked to the right. I was now being pressed into the seat. My head nearly collided with the side window as we were jerked sideways.

With the jet on its side at twenty-eight thousand feet, I pulled back farther on the throttles and twisted the yoke to the right while pushing forward, leveling out the aircraft.

In a terrorized pitch, my co-pilot asked, "What was that?"

"Clear air turbulence—or maybe we passed through that jumbo jet's vortices," I replied as calmly as possible, glancing back through the passageway at our passengers to make sure they were still in their seats. "That's why we wear seatbelts."

Having been through a similar event several months ago, when the aircraft's weather radar became useless as I made a series of tight turns trying to weave through several thunderstorms hovering over Manila, it was not the first time I had been awed by the power of Mother Nature. At the time, I was also trying to respond to directions from the approach controller, who was obviously not paying attention to her weather radar as she instructed me to fly directly through the center of a furious storm. Like this incident, the aircraft had been viciously tossed about, so violently the autopilot had been knocked off line. The difference in that incident was that I had been prepared for the possibility we would find ourselves getting bounced around. The clear air turbulence we had just flown through hadn't given us any clue as to what was in store.

After a few moments of silence, my co-pilot remarked, "That's why I like flying with you."

"What do you mean?"

"You never get shaken. You're always calm."

Tucking my trembling right hand between my thigh and the bulkhead next to me, I asked my co-pilot to reengage the autopilot, not wanting to advertise just how wrong he was about my calm demeanor.

My calm façade during frightening events was much like the veneer I had spent years hanging over my posttraumatic stress. While I constantly felt the emptiness created from memories collected over a career of violence nibbling away inside, I became well-practiced at hiding it from those around me. As I lay on the bed in our hotel room recalling that flight, it dawned on me that my shaking hand was yet one more indication that my emotionless shroud was crumbling and I would someday need to come to terms with my past.

Turning my attention back to the NCIS program, I felt my eyes lids becoming heavy as I watched Mark Harmon and David McCallum discuss the toxicology report of a cadaver lying on a stainless steel table between them. Several minutes later, listening to David McCallum's calming English accent, I fell into a deep sleep.

Unaware of how long I had been asleep, I felt the mattress shift as someone sat down next to me on the bed. Instinctively knowing who was sitting next to me, I kept my eyes closed as she began unbuttoning my shirt before working on taking my shorts off.

Opening one eye, I spied Supattra, completely naked, kneeling at my feet and pulling at my shorts. The sight of her naked golden body immediately aroused me and I reached out, gently taking her forearms and pulling her toward me.

We made slow and silent love. When we were finished, she nuzzled up to me, draping one of her legs over mine.

Shifting in the bed, her naked skin rubbing across mine, Supattra placed her head on my chest. "I went and talked to a monk today. There is a big temple not too far from here and that is where I went this afternoon."

Knowing that she had likely visited a temple during her mysterious exodus, I assumed there would soon be an admission that she was having a hard time coming to terms with my departure the next morning and, prompting her, I asked, "Why did you go see a monk?"

"You have told me a lot about your war this week, and I was having a hard time making sense of everything—about you and me, and our pasts. You have begun to heal and I have been concerned that you will never come back. This monk was very wise."

"What did he say?"

After a moment of silence, she answered, "What he said made a lot of sense."

Wrapping my arm around her bare shoulders and looking down at the top of her head resting on my chest, I asked again, "What did he say?"

"He told me that our lives are like islands and when things are good we spend the days walking its beaches, feeling the sand between our toes and the warmth of the sun on our backs, enjoying our paradise."

"That makes sense."

Continuing, she explained, "He told me that when bad things happen, it is like a big storm knocking us from the beach into the water, and shifting waters and winds take us from our island."

"The current."

"What?"

"Currents are fast moving water."

"Yes, shifting currents and strong winds move us from our island. How far we are taken from our island depends on how bad the thing was that happened. If it is not too bad, we swim back to our island and walk the beaches as if nothing happened. The beaches might be a little different shape from the effects of all the wind and rain, but it is the same sand under our feet and the sun comes from the same direction. If it is very bad, then we find ourselves far from our island and the current and winds keep us from swimming back to the beach where we were once walking."

"Wow! That's pretty deep."

"He said that we all want to swim back to our distant island because that is what we are comfortable with. It is what we know."

"Wow," I said again. "And he called it our distant island?"

"But he said sometimes we can't," she continued, ignoring my question. "Sometimes it is impossible to swim back to that distant island in this lifetime. He said that when we find ourselves swimming to a distant island and know in our hearts that we can never reach its shores, we should stop."

"We just need to tread water and watch the island languishing in the distance?"

Once again ignoring my question, she continued. "He said that we should stay in the same place and, without forgetting what has happened to us, focus on all the good things in our lives—focus on all the good inside of us."

"And what happens to our island? Does it move?"

"No, it will always be on the horizon in the distance and we can look at it and remember what it was like. He said a new island will slowly rise beneath us." She twisted her head so she was looking up at me. "He said sometimes when something very bad happens to us we can never return to what was before, and we must build a new island and walk on new beaches, feeling different sand between our toes and the warmth of the sun on our back from a different direction."

Looking down at her sparkling brown eyes, I asked, "Did what he say make you feel better?"

"It made sense to me. It made sense about you. I have listened to you tell me about what happened to you and I have seen how you no longer want to swim back to who you were before your war. You have stopped trying to swim back to that distant island and have focused on the good around you, watching the old island in the distance. You have built a new island and are walking its beaches."

"And what about you?"

"He explained that it is more difficult for me because I never had an island with beaches to walk on. He said that it is as if I am lost, swimming around in circles, looking for something that I have never seen—something that I might not recognize. He told me I should stop swimming and look at what is good in my life, building my first island. He explained that I should stand next to you and your island would become the foundation for mine. He said you could teach me about islands and how to build them now that you have begun to build a new one."

Lying on the bed, I looked up at the ceiling and pondered what she had just told me. Had I built a new island? Was I walking new shores?

Would this new island I had built be the basis for Supattra's island? Could I teach her how to build an island and be content with her life when I wasn't sure how I accomplished the task myself?

"He claims you can you share my island?"

"He says each of us will have our own island, but they will share the same space, and we will walk the same beaches together."

Taking my shoulders in her hands, she twisted me over so we were facing one another. I could see her love for me sparkling in her eyes. I could feel a wave of love for this beautiful woman surge through my body. Leaning down, I kissed her on the lips.

Looking into my eyes, she whispered, "Please come back to me."

Visualizing us walking along a white sandy beach with the warmth of the sun on our backs, I placed my mouth next to her ear and softly said, "I could never leave you."

CHAPTER 20

The Awakening

Twenty-three hours after taking off from Suvarnabhumi International Airport just southeast of Bangkok, with a two hour layover at Tokyo-Narita, my flight landed at Dulles International, just west of Washington, DC. After a short ride in a cramped, standing room only bus, I trudged through a long line that would eventually led me to a chest high counter and a uniformed customs agent.

A unique mixture of body odor, aftershave, and perfume wafted the air in the long line of fellow exhausted travelers. An eternity later, I found myself standing at the counter looking up at a bored customs agent in a blue uniform. Several flat-toned questions later, the agent scribbled a secret code onto my blue and white declaration form with a stroke of his hand, leaving me wondering if he had decided I needed a second screening and search or not. Picking my single black suitcase from a rattling silver carousel, I wearily stumbled through the crowd of fatigued vacationers and businessmen and women up to the final customs checkpoint where another agent glanced at my declaration form with the mystery mark. Having been sidetracked to the back offices for a protracted and laborious search on one previous occasion, when the final agent nodded an approving release from the confines of the customs area, I sighed in relief and quickly escaped, finding my way to the nearest exit.

Standing outside the passenger pickup door, I found I was severely underdressed for the chilly weather, a climate I had become completely unaccustomed to while living on an island in the Gulf of Thailand. While former airline passengers and airport workers, wearing thick jackets, scarves, and gloves eyed me suspiciously in my short-sleeved shirt and flip-flops, I attempted to fight off the cold that was quickly penetrating my bones and the overwhelming exhaustion from the lack of sleep and time change. Fortunately, John, one of the few friends in the United States I had maintained a friendship with over the years, arrived to pick me up within ten minutes.

After the customary shaking of hands and greetings, John and I climbed into his ancient, dark green Jaguar XK6 and began the thirty minute drive back to his house in Arlington. Sinking down into the Jaguar's well-worn leather passenger seat, I pushed my hands up next to the vents on the dashboard in hopes of feeling warm blowing air. Sadly, the bear of a man sitting next to me had a higher tolerance to the cold and hadn't turned the heat on.

Looking over at me reclining in the seat next to him, in his taunting English accent, John asked, "How was your flight?"

I sighed. "Long."

"You look absolutely wretched."

"Thanks for the vote of confidence." I laughed, tucking my hands into my armpits. "I've just spent the better part of a day squeezed into an economy size seat on an airplane—not to mention I've also undergone an eleven-hour time change."

He chuckled. "Just calling as I see it."

Knowing that our primary means of communication, the Internet, would not be available in Isaan, I had arranged the week before for him to pick me up, explaining that I would be traveling around the country.

"How was your Thailand excursion?" John asked,

"It was an amazing week." I thought about Supattra's visit with the monk on our last day and his words of wisdom about the distant island.

"Why was that? What happened?"

"It was a week that I will likely never forget. I think I may write it down so my kids can read about it someday."

"Another book in the works?"

Having self-published an espionage thriller several years

ago, I found writing enjoyable and relaxing. That first shot at writing a salable story was full of lessons, but mostly allowed me to begin discovering a personal style that included sentence and story structure, none of which found its way into the that initial attempt. Since then, I have written two more spy style novels but, unable to afford another self-publishing venture, I have limited their distribution to printed out paper copies to friends who have enjoyed my past efforts, with dreams of publishing them at a later date.

To tell the truth, I had considered writing a book about my final week in Thailand during the trip from Bangkok to Washington DC but quickly dismissed the idea, due to the intimacy of the topic. I also rejected the notion of a book about the week because I felt it might give people the impression I was attempting to solicit sympathy or make excuses for my past decisions.

I closed my eyes. "I don't think so."

"Why not?"

"The subject," I muttered. "I'm not sure I want to air my dirty laundry."

Once again, his cutting English accent grated across the Jaguar's interior as he asked, "Concerning an expedition in Thailand? How could that possible qualify as airing your dirty laundry?"

"It was more than just a trip in Thailand. I've been struggling with posttraumatic stress for years—"

"I knew that," he interrupted, chuckling again in some Irish-Welsh mixture of an accent. "Everyone knows you were affected by the war."

Opening my eyes and looking over at him as he maneuvered the Jaguar onto the Dulles access road, I asked, "You knew? How could you know? We didn't meet till years after my experience in Iraq."

"You may have tried to keep it a secret but your ex-wife informed everyone." Then, chuckling one more time, he added, "Of course that was while we were still on speaking terms with one another."

"She was desperate and trying to hold our marriage together. At the time, I was incapable of any emotion. When I wouldn't listen to her claims, she began to tell anyone who would listen that I was suffering from posttraumatic stress. While slightly misdirected, her intentions were honorable," I mumbled, dropping my head back down on the seatback and closing my eyes again.

"You should write about posttraumatic stress. With Iraq finished and Afghanistan coming to an end, it's a popular topic nowadays. You could actually earn some money."

"Yeah, I might have better luck with a story about posttraumatic stress. The espionage thriller market is a tough one to break into."

"People want to hear about posttraumatic stress. Who better from than someone who knows the topic first hand?"

"Like I said, it might be a little too close to home. I'm not sure people want to hear about all the skeletons in my closet."

"Of course, they want to hear about your skeletons. Everyone wants to hear about skeletons, as long as they aren't theirs. Use your penname, Pat whatever. The name you used on that first book. If it makes you feel better, don't put your name on it."

"Ashtre. Pat Ashtre."

Twenty minutes of small talk later, discussing current events and politics, John pulled his Jaguar across the gravel path of his driveway, coming to a halt next to a two-story, rectangular, white-wood clapboard home. Two enormous trees grew in the front yard on a near-barren lawn of short, unsightly grass that struggled to survive in the shade. With short eaves, the home's rain gutters and vinyl siding were missing from the backside of house, revealing the roof's aged wooden joists. A small wooden deck, covered in Astroturf, with a pair of French doors to receive guests at the rear of the house provided a view of a lush garden and a newer outbuilding at the back corner of the lot.

With my single black suitcase in hand and my black carryon backpack slung across my shoulder, I walked across his backyard and entered the large outbuilding. The outbuilding was what most of John's, and his wife Kathy's, friends and acquaintances referred to as the backyard bar. A large single room, whose unfinished walls were decorated with objects gathered over decades of living and working in the nation's capital. One side of the room had several gray filing cabinets, presumably filled with John's professional records, and a long bookcase loaded with mostly non-fiction works documenting wars and political intrigue. On the other side of the room stood an ancient and meticulously carved wooden buffet with half a dozen bottles of various types of alcohol on top. A large square mirror, encased a plain wooden frame, hovered on the wall above the buffet. A dark brown bar with two stools was situated so that a barman, or woman, could stand behind the counter and pour drinks from bottles on the buffet. Trinkets, pictures, posters, and several weapons adorned the walls or stood on the tables around the room. On the far wall was a well-worn beige futon sofa, allowing refuge for those guests who had had too much to drink—or a friend arriving from Thailand.

Dropping my luggage next to the door, I maneuvered over to the futon and sat down, pondering the thought of writing about my final week in Thailand. Sure, I had written several espionage stories, but putting pen to paper about something as real and important as posttraumatic stress would be far different. How could I take my limited experience of writing stories and use it to cobble together an account that adequately highlighted the importance of the week, presenting a narrative that readers would find both entertaining and enlightening. More importantly, could I create a story that didn't dribble with self-sympathy or appear to beg for absolution?

After a shower in the main house I wandered out the French doors to the small Astroturf-covered deck and found Kathy sitting just outside their backdoor. Leaning back in a faded blue plastic Adirondack chair with a glass of red wine in her hand, she was ignoring the early evening chill.

As I sat down across from her on an identical faded red plastic Adirondack chair, Kathy, absently pushed a strand of strawberry blonde hair from her face. "Considering what we just went through, this feels like a flipping summer evening."

"What do you mean?"

"You missed the coldest winter I think I have ever experienced. It was absolutely frigid."

"I was watching the weather reports. I waited to come back until it warmed up."

Hesitating a moment, as if not sure how to say what was on her mind, she said, "John tells me you're thinking about writing a story about posttraumatic stress. I think it's a great idea."

"I'm not sure I could do it justice."

"Why? You're a good writer and you know the topic better than most people."

Laughing, I asked, "So my ex-wife told you I had posttraumatic stress, too?"

"That was one of the first things she told me when we met. It was a bit of a creepy introduction. She told anyone who would listen that you had posttraumatic stress, along with a lot of other damaging tidbits."

"I imagine those tidbits had to do with me living with a woman half my age and her former profession. All true I might add. She somehow thought that if I suddenly grasped that I had posttraumatic stress all our problems would have been solved."

"Maybe they would have." Kathy took sip of wine. "Maybe if you had come to terms with having posttraumatic stress, things would have been different between you two."

"Did she tell everyone that she suffers from it as well?"

"She left that crumb of information out, but it still might have helped your marriage had you realized you were struggling with posttraumatic stress."

"It might have been the mechanism behind the downfall of our marriage but our problems were far bigger than me suddenly recognizing I had posttraumatic stress."

"Then you should write about that. You should put that into a story about posttraumatic stress."

Waking up the next morning, I had an indescribable sinking feeling that was somewhat familiar. Rolling over on the beige futon, I could smell the tequila John and I had drunk the night before, several shots to celebrate my return that had managed to empty an entire bottle. Sitting up and rubbing my eyes, I tried to remember when I had felt the glum feeling currently simmering inside me. The melancholy feeling wasn't overwhelming, just a slight sensation of something nipping at the edges of my emotions. Standing up, I decided that my somber disposition was the result of the looming reunion with my ex-wife.

Unable to shake the feeling, I walked the mile to the Knights of Columbus Club where my aged Chevy pickup was parked and drove to the house where my ex-wife and two youngest children lived—a small tan stucco home with an enormous tree growing in the front yard. My memories of living in that house were split evenly between good and bad. It was a Saturday so I assumed that everyone would be home. As I walked up the stairs to the front door, I saw a pair of men's running shoes sitting on the front stoop. Hesitating for a moment, I knocked on the door. Over the next thirty minutes I surprised my two youngest children, found out that my middle daughter was dating her first boyfriend, my son had grown to nearly my height, and that my ex-wife's boyfriend, who lived out of state, was staying at the house for the weekend. When I saw through the front window my ex-wife drive up, I said goodbye to my children and stepped out the house, greeting her with a hug and kiss to the cheek. I then introduced myself to her boyfriend, who I apparently had met years ago and, after a short conversation, I returned to John and Kathy's outbuilding.

Leaving my ex-wife and her boyfriend alone that Sunday with the children, I picked up my son from school on the following Monday, taking him to McDonald's for a late lunch. He sat across the table from me, sipping an iced Café Mocha.

"Dad," he asked, "how long will you be here this time?"

"That depends on how long my money lasts, or if I'm able to find a job."

He was unusually quiet for a moment. My heart sank when he looked at me, saying that he would pay me back for lunch when he got his allowance later in the week.

That same week, while I was driving him home from

school he began talking about a strange religion he had made up. When I asked him if he believed in God, he said "Not really. I used to talk to God but none of my prayers were ever answered."

My heart sank again, as I knew that he had been praying for me to come home. Turning onto the street where he lived, I said "God listens to everyone's prayers, but he has a bigger mission than just answering one person's request," hoping those half-hearted words would sink into his impressionable mind.

Several weeks after my return, I began taking my middle daughter to driver's education classes each morning, picking her up after each class. She would slip behind the steering wheel of my 1994 Chevy Silverado pickup, with paint flaking from its sides and expired license plates mounted on its bumpers, and drive. A career of instructing pilots to fly in absolutely treacherous conditions led me to become a comfortable and relaxed driving instructor for my middle daughter, as she learned to maneuver a poor turning radius and overpowered pickup while we causally talked about local events and life. I'm not sure a father could have asked for more.

My oldest daughter, a recent graduate from Colorado University at Boulder, her mother's and my alma mater, now working for Boulder County, eventually called me after several weeks. She had known I was back in the country but, understanding the gravity of my family abandonment, I knew she would likely never forgive me for my Southeast Asian disappearance, not to mention she was among the victims of my first marriage's demise that occurred shortly after the First Gulf War and the Jeff Couch incident.

Returning to John and Kathy's each evening, I would eat dinner with them before retiring to the outbuilding. The idea of a story about posttraumatic stress brewed inside my mind and I would ponder the best way to approach the topic each sleepless night.

Slowly building a routine, I began picking up my son at school each day, spending afternoons with him and my daughter at their home, leaving when my ex-wife returned from work. I had been back for two weeks when the growing strain between us erupted and my ex-wife told me to get out of her house, claiming that I had been trespassing. The tension that had driven us apart years before still remained, her believing that my every deed was a testament to my lacking reliability and responsibility, and my judging her conduct as evidence of her need to manipulate and control everything within arm's reach. Once again, we became the poster children for Robert Merton's concept of a self-fulfilling prophecy. Several days later, she gave me permission to spend the afternoons with the children in the house again and I tried to show my appreciation by cleaning the kitchen, doing the laundry, and any other handiwork needed, ensuring I was gone before she arrived home.

During one of our dinnertime discussions about the possibility of a book outlining my last week in Thailand posttraumatic stress, Kathy asked why some people seem to be able to deal with the memories and others not. I shrugged my shoulders, claiming I didn't know. Having given that question a lot of thought over the years, my feigned ignorance had been an outright lie. Why are some crippled and others not? Why was I the one who found himself in a downward spiral consumed with a hollow feeling? Why had others walked away from the same experiences seemingly unscathed? The reason I lied when asked by Kathy about the disparity of posttraumatic stress reactions among combat veterans was because it illustrated a weakness or sensitivity I wasn't prepared to reveal about myself, and another reason for not writing and publishing a story about my posttraumatic stress.

The title posttraumatic stress has been coined to describe the human response to those inexplicable events that we find difficult to come to terms with, generating reactions from its sufferers that are as varied as there are trees in a forest. It is evident to me that the wide-ranging experiences of taking part in a conflict or war are not necessarily commiserate with the follow-up reaction of its warriors, and I imagine that is true about every form of posttraumatic stress, created on the battlefield or not. Those trudging along the roads below me as I flew across the battlefields certainly must have felt a higher level of risk than I, but many seem to have been able to go back to their lives, abiding by the civilized constraints of our laws and customs. On the other hand, I have met former combatants who lived and worked in relatively safe surroundings during that same conflict who have had difficulty reintegrating back into society. Given that chaotic array of consequences to a wide ranging level of risk, I believe every participant is affected with posttraumatic stress and one's ability to reconform with society lies in some intrinsic ability, or lack thereof, to compartmentalize the memory of those experiences, based on some level of individual fortitude that is passed on through genetics or upbringing from generation to generation.

On my second week back, having just eaten dinner with John and Kathy, and returned to the outbuilding, I pulled my laptop from my backpack, turned it on, waiting for the desktop screen to appear while considering how to write the narrative of my final week in Thailand, explaining its significances to my posttraumatic stress. How could I write about Supattra that would allow readers to understand the importance that she, her tainted past, and culture had played during my healing process? When the desktop screen appeared, I moved the cursor to the Microsoft Word icon and with the press of a finger I took the first step in writing about my posttraumatic stress.

Staring at the opened Microsoft Word program for several minutes, its small black cursor flashing on the white screen, I then typed, *On the morning of September 11, 2001, I was a happily married man with a lovely wife, three children, and a house in Arlington, Virginia. I was a good father and husband, and looking into the mirror each morning I was happy with the reflected image. But all that was about to change,* as if it had been a repeating unconscious thought, hibernating in the recesses of my mind for years.

The act of writing this story became as pleasurable and as it was distasteful. Trying to remember every detail of my Isaan trip brought back wonderful memories, not just of the week but of my life in Thailand with Supattra. On the other hand, I found that trying to remember those same details brought the pain of the entire posttraumatic stress experience and each of the decisions I made while under its influence to center stage. Previously looking back on those events in tolerable snapshots or glimpses, having them coalesce into one narrative became a guilt ridden journey. The act of organizing and reflecting on years of meditative thoughts concerning posttraumatic stress revealed the sheer magnitude of both the disorder and how far I had strayed from my responsibilities.

Aside from the book, another issue arose when I arrived back in the United States, a feeling that I was a mere guest or tourist in this country. There is no expectation by those around me to remain here for any given length of time. My children, ex-wife, and—with a few exceptions—friends kept me at arm's length. I contributed to their expectation by feeling no more attached to my fellow citizens and these surroundings than if had I been in Nairobi or Paris. Complicating this nation-less sentiment, I have found myself pulled from one direction by the needs of my three children, and to the other by a woman halfway around the world who loves and needs me as much. The travesty of the situation is that those two worlds will likely never mix.

All the while, the sinking feeling I had felt on my first morning back in the United States continued to smolder, and I continued ponder its familiarity. Then one day, as I was toiling away with this story, its origins dawned on me, and I recognized that the sensation was the same hollow feeling I had attempted to escape from all those years ago. The emotion I experienced while struggling with posttraumatic stress had been analogous to that of being lost—and I once again felt lost. This enlightenment made me momentarily wonder if I wasn't slipping back into a posttraumatic stress state.

While it was easy to surmise that I was skidding back into the posttraumatic stress quandary, it was Supattra who diagnosed the source of my problem, when during one of our daily conversations she said, "You are lost because all your reeds are here with me."

She was right. In an attempt to leave the hollowness behind, I had moved to an island halfway across the world, tossing my entire support structure aside in this country and building a new one overseas. With that, I had made myself a tourist or a visitor in my native land. I felt lost because I had constructed a new support structure in a foreign country, and on difficult days, short of a cell phone and long distance call, I had no reeds to lean against.

The final issue that I found myself confronted with was that during each call back to Thailand, I felt Supattra slipping away from me. I could hear her preparing for the conversation when I explained that I wouldn't be coming back. My heart slowly began breaking as I listened to the woman I loved stop believing in me, all the while realizing that it was inevitable. I had to make a choice between this life or that. My two worlds could not coexist.

I am not Buddhist, nor have I spent much time studying Buddhism, but I did use those elements of the religion Supattra taught me to help understand what had happened to me after the Pentagon, Iraq, and my Southeast Asian cruise. Buddhism speaks of the four noble truths: suffering is an inherent part of life and is the result of our ignorance about the world around us; we are able to discover the source of our suffering; we are able to learn the path to end our suffering; and we are able to travel that individual path, ending our suffering.

I was ignorant of the horrors of war and lost my innocence. Searching for a solution to rid myself of the hollowness that plagued me, I discovered a country, a woman, and a mindset, and while I will never be completely cured from what those events did to me, I began traveling that individual path to heal several years ago.

Piecing memories and conversations together that occurred during that last week in Thailand, I came to realize that my posttraumatic stress was not the result of an airliner colliding into the Pentagon, the drive north in Iraq, or that final Southeast Asian cruise. The foundation of my posttraumatic stress began during training missions like the one I shared with Mike Lueck off the coast of Southern California as I began to educate myself to control fear in the face of disaster and sorrow in face of death. As I cultivated those aptitudes in an environment seeped in danger and death, they flourished. During sorties like my unaided night flight over the Mariana Trench, I began to educate younger marines to perfect the same skill sets. Refining my sentiment dulling expertise in conflicts like the First Gulf War, and places like Liberia and 9/11 at the Pentagon, I had perfected those talents by the time I was flying over some nameless city in Iraq as I emotionlessly pondered how many civilians we were killing while trying to extract the wounded marines. The first crack in the veil I had trained myself to drape over my sentiments occurred when I orchestrated the destruction of two fleeing cars and the death of their occupants, when my actions in destroying one vehicle shocked me into not chasing down the second. Damaged but not destroyed by that one event, I still was able to rely on those same skills in locations such as An Nasiriyah and Tikrit.

Writing this story, I have come to realize that posttraumatic stress was the result of learning to suppress fear and sorrow with such precision that those same emotions had nowhere to go, no release, and began festering away at my soul. It was not until an event involving a simple case of clear air turbulence over the South China Sea that I realized I could no longer rely on those skills. That flight, as I hid my trembling hand from my co-pilot, became the prelude to the eventual necessity of confronting every one of my past woes and regrets.

That final week in Thailand also amplified my understanding of the boundlessness of posttraumatic stress and how its effects are far wider than we can imagine: destroying strong marriages, forcing an intelligent young woman to sell her body, disorienting another reeling from sexual abuse at the hands of her father, and even causing a famous mountain climber to write about its intimacies in one of his books. I have come to believe that Edward Whymper's words: *Still, the last sad memory hovers round, and sometimes drifts across like floating mist, cutting off sunshine and chilling the remembrance of happier times,* as to close an emotional descriptor of the posttraumatic stress state of mind as I have ever come across.

Finally, during that last week I began to understand my move to Thailand, leaving behind all those reminders of who I had become, allowed me room to contemplate each of my regrets in singular form without the daily reminders and distractions of all the other misgivings plaguing my consciousness. Surrounded by the simplicity of a Buddhist culture I learned that whether you were born into riches or poverty, life is a struggle nonetheless. I discovered that while manmade lines delineating right and wrong are a needed restraint, they are nonetheless flawed. Like three reeds holding themselves up, I realized that everything we do in life is dependent and we never make our way along life's path alone. I began to understand that one's belief in any religion can be a powerful reinforcement against the consequences of a not so fair life. I witnessed and came to appreciate that hypocrisy is just one of many tools we use to survive. I realized we should never dismiss anything on its visible merits because sometimes the things that make the most difference can sometime come in strange and unexpected packages. And finally I came to understand that the life we envision is nothing more than an illusion. Everyone has a distant island in their future.

By no means did I write this story as a vehicle to make excuses for my decisions or profess that an acceptable solution to dealing with traumatic events is to leave one's family, move to a foreign country, and shack up with a woman half one's age. On the contrary, I have simply attempted to describe that moment during which I began to understand the world around me being far more complicated than that defined by the most intellectually promising hypothesis and theories. That complexity can only be truly witnessed over the course of a lifetime: falling into a deep love we thought could stand the test of time and then watching that passion wither or be involuntarily jerked from our grasp; a premonition about a future event that comes true, shaking the very fibers of our beliefs about the world around us; or encountering a traumatic event that casts us into a sea of despair in which we question mankind's true nature, sending us along a path that seems endless and without explanation. Our ability to recover from these experiences become even more convoluted when we stamp manmade lines of right and wrong onto the path leading back to constancy. The lucidity of those events and our recollections of the experiences are normally a hazy quagmire of guesses and suppositions but, on occasion, seemingly at the darkest hour, we can come to an epiphany that allows crystal clear clarity, limited only by our human intellect.

Before American Airlines flight 77 was flown into the Pentagon, the drive north in Iraq, and a cruise hunting for terrorists on the high seas, I was a happily married man and my future path was as clear as one could expect. My wife's and my relationship could have only been described as idyllic by those around us, and I was sure that she was the woman I would live with for the remaining days of my life. The events that unfolded, setting us on a diverging course, shattered the notion of endless and boundless love. I can now look back fondly at the memories of building a family with my ex-wife, knowing that the end of our marriage was simply a part of the inevitable suffering we all endure in this life.

Prior to Jeff Couch's premonition, I believed we were all on a self-determined journey, the forks in the road and paths we selected shaping our future. Since that day, I have often asked myself how Jeff Couch knew, whose premonition about his death in a helicopter came true, that I was the one to fly with. Did Charles Darwin's theory of biological evolution and his concepts on natural selection only hit tip of the iceberg? Is there a genetic human trait passed down from generation to generation that allows its benefactors insight into the future? Or maybe David Mitchell's 2004 fictional novel, *Cloud Atlas*, describing how history repeats itself and connects people across the ages, is closer to the mark and Jeff had been through an age-appropriate version of the same fateful day many times over, throughout the centuries. Or maybe the biblical verses of Ecclesiastes, describing that *to everything there is a season and a time to every purpose,* and *there is a time to be born and a time to die; a time to plant and a time to pluck up that which has been planted*, are true in their most literal form and every stage of our lives predetermined? Have Supattra and I shared many lives together, and will we continue to do so? In the end, I learned that it really doesn't matter whether its glimpses into the future, connected worlds, biblical verses, or countless lives shared with the same person. Life is what it is, and attempting to unweave its complexity only leads to more confusion. Like driving down the center line on a Thai highway, it's okay to be oblivious about some things because it really won't make a difference if we do or don't know.

Before witnessing primitive acts during the numerous conflicts I participated in around the globe over the years, I believed that good things happen to good people. Years of watching mankind at its worst during those same conflicts showed me just how truly cruel and primitive humanity can be and taught me firsthand the inherent unfairness of life. The proverbial straw that broke the camel's back started in the Pentagon and ended on the high seas of Southeast Asia, pushing me over an invisible edge and throwing me into a mire of confusion, selfishness, and self-denial that has been christened Posttraumatic Stress Disorder. What I have learned over the last eight years, with a former bargirl at my side, is that life is a dependent struggle supported by reeds of our choosing, and all we can do is our best, hoping for an easier time on our next go round.

My final week in Thailand was a memorable experience that I will never forget, but it was not my awakening from Posttraumatic Stress Disorder. While I began to feel a peace that week which had eluded me for years, as the chaos that accompanies posttraumatic stress slowly began to tumble into place, my memories and misgivings remained singular and out of order. And while that week allowed me to begin to understand the repercussions of life's struggle, the knowledge didn't suddenly band together with the realization that life's not fair, bad things do happen to good people, and the inadequacies of manmade lines delineating right and wrong, making sense of it all.

My awakening occurred as I realized that the minute we think we've figured things out, life will throw a curveball. My true awakening occurred as I wrote this story about discovering that every experience in life changes us just a little bit, and how harrowing experiences change us a lot. My awakening transpired as I stopped examining my life in bite size increments and scrutinized them as an entire narrative: my former profession and its associated training, conflicts, and wars; a loving and happy marriage that dissolved into a living nightmare; a healing process that took place in a foreign country with a damaged woman at my side; and the good and bad decisions I made along that path. Writing this story became that epiphany as I collated the events of the previous week, a lifetime of experiences, and years of meditative pondering, discovering that a Bangkok monk that I would likely never meet had been right. You can't always swim back to that distant island.

EPILOGUE

Farewell Noojan Phundet ~ September 14 – 18, 2014

Rain pelted the overhead tile roof and the sound of crashing waves reverberated through the concrete walls of my beachside abode. An occasional strobe of light flashed through the room's single window followed by a distant clap of thunder and Mother Nature's fury harmonized into a calming composition. Lying back on a bed that I had not enjoyed for just over four months, I felt myself falling into serene sleep as another wail of far-away thunder seemed to momentarily punctuate the clatter of the overhead rain and roar of waves. Just as I began to drop down into deep recesses of unconsciousness the door of the bedroom burst open and the lights came on, revealing my long-time partner Supattra standing in the doorway with long, pitch-black hair, glistening dark brown half-cloaked eyes, and tear-stained cheeks.

"My uncle is dead," she cried out in a trembling voice, pushing several strands of hair from her face. "Noojan Phundet has died."

Sitting up on the bed while rubbing my eyes, I replied, "I thought your mother said he was getting better?"

"Yes, but he is dead."

Surrounded by the Buddhist culture of Thailand for many years, I learned long ago that it was nearly impossible to get accurate information in this vibrant and culturally rich country. The facts always seemed to be obscured by an entirely different level of awareness, foreign to my Western upbringing and education. Their religion and way of life mold their perception of events unfolding around them in ways that make it hard for a Westerner to understand, with reality playing a minor role. The health of an ailing uncle was no exception.

"But your mother said he was getting better," I repeated, sheathing my anticipatory fervor in a cloak of calmness.

"He was getting better. She saw that he had begun to prepare himself and find the peace necessary to move on to his next life."

Scratching my head, trying to uncoil her Buddhist logic, I asked, "So she knew he was preparing himself to die but told us that he was getting better?"

"I must leave tomorrow," Supattra added, ignoring my question. "You don't need to come if you don't wish to."

"You know I should go," I muttered, trying to not show my exasperation, having arrived on the island of PhaNgan in the Gulf of Thailand, my home, less than twelve hours earlier.

Only just returned from an extended hiatus in the United States, paving the way to take Supattra back to my native country, I had no desire to leave the comfort of a house I had called home for over eight years but knew that my place was by her side as Noojan Phundet was put to rest. As his life waned, Supattra's family had been keeping vigil over him for several weeks in the small rice farming village of Yuan Kom City in northeast Thailand. Taking turns, they would watch over him during the day, feeding and cleaning him, and each night the entire family would sleep on the floor around him, letting him know he was not alone as he began to make the transition.

An uncle on her mother's side of the family, Noojan Phundet had been a short man with a thick torso, whose once thick arms and legs had become skeletal in his later years. With a weathered face, bushy eyebrows, and large innocent brown eyes, his leather-like chest and back had been festooned with faded Buddhist tattoos. I had known him for nearly as long as I had been in this country.

Thai families are incredibly close, even more so when they hail from the poverty-stricken Northeast or Isaan. Unable to make an adequate living off the rice harvested once a year in the seasonably dry northeast, most Isaan people move away to low-paying jobs in and around Bangkok. As a result, Isaan children are typically raised by their grandparents in the rice-farming villages of the northeast. Noojan Phundet's daughter and Supattra had grown up together under the tutelage of her mother's parents. While Noojan labored at construction in Bangkok, his daughter had been raised with Supattra and he had played an important role in her life.

The next morning, I found myself sitting in our idling four-door pickup waiting for the early morning ferry from the island of PhaNgan destined for the port of Donsak on the mainland. After the two-and-a-half-hour ferry ride across the lower Gulf of Thailand, we drove the eight hours to Bangkok where we picked up Supattra's two older sisters before continuing north. The three sisters babbled in their native language of Isaan, closer to Laotian than Thai, as we ascended the Khorat Plateau to rice country.

During a lull in their conversation, Supattra turned to me and commented, "My sister Aae did not want to come."

"Why's that?" I asked, while weaving past several slow-moving buses as they struggled up the freeway's steep incline leading to the rolling hills of the Khorat Plateau.

"She had an argument with Aae and did not know whether she would be welcome."

Breaking into a grin, I replied, "Aae had an argument with Aae."

Thai is a difficult language to master because what we Westerners hear as one word can actually have up to four different meanings, simply based on the tonal inflection. These inflectional differences carry into Thai names. Aae with a flat inflection was Supattra's sister and Aae with an ascending inflection was Supattra's cousin. Or is it the other way around? I can never remember. I can't tell you how many times I have asked some question about either her cousin or sister and confused the inflection, perplexing Supattra as to who I am inquiring about.

Looking over at me with flashing brown eyes, Supattra said, "Aae did not know whether she should come with us. She had a very bad disagreement with my cousin Aae two years ago and they have not spoken since. But last night she was visited by Noojan and he took my sister's hand while she slept."

"He wanted her to come?"

"Yes, he wants her to be with him when he moves on to his next life."

Six hours later, as the sun was beginning to peek over the horizon, I turned our truck onto a dirt road that led away from the freeway. A refreshing and brisk morning breeze blew through the truck's open windows as we twisted our way through thick lush foliage that suddenly opened up to a shimmering checkerboard of rice paddies. There is something magical about the Isaan air, its delicate mix of fragrances filling its beneficiaries with a soul-gratifying sensation. A vast horizon of bright green rice paddies outlined in tall trees, waist high grass, and colorful flower-topped bushes surrounded us. As Supattra uttered some indiscernible Isaan axiom and *waied*, we arrived at Yuan Kom, a small village situated on a low knoll amidst the vibrant scenery. Turning through a narrow gate, we entered the village and were immediately engulfed into a maze of narrow streets lined with two story concrete and wooden homes surrounded by a sea of tropical plants, papaya, and mango trees. Tall vine covered concrete poles lofted hundreds of twisted black wires that carried intermittent electricity to the homes. Mother hens led their small fluffy chicks along the shoulder of the road. Red capped and bearded roasters cackled from fence posts. And an occasional water buffalo looked up with large quizzical eyes from pens tucked away between the homes. It was like stepping back in time. Several scraggly looking dogs lay in the dirt here and there, watching our truck ease down the tight lane. We passed the temple grounds where an ornate white building with a steep red roof stood center stage. Trimmed with an undulating gold feathered serpentine shape that turned up and faced away at its apex, this structure was likely the oldest in the village and was considered its heart. A newer and larger dark gray structure with wall to wall aluminum windows and a similar red roof, lacking the ornate trim, stood in the background. The two similar but starkly different buildings, standing side by side, elicited thoughts of old verse new, and life verse death. Passing through an intersection, with slim dusty lanes thrusting out like the spokes of a wagon wheel, we drove down a dirt road on the far side of the village and arrived at Supattra's child-hood home.

I stopped in front of the house. The truck doors popped open and the three sisters jumped from their seats sporting wide grins, leaving me with the luggage. Supattra's mother, father, and a neighbor woman met the sisters at the home's wide, double front doors with toothy smiles. Family is the core of any Thai's life and as many times as I have come to Yuan Kom with Supattra, I have never seen her anything but elated to be back in her childhood stomping grounds, no matter the occasion. After unloading our luggage and dragging it up onto a large covered blue tiled patio that reached from one side of the house to the other, I drove the pickup to the base of the hill, at the edge of the village, and parked next to an open sid-ed thatched-roof hut that looked as if it had been constructed of fallen branches and left over building supplies. A small wooden stall next to the hut housed a single black water buffa-lo that peered at me with wide innocent eyes as it nibbled its morning meal.

Walking back up the road and greeting the villagers that I recognized from previous visits, I took a seat at a concrete picnic table shaded by a tall mango tree, adjacent the covered patio, waiting my turn to take a shower and scrub off the long drive. As I sat at the picnic table, the neighbor and Supattra's mother began babbling in Isaan with the word *farang* seem-ingly the focal point of the conversation. I knew they were talking about someone who was not Thai and more than likely me. Being the only Southeast Asian country to not be con-quered or colonized—there is that pesky little fact that they sided with the Japanese during WWII to avoid that particular fate—Thai's are incredibly nationalistic, and tend to look down on other countries and cultures. Their Western industri-alized allies are no exception. Long story short, Thai's use the term *farang*, usually pronounced *falong*—R's a difficult letter for them—to describe any fair skinned foreigner. It is not meant as either an endearing or demeaning description. It is simply their way of saying "the guy or gal with white skin that's not from around here." Of course they have different expressions to identify Japanese, Africans, Arabs, and likely any other race that can be distinguished by the some physical characteristic, such as the color of their skin, but once again these terms are not meant to be disparaging. They are simply a general descriptor to the fact that someone is not Thai.

After a quick Isaan shower and change of clothes, the three sisters, their mother, and I began walking back down the dirt road toward the thatched-roof hut and our pickup. Turning to the left at the bottom of the hill, we rambled along a cracked concrete road that marked the edge of the village and passed by small homes constructed of cinderblock, faded wood, and corrugated metal, all entangled in vines and lush vegetation. Tall trees, with thick foliage-covered branches, bordered the road, while waist high grass and bushes bearing vibrant purple and yellow flowers grew between their trunks. Beyond the trees and bushes was an ocean of bright green square rice paddies, shimmering under the hot sun, separated by low dirt mounds wide enough for a single man or woman to negotiate. Several hefty blackish frogs hastily hopped out of our way, seeking refuge in the tall grass from the potentially threatening carnivores.

The cracked concrete road came to an end as we stepped around several deep puddles of brown water and we continued down a dirt road. Looking up, I spied Noojan Phundet's home across a small field filled with clumps of short grass. After years of toiling away at his low-paying construction job in Bangkok, Noojan had just recently moved back to Yuan Kom, and with the money he had saved over a lifetime of hard labor, bought a small plot of land on the southwest side of the village. The home he built was anything but extravagant, a small concrete building with a corrugated metal roof that included one bedroom, a living room, and kitchen, designed to house his family of four. Other than a white porcelain Thai style squatting toilet, the small bathroom attached to the building had one spigot of running water mounted halfway up the wall and a small hole at the base of another wall to allow spillage to run out into the yard. The floors of all the rooms were untreated gray concrete, allowing sanctuary from the daily heat as coolness radiated upward. Noojan's home remained unpainted, and rather than glass windows several openings on the side of the building were covered with simple wooden shutters that could be opened during the day to allow air to flow through.

A white pickup was parked along the road next to the home, its bed packed with a sound system and four enormous speakers blaring out tinny sounding, undoubtedly sad, Isaan songs. A large overhead canopy stood in the front yard filled with people milling around ten or twelve folding tables topped with platters of food and surrounded by red plastic chairs.

Slowing my pace, I allowed Supattra, her sisters, and mother to precede me into the throng of mourners. My female companions weaved through the crowd, greeting friends and relatives they hadn't seen in years with a *wai*. At one point we ran into Aae, Noojan's daughter, and she began crying when she saw me bringing up the rear of our small procession. I had known Aae for years, and at one point she had come down to Koh PhaNgan to work for me and Supattra. After the tearful greeting with Noojan's daughter we worked our way through the rest of the gathering and the four women disappeared inside Noojan's house.

Peeking through the doorless opening of the house, I saw the room beyond was filled with old women dressed in faded sarongs and floral patterned muumuu-like dresses, with a smattering of old men between. Sitting cross-legged on the floor next to them was a large white casket with gold ornamental facets and a matching elaborate tiered top. String lights had been draped over the casket, flashing in a nonsensical rhythm, and gifts to the family were mounted onto decorative cardboard backings and hung on the walls above. The value of gifts were commensurate to the average income of the village, included plastic clocks, dinner ware, and decorative pillows—inexpensive offerings but nonetheless an important element of the ritual. Vivid flowers decorated the edges of the scene, giving it a tropical air. On either side of the casket stood thick yellow candles on low tables, their burning wicks flickering and dancing in the dimly lit room, producing a seemingly chaotic tempo when mixed against the flashing lights. A pot filled with sand sat on the floor directly in front of the casket, holding the remains of a hundred sticks of incense, along with a reed mat.

Supattra and her sisters dropped to their knees at the doorway and scooted across the floor onto the reed mat. Each taking a single piece of incense, they lit the end on one of the burning candles and clasped it between their hands, before raising it to their foreheads, once again *waiing*. After a moment of silence, they bowed in respect to Noojan Phundet before placing the burning incense in the sand-filled pot. Turning, Supattra gestured for me to join her. Mimicking her actions, I dropped to my knees, scooted across the floor onto the reed mat, and pulled a single piece of incense from a nearby package.

When I looked at her with questioning eyes, she whispered, "Tell Noojan who is kneeling before him. You don't need to say anything. Just say it in your heart."

Lighting the end on the burning candle to my left, I cupped the incense between my hands and raised it to my forehead before bowing.

"Did you tell him who you were?" Supattra asked.

"He knows it's me," I whispered back, slipping the burning incense into the sand.

Ceremony complete, I glanced around the room, taking in the details of the setting. The beautiful tropical flowers decorating the casket caught my attention as I suddenly realized that they were all plastic. Silently chuckling to myself, I thought *only in Thailand, a land filled with an abundance of beautiful plants and flowers, would you find plastic replicas trimming such a scene. These practical people would rather reuse imitation flowers than worry about watering or replacing them during a several day long ceremony.*

To one side, a large black and white framed picture of Supattra's uncle in his youth stood on a tripod. The picture showed him with a Fu Manchu mustache that made him look more like Poncho Villa than a Thai construction worker or Sax Rohmer's evil fictional character. The sight of Noojan Phundet with the Spanish looking mustache made me momentarily wonder if he hadn't been a Mexican bandito in a past life. As I examined the picture, I recalled the last time I had seen him, four months earlier.

His eyes had been glossed over in what I thought was a mix of drunkenness and cataracts at the time, and he seemed frail and had a distended belly. While he spoke no English, we had a short conversation in Thai, limited by my vocabulary. When I asked how he was doing, '*Sa baai dee mai*' he had responded, "*Mai sa baai*,' or not so well.

Supattra explained to me later that he was very sick, his liver was failing him. Not an uncommon ailment for Isaan men, where the strength of *lao kow* tested even the best of livers.

Scooting over to the crowd of women, in their sarongs and muumuus, and the old men, I leaned my back up against the wall and crossed my legs under me into a painful knot, while continuing to take in the tranquil scene. One woman chattered something in the Isaan language while pointing to the base of the casket. Another woman quickly stood, grabbed a piece of dirty laundry from the corner of the room, and placed it on a puddle of water that was obviously leaking from the casket.

Whispering into Supattra's ear, I asked, "Is something leaking from the casket?"

Replying with a simple unconcerned nod, she went back to her conversation with the woman to her left.

Studying the casket, I then asked, "How do they keep your uncle from smelling? Is the casket filled with ice?"

"Yes, ice, and they put him in the same water that keeps plants fresh. Chlora…chlora…chlora something."

Scratching my head, I asked, "Chlorophyll? It can't be chlorophyll. How about formaldehyde?"

"It is whatever they use for plants," she offhandedly responded, patting me on the knee. "He will stay fresh for many days."

Thankful that it wasn't pure body fluid leaking from the casket, I still wondered how much of Noojan Phundet was seeping onto the floor amidst his farewell celebration.

After another thirty minutes of conversation with the old women and men in the house, Supattra patted me on the knee again and gestured toward the door with her chin, indicating it was time for us to leave. Standing up from the concrete floor my hips, knees, and ankles wailed in pain as I unraveled them from the appendage tether I had tied earlier. Attempting to disguise my stiff joins from the limber elderly villagers around me, I moved from the room in a slow and methodical cadence. An old lady to my right cackled and said something to the crowd sitting on the floor that included the word *farang*, to which they all began laughing.

Looking to Supattra as I stiffly walked towards the door, I asked, "What are they laughing at?"

She smiled and shook her head, saying, "They think *farang* bodies are spoiled."

"Spoiled?"

"Yes, *farangs* always sit in comfortable chairs and lie in restful beds. *Farang* bodies are not tough like Isaan bodies."

"So they're laughing at me?"

"They are laughing at your spoiled body."

Taking a moment to articulate a response to this somewhat impolite claim, I turned to the old woman who had made the comment and smilingly said, "*Yaawng yaawng niu meuuay*," attempting to tell her my legs and hips were stiff from sitting, and the entire room of old men and women began laughing and clapping their hands.

Supattra looked over at me and giggled, saying, "The words were out of order, but you just told them that when you sit cross-legged your fingers and toes get stiff."

As we stepped out the front door, I placed my arms around Supattra's waist and whispered, "It could have been worse."

Having lived here for as long as I have, two opposing lessons concerning communicating in this country have been emblazed into my psyche: First, conversing through words, no matter the tongue, or body language is much like handling a

live grenade with the pin already pulled. What might be considered appropriate in the Western world could very well be
measured as offensive in Southeast Asia. Second, Thais have
good souls and a *farang* attempting to communicate in their
language gets a lot of latitude.

Outside Noojan Phundet's house, the tables and chairs
were filled with a morning crowd eating and drinking, with
eight teenage boys acting as waiters delivering food, and busboys removing used plates and silverware. Taking a seat at
one of the folding tables I noticed an old, frail, white-haired
woman with a hunched back emerge from a shed-like building
constructed of cinderblock and a rusted corrugated steel roof.
Wrapped in a sarong, the old woman carefully made her way
across the small field between the shed and Noojan's house.
Several of the women tending the kitchen saw her coming and
chattered together before filling a plastic container with rice
and a thick bamboo soup. Taking the container, one of the
women delivered it to the old woman, who upon receiving the
food, turned and began shuffling back toward the shed. Sitting
down next to me, Supattra took up another conversation with
more villagers as I began nibbling at what was likely the same
bamboo soup given to the old woman, along with chicken
wings and a fried fish that had been laid out for visitors.
Sometime later, I watched the old stooped woman remerge
from the shed and drop onto the ground the remnants of her
meal, which several chickens immediately began devouring.

Nudging Supattra, I asked, "Who's the old lady?"

Glancing up at the elderly woman as she reentered the
shed, Supattra commented, "She is a villager."

"She lives in a shed?"

"It is her house. Her husband has been dead many years
and she has no money. So the villagers feed her when they
can."

"And when they can't?"

"She finds food in the countryside."

"She forages?"

Looking at me with quizzical expression, Supattra said, "I
don't know what that means—forages."

"She lives off the land."

"Yes, many people in the village live off the land. There are many frogs, birds, and plants you can eat that grow between the rice fields."

It is true, while visiting Supattra's village over the years, I have seen many people wandering between the paddies, picking plants, catching frogs, or harvesting ant nests, to name a few. While Supattra's family is considered well off with seventeen *rai* of farmland, or nearly seven acres, many villagers have no land to speak of and must rely on low-paying jobs, foraging, or both to survive. Isaan people consider many of the items that are scavenged in the countryside delicacies, and a popular destination for Supattra and her family is to be found on the back roads of the countryside where those same items can be purchased for a small price. Supattra refers to that marketplace as the "jungle market."

Feeling a hand on my shoulder, I turned and was met with the sight of Noojan's son *waiing* me. Standing, I returned his *wai* and then shook his hand. Noojan's son was a replica of his father in his youth, with muscular arms and legs attached to a thick torso. His son had the same bushy eyebrows hanging over wide innocent eyes.

Looking into his eyes, I said, "*Siia Jai,*" telling him I was sorry.

Nodding his head, Noojan's son spoke with Supattra in Isaan and she, in turn, looked at me and translated, "He is glad you are here. It means a lot to their family."

Traversing the same cracked concrete road we had walked down two hours earlier, the family meandered back along the village boundary, passed the thatched-roof hut and our pickup, turning up the dirt lane to their home. The three sisters immediately began pouring drinks and preparing for a late morning lunch. Sitting down at the concrete picnic table, I began sipping at a beer delivered to me by Aae. A rotund woman with wide face and a small impish nose dressed in an oversized floral blouse and blue pants and an older man with thick black-framed glasses had joined the family and lay on reed mats on the far side of the patio. The woman, lying on her side, glared at me with an unsmiling face, which is unusual in this region of Thailand. The old man, lying on his back with his head resting on a pillow, smiled at me each time I looked at him, which is a Thai's normal response to a foreigner. Having never met these two before, I hesitated in introducing myself in order to break the ice, as I normally do in Isaan, due to the language barrier. Rather than using my limited Thai to greet strangers, I have found over the years that it is better to let someone educated in both languages to do the honors, thereby avoiding my inevitable mispronunciation, incorrect tonal inflection, lousy sentence structure, or just plain wrong words that could change my intended goodwill into an unfortunate international incident.

Smiling back at the old man, while glancing at the unsmiling woman, I wondered if this was a father-daughter team or husband and wife. Eventually, I surmised that these two were obviously relatives of the family and, based on the intimacy of the couple, that they were husband and wife. As she moved to the side of the house to help prepare the meal, I watched in interest at the rotund woman's aptness in the kitchen, moving from chore to chore without supervision or guidance. She would occasional glance over at me with the same unsmiling face as I watched her dig a fresh ginger root from a nearby bush or slice through stalks of lemon grass, as she assembled what would undoubtedly be Thai chicken soup. She continued her surveillance of me, likely trying to decide whether I was worthy of a smile. As we sat down for our meal on the patio's hard tiles, once again forcing me to tie myself into an uncomfortable cluster of limbs, she sat back down next to her husband, and pushed the bowl of chicken soup in front of me. It was then I realized that her selection of chicken soup was in deference of me. *Farangs* are stereotyped in this wonderful country. They can't sit cross-legged too long and they hate spicy food, to name a few common perceptions or misperceptions. The unsmiling rotund woman, who spoke no English, using her limited knowledge of *farangs*, had chosen a meal that she thought I would appreciate as a guest in Isaan. And while I was never afforded a smile by the woman over the next day and a half, it was apparent that her unsmiling face was not meant as a sign of disrespect. It was an indication that she had spent very little time around fair-skinned folk from the West, and she was simply trying to cautiously figure me out.

With food-and-liquor-filled bellies combined with a night-long drive, Supattra and her sisters began to show signs of sleepiness, and one by one excused themselves for an afternoon nap on the cool tiled floor just inside the front doors. Feeling the same drowsiness overcoming me, I decided on a short walk to stretch my legs before laying my head on a pillow that would be followed with a well-deserved snooze.

Walking back down to the road to our pickup, I turned right and found the road leading out into the rice paddies. Wandering down an intersecting dirt trail that weaved its way between the vibrant green paddies, I passed more thatched-roof huts that had faded into a silver hue from years under the hot Isaan sun. The wet rice paddies seemed to coalesce with shade provided by the tall trees bracketing the trail and provided an unusual coolness to my journey. The air smelled of freshly turned soil, stagnant water, tender rice stalks, and fragrant flowers. It was a calming aroma that filled me with unqualified bliss and an unrestrained smile spread across my face.

Five minutes later, I arrived at the edge of Supattra's family farm. Years before Supattra's father had dug out one of the paddies to create a pond in order to raise fish. While he lacked the technological knowhow and his attempted venture had failed, he had unintentionally created an ecological and visual masterpiece that blossomed each wet season. Several tall trees lazily hung overhead casting the pond into a mosaic of shade and sun, its soothing green waters were topped with five or six wide lily pads and large purple, blue, and red flowers. Frogs and birds flocked to the pond, searching out meals of water bugs, tadpoles, and minnows. Lying down on the wrapped plank floor of the family's thatched covered hut, I placed my hands behind my head, felt, and smelled an aromatic cool breeze waft across me. Closing my eyes, I immediately fell asleep.

Waking some hours later, I stood and stretched my limbs, trying to discern how long I had slept. The sun was just above the horizon to the west and Yuan Kom stood like an island in a sea of vibrant green to the east. Raising my hands above my head, I stretched my back, before ambling back down the dirt path surrounded by the rice paddies and bracketed by the tall trees.

As I strolled up to the house, Supattra anxiously called out, "Where have you been? I have been worried about you."

"I fell asleep at the farm."

With a wide smile on her face, Aae called out from behind Supattra, asking, "You went out to the farm? I wanted to go out there. You should have told me where you were going."

"You were sleeping."

Smiling, all signs of concern vanishing from her tone and expression, Supattra asked, "Did you sleep well?"

"Like a baby."

"We need to get ready to go back to my uncle's house. You need to take another shower."

With visions of ice-water-induced goose bumps and shivering flashing in my mind, I begrudgingly nodded my head and moved toward the bathroom with its waiting barrel of cold greenish liquid.

Stripping my clothes off and hanging them on the dormant showerhead, I nervously moved over to the barrel and dipped the plastic bowl into the shimmering murky water. Taking a deep breath, I poured the water directly over my head, sending shivers down my spine and through my limbs. Dousing my right arm pit with the second bowl of water, a particular sensitive area, it felt as if I had just been struck by a low voltage cattle prod. Four more lung-gasping bowls of water and I dropped the bowl back into the barrel. With all the hairs on my body standing erect, I found a piece of soap and scrubbed myself down. The next dousing was less painful, as all my nerve endings had already surrendered to numbness. Wrapping a towel around my waist, I stepped from the bathroom to find Supattra waiting with a pair of blue jeans and a dark blue shirt.

"You must be dressed in a dark color."

Taking her choice of clothes from her outstretched hand, I nodded and in a chattering mumble replied, "These are fine."

Giggling, she commented, "The water is not that cold."

"You don't sport a spoiled *farang* body. It's cold to me."

After dressing in our small room, I moved out to the shaded patio and took a seat at the picnic table. Sitting on the bench, sipping another beer, I began examining a swarm of red ants at my feet, scavenging next to the edge of the patio. Having had a painful run in with these ants last time I was here, at this very same table, I daintily moved my feet away from their search pattern and inspected the bench next to me to ensure they weren't planning a classic surprise envelopment attack on my position. As I was carefully scrutinizing the ants, Supattra emerged from the house wearing a black, knee-length dress. In what I assumed was an unaware move, she stepped up barefoot next to me into the middle of the horde of hungry ants.

"Supattra," I nervously pointed out, "There are red ants all around you."

Looking down at the ants swarming around her feet with an unconcerned expression, she calmly replied, "If I don't bother them, they will leave me alone."

Watching the ants keep their distance from Supattra's bare feet, as if there was some unseen force-field at work, I shook my head in disbelief, asking, "Is there some Isaan Buddhist agreement with ants? Have they agreed to keep their distance if you feed them once a day? Last time I was here, they nearly pulled me down and dragged me to their lair."

Giggling, Supattra replied, "May be they like sweet *farang* skin more than tough Isaan skin."

"That must be it." I chuckled. "It's the spoiled *farang* body versus the tough Isaan body, again."

A short time later, we began retracing our earlier route along the now darkened road back to Noojan's house. Dim lights from several of the houses along the road illuminated the way and an overhead full moon revealed the outlying rice paddies in shades of gray, as a warm soft breeze brought with it the same aroma I had smelled on my walk to the family farm and during my afternoon siesta. As we drew close I could hear the tinny music still being played from the massive sound system mounted in the back of the pickup, and looking across the small field I noticed the mourners who had flocked under the overhead canopy earlier seemed to have never left, still eating, drinking, and talking to one another. While everything on the outside of the house seemed to be trapped in a time warp, the atmosphere inside the house had dramatically changed. The room was now filled with men and women sitting around reed mats playing cards and drinking.

Following Supattra's lead, I re-entered the house and once again dropped to my knees, scooting over to the reed mat in front of the casket, paying my respects to Noojan Phundet with burning incense. From there we moved over to the closest card game, wiggling between several other players, and the fun began.

It was a game I had never played before and seemed to be based loosely on black jack where the players were competing against the dealer. After slapping twenty baht down on the mat, I was dealt two cards and given a choice of a third or holding. It took several rounds, and the loss of about a hundred baht—just over 3 dollars—to conclude that, whereas in black jack, your goal is the number twenty-one, this game was built around the number nine.

At some point, between the cheers of winners and moans of losers, I was delivered another glass filled with beer. At some even later point, Supattra became the dealer and my losses began multiplying. Not because I was losing, but rather, she as dealer was taking a financial beating by the other players. Watching our money spilling across the reed mat, I removed myself from the game and walked outside, not wanting to witness the monetary massacre taking place at the hands of my partner. Sitting down on one of the red plastic chairs, I immediately realized I had inadvertently chosen a table filled with inebriated men.

Reading this story, you should have already come to the conclusion that, while I may poke fun at Thailand at times, I truly love this country and its people. With that said, everything I find myself doing on a regular basis in this wonderful and culturally rich region of the world, I attempt to walk away with two lessons. Those lessons can be opposing in nature or not.

The first lesson I learned about alcohol consumption in Thailand was that nothing good happens after midnight. A late night of over indulgence in the spirits while patronizing one of my favorite local pubs leads to one of two things, or both most of the time. I will wake up and regret the previous evening for physical and/or psychological reasons. I will either find myself lying on a bed, drenched in sweat, as the countless drinks I consumed leach from my body with my head pounding like a jackhammer and/or find myself recalling the things I said and did, whose memory fully dilutes any fun I might have perceived.

The second lesson I have learned while living in this country is to avoid groups of intoxicated Thai men at all costs. If I were to choose my least likeable scenario in Thailand, it would be having a conversation with a drunken Thai man who believes and wants to prove he has mastered the English language. Over the years I have found that being alone with a group of drunken men is a guaranteed trip into my least likeable scenario. There will be at least one in the crowd who will want to demonstrate that he can communicate in my native language and it will normally be the one least capable of the act. It is interesting to note that Thai women do not pose the same threat. For whatever reason, a drunken Thai woman never feels the need to prove her vernacular aptness. As a result, I normally am very cautious and always on the lookout to avoid gatherings of intoxicated Thai men.

Unsurprisingly, the man to my left looked over and mumbled, "*Hallo, yu num Sewat. Oow me num?*"

Trying to keep the immediate wave of regret about lowering my guard concerning finding myself surrounded by drunken Thai men from showing, I smilingly and politely replied, "*Mai khao jai, khrapp,*" or I don't understand.

Leaning forward in his chair to within inches of my face, obviously thinking that our distance from one another had something to do with my inability to comprehend his English, he repeated, "*Yu num Sewat. Oow me num?*"

With the smell of hot whiskey and stomach acid wafting the air around me, I suddenly wondered if I hadn't mistakenly though this man was trying speak English when in fact he was simply slurring his native language. With a questioning expression, I asked if he could please repeat what he had said, "*Saam saak.*"

It was his turn to look at me with quizzical expression. Moving his face a tolerable distance from mine and cocking his head to one side, he replied, "*A rai?*"

Now, my Thai should be far better than it is after eight years of living in this country and when asked why it isn't, I normally reply that with Supattra always by my side I am never placed in a difficult situation requiring communication to extract myself. She always saves the day.

Several years ago, Supattra and I came to Isaan and spent two weeks with her family in Yuan Kom and my Thai flourished. Her mother even commented that if I were to stay another month, I would be fluent. This was because during that visit, I often found myself without Supattra and had to rely on my ability to speak Thai to communicate. The other side of learning Thai while in Isaan is that I was actually learning two languages, thinking they were one. The Thais in this region of the country speak exclusively Isaan to one another. If I asked questions or tried to communicate in Thai they would obviously talk to me in that language. But all the other words and phrases I was picking up as a bystander, was in the Isaan dialect. So upon my return to Koh PhaNgan, while trying to impress my Thai friends how much of their language I had learned, they would give me the same quizzical look the drunk across the table had just given me.

All this aside, I immediately translated what the drunk had said as, "What?" and repeated my earlier request, "*Saam saak.*"

Shaking his head, the drunken man across from me turned and laughingly said something to his equally inebriated friends that included the word *farang*. The other drunks became hysterical, laughing and slapping their thighs, and pounding their glasses and bottles on the table top. While this situation might cause the typical person to become embarrassed, I smiled at my mysterious victory in avoiding an English conversation with the drunken man and quickly made an escape from the table. I found out later from Supattra that rather than asking him to repeat his question, I had been saying the word, "Repetitiously."

Walking over to an open window with a beer in my hand, I looked into the house and saw that Aae, Supattra's sister, had joined in the dealing duties. Much to my delight, Aae was skillfully winning back all the money Supattra lost. Game after game, Aae and Supattra were seemingly clearing all the bets off the mat, while the players grumbled and moaned.

Looking up from the floor, Supattra smilingly handed me several thousand baht, saying, "Aae is very good."

Supattra's uncle, sitting next to her on the floor, looked up and said something in Isaan to me and Aae turned, translating, "He says he wants me to go away and let Supattra deal again."

Chuckling, I replied, "Tell him I don't want you to go anywhere. I was losing my hat and ass without you."

Her uncle laughed, and held his beer glass up to the window for a toast after Aae translated my reply.

After emptying the pockets of all the gambling mourners and saying our farewells, Supattra, her sisters, mother, and I began walking back down the dirt road leading away from Noojan's house. As we passed the tall trees marking the edge of the village with the rice paddies glistening under the moon, Supattra silently took my hand and smiled. Her beautiful oval-shaped face looking up at me, cast in shadows, brought an instinctive smile to my face. Looking over my shoulder when Aae began anxiously babbling something behind us, I asked Supattra what was going on.

As I watched her mother pull a Buddhist medallion from around her neck, Supattra replied, "Aae says Noojan is walking next to her."

"Noojan's walking next to her?"

"Yes, she feels him next to her."

"Is that bad?"

"No, but it has frightened her. She does not know why he is there."

Watching Supattra's mother place the medallion around Aae's neck, I said, "But Noojan was a good person."

"Yes, but Aae does not know why he keeps coming to her."

"There might be a bad reason he's hanging out with Aae?"

"Yes."

Realizing, by the shortness of her answer to my question, that was all I was going to get out of Supattra concerning her uncle coming to Aae, I turned away from the scene behind us and began contemplating the day. I have lived in Thailand long enough to stop visiting the standard tourist destinations that populate this beautiful country. Their allure long since faded; the enchanting elephant farms, spectacular temples, and astounding waterfalls now seem dull and their hidden secrets obvious. That doesn't mean that I am not still in awe of this country, for each time I think I've seen it all, I witness something that reminds me why I live halfway across the world from my native land. As I walked from his unpretentious house that evening, I realized that Noojan's funeral was one of those moments.

The next morning, I took another frigid Isaan shower and stepped out onto the shaded patio, taking a seat at the concrete picnic table. Relieved to see that the ants were no longer swarming on discarded morsels, I watched as the women began preparing our morning meal. Firing up the small charcoal cooker, Supattra's mother heated up yesterday's leftovers. The three sisters began rolling sticky rice and a sweet soybean paste into banana leafs, talking and laughing about something in their regional dialect. I watched them meticulously bind each wrapper with a strand of fiber from the same leafs, before setting them in a large pot.

While learning to love the fiery food of Thailand, I have never been an enthusiast of Isaan cuisine. When asked to describe Isaan food, I usually begin by saying it's very earthy. Actually, Isaan food smells so unpleasant to me that I have a hard time getting it past my nose and into my mouth. Also, many of the ingredients seem repugnant to my Western palate. I'm not your typical American food sissy by any means. I enjoy liver and other organs most Westerners find distasteful, but the sight of a small intestine or coagulated blood floating in my soup is a surefire method of dispelling any hunger I might have. So when the rotund woman who didn't smile made me chicken soup the day before, I was truly appreciative.

Walking back to Noojan's house after we had eaten, the mourners continued to crowd under the tent still seemingly trapped in an endless time warp of talking, eating, and drinking. Several bald and eyebrow-less boys wandered passed me as I sat down on one of the red plastic chairs. A shaved head and loss of eyebrows made such an extreme change to their appearance, it took several minutes to realize they were the same teenaged boys who had been acting as waiters and busboys the day before.

With the Isaan sun relentlessly pounding down on Yuan Kom, the overhead canopy quickly turned into a tropical greenhouse run amok. Even the squadrons of flies that had been skillfully dive bombing the plates of food earlier seemed to now be circling above in disarray, their internal sensors malfunctioning in the extreme heat.

Supattra pointed to the thick grass and tall trees along the road marking the village boundary, silently indicating that we should move out from the crowd and seek refuge in the coolness of the trees. Carrying several red plastic chairs to edge of the road, we sat down under a stand of three large trees and watched as the teenaged boys began moving the tables and chairs off to the side.

Sitting in the shade next to me, Supattra reached out and took my hand and said, "Thank you."

"Thank you for what?"

"Thank you for being here with me," she replied. "My family and the villagers all like you. They say you are good because, while you don't understand our language, you don't need to be involved in everything going on around you. You have patience and patience is a valued Isaan quality. Thank you."

Flushed with a warm feeling of acceptance, I asked, "Who told you I have patience?"

"Many people have told me that. The woman who cooked you chicken soup yesterday, my uncle, my mother, and many more have talked to me about you. They say I am very lucky to have you."

Smiling, I responded, "We are together because we belong with each other and no one else." As Supattra leaned over to give me a *hom noi,* I saw a single tear working its way down her cheek and asked, "Why are you crying?"

"I am happy."

A short time later, a man on a scooter arrived with five or six coconuts wedged between the seat and handlebars. Seeing the man on the scooter in front of this father's house, Noojan's son jogged over and passed him small amount of money, taking the coconuts back to the kitchen.

Watching the transaction between Noojan's son and the coconut bearing man, I asked, "What are the coconuts for?"

"To wash Noojan," Supattra replied. "Noojan's son has asked me and my sister Aae to help wash his father's face."

"His face?"

"Yes, it is very important and not everyone is allowed to wash his face."

"Does everyone get to wash the rest of him?"

"Whoever wants to can help wash him, but only those asked can wash his face."

"When do you wash him?"

"Just before he is placed in the fire."

Thirty minutes later a bright red pickup truck, filled with five color-clashing orange-robed monks, passed by our road-side lookout and turned onto the intersecting road toward Noojan's house. As if receiving a silent communiqué, Supattra's family stood and began walking toward the house. As I stood to follow, Supattra turned, placing a hand on my shoulder, and said that I could stay in the shade under the trees. Sitting back down, I noticed her father, who had been sitting two seats to my left, hadn't moved, and I realized whatever was going to take place was for blood relatives only.

Looking back up at the house, I noticed that the teenaged boys with shaved heads had changed into orange robes and began lining up, as if preparing themselves for a military inspection. The red truck came to a halt in front of Noojan's house and monks climbed from its bed, glancing at the teenaged boys as they lazily strolled past. The monks, the orange-robed teenage boys, followed by Supattra and her family, walked into Noojan's home. A gentle breeze blew across my back, surrounding me with that familiar and uniquely calming aroma that had conjoined over the rice paddies behind me, as the monks begin chanting in a singsong melody that slowly developed into soothing countermelodies. It was beautiful, peaceful experience, listening to the monks' voices echoing from Noojan's house as I sat in the shade under the trees, next to the sea of rice paddies surrounding this small village. Another silent communiqué was received and Supattra's father stood and walked over to a pole that had been erected in the center of the small field next to Noojan's house. The chanting ended a moment later and the five monks stepped from the house, followed by Supattra's family.

Seeing the monks emerge from the house, Supattra's father lit the end of a string of firecrackers that had been hanging from the pole. As they began loudly bursting and exploding, I thought of the fishing village on Koh PhaNgan where Supattra and I live, and how the fishermen use firecrackers to ward off evil spirits as they pull away from the pier, and I assumed that these where being used in a similar fashion. No evil spirits would be following Noojan Phundet into his next life.

The monks climbed back into the bed of the red pickup and were driven off as the orange-robed teenagers hefted Noojan's casket from its former perch and carried it out of the house. Another gold truck arrived with an elaborate pink and white silken shade strung over the bed. Walking out under the overhead canopy in front of Noojan's house, the teenagers placed the casket in the pickup's bed and the mourners began lining up behind, as if forming up for a parade. I caught a glimpse of

Supattra in the crowd carrying a wooden box while her sister held the large black and white picture of Noojan with his Fu Manchu mustache. Standing, I joined the end of the procession, and the truck filled with the sound system, followed by the one carrying Noojan Phundet began to slowly drive down the narrow road. With a background of tinny Isaan music the small parade of family and friends began following the two trucks as they wove their way through the narrow streets of Yuan Kom City.

Other villagers appeared in their front yards, observing us and paying their respects to Noojan, as his small parade passed by. Some waved and called out to people in the following crowd, as if we were simply out for a Sunday walk. Others watched in silence as the procession wended its way through Yuan Kom City and past their modest homes. Making a left turn onto one of the two main roads bisecting the village, I noticed that Noojan's family had mixed in with the mourners, with no precedence as to the order of the parade. Children joined the procession, skipping and chatting with each other, the family, and mourners, obviously wanting to take part in the rare excitement that transpires in this quiet village from time to time. The procession entered the temple grounds through a back gate, the new dark gray building with aluminum windows to one side and a thick grove of thin trees and vines to the other. I caught a glimpse of the ornate steep red roof of the main temple to my left as a large pond appeared next to the road on my right. As many times as I had been to this small village, I had never known there was a pond tucked away on the temple grounds, hidden by thick jungle. Supattra appeared by my side, explaining that the pond is the village water supply.

Looking down at her walking next to me, I said, "I recognize the greenish tint."

"What do you mean?"

"From the barrel. It's the same green water in the barrel in your family's bathroom."

Finally the procession arrived at a small white building with three sets of steep stairs positioned on separate sides of the structure leading up to the ancient iron door of the furnace. The building was topped with a four-story, narrow red brick chimney the same height as the main temple. A shaded seating area stood next to the furnace where the five orange-robed monks sat on a stage inside, scrutinizing the passing parade. Reed mats had been laid out next to the stage and fifty or sixty blue plastic chairs were positioned just behind them. A small group of well-dressed Thai men and women sat huddled to one side of the rows of blue chairs. The procession slowly began circling the furnace and, on its third turn, we came to a halt next to the shaded seating area.

With family and friends standing around, the orange-robed teenagers pulled the top off the elaborate white casket and gently lifted a smaller one from within, setting it on a silver metal table that stood next to the stairs leading up to the furnace. Walking over to the shaded seating area, I watched the teenaged boys then lift the top off the smaller casket as Noojan's friends and family crowded around.

Supattra, her sister, and Noojan's son positioned themselves near the head of the casket as buckets of coconut water appeared. It would be the last time they saw Noojan in this lifetime, and his friends and relatives all took part in washing him down. One by one, after one last glimpse and touch, Noojan's family and friends moved to the shaded seating area. The family sat on reed mats next to the stage and Noojan's friends moved to the rows of blue plastic chairs behind them. I took a seat in the last row of blue chairs.

The orange-robed teenagers picked up Noojan's casket while four men began moving the table up the furnace stairs. Watching the teenagers humbly hold Noojan's casket high on their shoulders as the table was repositioned filled me with wonderment at this one small piece of an entire ceremony. Sitting in the back row of blue chairs, I speculated as to the centuries had it taken for this one element of the ritual to develop.

Its calm cadence was somehow hypnotizing. Once the table was positioned next to the ancient iron furnace door, the orange-robed teenagers carried the casket up the stairs, as if a

well-practiced military color guard, and once again gently
placed Noojan on the table.

Three young girls began handing out folded paper flowers
to the friends and family, and several men began stringing cotton twine from Noojan's casket to the stage. The orange-robed
teenagers moved onto the stage and sat in front of the monks.
The end of the twine was laid across the laps of the five monks
and then wrapped loosely around the boys. I'd seen the string
rite before—a highway for spirits connecting Noojan Phundet
to the monks and teenaged boys on stage. Noojan's son remained next to his father near the furnace door.

The monks began a chanting melody that once again slowly developed into countermelodies as the family and friends
held their clasped hands in a *wai* next to their foreheads. It was
an experience that seemed to wash away any anxieties that
might have been hiding out in the recesses of my mind and I
wandered if it had the same effect on Noojan's family and
friends. When the chanting finally ended, the string was removed and, with Noojan's son still positioned next to his father and his sister at the base of the furnace steps, the monks
began to stand, one by one.

A small black and brown dog joined the first monk as he
stepped from the stage. Having seen this elderly monk many
times before, I couldn't help but silently chuckle to myself.
Each and every time I had seen him, he had one animal or another following him everywhere he went. The year before,
while attending a ceremony for Supattra's grandmother, the
monk had a black cat following him. The time before that had
been another dog, with a white and brown coat of fur.

Walking up to Noojan's daughter with the black and brown
dog at his feet, the elderly monk received a new set of orange
robes, still wrapped in plastic, before turning toward the stairs.
The dog, instinctively knowing not to follow, stood panting at
the base of the furnace as the old monk slowly made his way
to the top, supporting himself on a thick concrete banister. The
elderly monk then placed the new robes on a small table positioned at the foot of the casket and began calling out more
chanting melodies as he clasped his hands together in a high

wai, saying his final valediction to Noojan Phundet. When he finished he *waied* Noojan's son and slowly made his way down the side steps to the awaiting dog. Returning to the shaded seating area, the monk took a seat above as the dog sat down at the base of the stage, once again patiently waiting for his master.

The four remaining monks followed, without any animals in tow, and mimicked the first monk's actions, returning to the stage when finished. As man at a podium began calling out names, people in the shaded seating area stood, walked over to Noojan's daughter, Aae, and gave her a *wai*. Aae would then give them a gift commensurate with their official standing and they would climb the steps to the iron furnace, place their origami flower onto the casket and gift onto a small table before *waiing* Noojan's son. When they finished, they climbed down the stairs on the side of the building and return to their seats in the shaded seating area.

The well-dressed men and women, who I would learn later were district officials, were the first to be called, and given orange pillows. The district officials were followed by the orange-robed teenagers, friends, and finally Noojan's family. Hearing Supattra's name called I watched her stand and make her way toward her cousin at the bottom of the stairs leading to Noojan's body. In a halting tumble of tones, as one does when they suddenly change from one language to another, the man at the podium then called my name. I raised my eyebrows in disbelief as the surprising panegyric swept across me like an unforeseen wave. As the only *farang* in the crowd, I was both astonished and honored to be considered a member of Noojan's family and a part of his farewell. As I stood, nearly knocking over my blue plastic chair, the entire enclave of district officials twisted in their seats to catch a glimpse of the strange name's owner and lone *farang* given such an accolade. Approaching Aae and giving the best *wai* I could conjure, I smiled a silent thank you. I could see that her eyes were red and her cheeks were stained with tears. She handed me a simple orange terrycloth towel. I climbed the steps to the furnace and looked at Noojan's son, who stood stoically next to his father. Placing the towel on top of Supattra's and my flower onto the casket, I turned to Noojan's son and presented him with another worthy *wai.*

As the last of the family were called, the mood of the ceremony began to shift from solemn to jovial, as the attendees became aware that it would soon be time to return to Noojan's house and resume the celebration. The monks filed off the stage, followed by the teenaged boys, both factions splitting up and wandering away in separate directions between the temple buildings. Once again, I silently chuckled at the sight of the black and brown dog, its tail briskly wagging from side to side as it followed the elderly monk. Supattra soon joined me and took my hand, leading me toward the main temple, its bright red roof highlighting both its white walls and the surrounding emerald green flora and shrubbery.

Walking past the elaborate red roofed temple, I asked, "Considering I was named with the family members, shouldn't I have sat with you on the floor next to the stage?"

"Yes, but people understand that *farangs* have difficulty sitting on the floor for long periods."

"But I could have done it." I chuckled. "My body is not that spoiled."

"It doesn't matter." She looked up. "People just want you to be comfortable and feel welcome."

Shaking my head, I smiled. "I could have done it for Noojan."

Then, after a brief hesitation, she whispered, "He would not close his eyes. I tried many times to close them but Noojan would not let me."

"What does that mean?"

"He is not ready to leave. There is something else he must do."

"What could it be? May be something about your sister?"

"I have no idea."

Walking out of the temple grounds, we turned down one of the narrow dirt lanes and strolled through the village. Several villagers recognized us, waving and calling out. Others silently watched our passage. Passing the spoke-wheeled intersection, we wandering down the dirt road toward the thatched roof hut and our pickup, stopping in front of Supattra's childhood home. With the Isaan sun bearing down on us, she looked up at me and smiled.

"Is Noojan at rest?" I asked.

"Not yet."

"When will we find out?"

First glancing down at her feet, Supattra looked back up and replied, "Noojan will move on when he is ready."

"But not now?"

With smiling eyes, she said, "His family and friends will stay at his house with his spirit, and when he is ready he will move on."

Walking up to the covered patio, past the tall mango tree, Supattra poured us two beers on ice as I sat down at the concrete picnic table, inspecting the ground at my feet for red ants.

As she delivered me the beer- and ice- filled glass, already sweating with condensation, I asked, "Have you ever considered moving back here? Back to Yuan Kom, I mean."

"I would love to have a small house in this village but I do not want to live here. It is peaceful and quiet but we would become bored—and there is no way to make money in Isaan. I would like a small house with one bedroom and a nice kitchen to stay when we visit, but nothing more."

Chuckling, I added, "And air conditioning?"

Giggling as she sat next to me on the concrete bench, she replied, "And at least one air conditioner."

As we sat sipping beer, Supattra's mother and father, then her two sisters walked up to the house, sitting down cross legged on the patio and pouring more glasses of beer. The unsmiling rotund lady with her elderly husband were the next to join us, followed by woman carrying a bag of fried bugs that looked to be grasshoppers. The sight of the bag of bugs made me wonder if they had bought them at the jungle market. The conversation and laughter continued to grow as several more friends and relatives arrived. At some point the bugs were poured into a bowl and the crowd lying and sitting cross legged on the hard cool patio began eating the small crispy insects as if they were snacking on popcorn.

The unsmiling rotund lady said something to Supattra who, in turn, looked at me, translating. "She wants to know if all *farangs* are like you."

Laughing, I replied, "No, *mia chia.*"

Another question from the rotund lady and Supattra translated, "In what way are you different?"

Taking a few moments to consider her question, I finally responded, "I have learned that watching and listening, waiting for the answer to present itself, is preferable to asking a lot of questions."

Thais are a proud people who dislike being wrong or looking weak in front of peers. Rarely will they admit to making a mistake, no matter how blatant. As a Westerner, on first arriving in this country, I interpreted this as not taking responsibility for one's actions. While I can't say which came first, the culturally taught mannerism of not judging one another for their misdeeds or not outwardly recognizing their culpability, these two traits are connected in a complex web that are lost on most outsiders—and probably the Thais themselves. Beyond this question of which cultural trait, not pointing out faults or acknowledging one's failures, preceded the other, I have learned that Thais do feel guilty for their transgressions, no matter how small. This need for not looking weak extends beyond not admitting failure in their personal interactions with one another. For example, Thais do not like to ask a lot of questions because, once again, making too many inquires generates the impression that they don't know what's going on and creates the appearance they're out of the loop or unable to comprehend their surroundings. I attribute my success in this country to the fact that I have fully taken on this particular trait, although for an entirely different reason. I want to fit in and be accepted. What was the significance of the teenagers shaving their heads and eyebrows and donning orange robes? I have no idea, I didn't ask. Why wasn't I asked to join the family and the teenagers in Noojan's house with the monks? I don't know and chose not to inquire. Why did the procession take three turns around the furnace? I never asked. Why did the villagers wash Noojan with coconut water? Beats me, but it was pretty interesting. On the other hand, by keeping my eyes and ears open and my mouth shut, I already knew about the firecrackers and the thin cotton string strung from Noojan's casket to the monks and teenagers. That's not to say I never ask questions, but when I do, they're normally about general issues that momentarily stir my curiosity, and the answers provided normally reveal far more than a series of pointed and prying queries. Is the casket filled with ice? Who's the old lady living in the shed? What're the coconuts for? What I have learned in this incredibly colorful country is that with patience all my questions will eventually be answered, and with my silence, the Thais around me are more tolerant of the foreigner in their midst.

As Supattra translated my reply, my onlookers sitting cross legged on the patio all broke out in wide grins, clapping their hands and laughing. She placed her arm around my shoulders and pulled me close, saying, "You have learned much."

Another question came from the rotund woman's husband, lying on his side and leaning against his elbow, his thick black-framed glasses threatening to fall off the end of his nose at any moment. Supattra quickly regained her composure and translated, "What is it about Thailand that you like the most?"

Taking a long sip of beer, the ice cubes in the glass faintly tinkling against one another, I replied, "*Jai yen.*"

Rather than laughing at my answer, the cross-legged crowd all began nodding their heads, muttering a mix of, "*khaas,*" and "*chais,*" which I immediately translated as agreement.

Southeast Asians dislike confrontation, and one of the most important and difficult lessons I have learned over the years is what Thais refer to as *jai yen*, or a cool heart. The opposite of *jai yen* is *jai rawwn*, or a hot heart. I would go so far as to say that *jai yen* is one of the underpinnings of their entire culture. A good example is my dealing with employees over the years. An angry or disgruntled employee will rarely confront their manager directly but rather send an emissary to avoid a possible altercation in order to ensure a cool heart. I learned very quickly with Supattra that couples don't prefer to quarrel in her culture. They simply state their grievances in a calm manner and follow the assertion with silence. The silence allows the accused to ponder his or her infraction and make the next move. If a dispute follows, silence becomes the battleground of the argument. Whoever can remain voiceless the longest, before the other either exhibits some level of *jai rawwn* or capitulates and presents an apology in the form of an unrelated act of kindness, becomes the victor.

Western psychotherapists specializing in marriage counseling will likely find this method absurd, not directly airing one's grievances down to the infinitesimal detail, but in this region of the world it works, and the tentacles of *jai yen* have found their way into every fiber of their religion, culture, and lives.

To live fruitfully among the people of Thailand, one must learn to never place someone else in the position of losing face. *Jai yen* and its most notable champion, silence, becomes either the workbench or battleground of success.

Sitting on patio, we drank and ate, and then we drank some more. Day turned into night as a cool breeze blew across the patio, bringing with it the sweet scent of the rice paddies and the intangible soul-fulfilling sensation it provides. As I lay back on the cool tiles, taking in the stars while listening to the family converse in their native language, I could hear the sound of a scooter turning down the dirt road that led to Supattra's childhood home.

Like a Thai version of Paul Reverie, the celebrated American patriot alerting the Colonial Militia to the approach of the Red Coats as he rode his horse across the Massachusetts countryside, a man drove his motorcycle through Yuan Kom City bringing news to Noojan Phundet's family members of a problem at the temple. Stopping out in front of the house just long enough to sound the alert, the man throttled his small scooter and continued on down the road to the base of the hill, before turning left in the direction of Noojan's house.

With troubled expressions suddenly appearing on their faces, the family members began babbling in a fretful tone.

Looking over at Supattra sitting cross-legged between her two sisters, I asked, "What's going on?"

"Noojan Phundet did not burn," she said in a hushed and trembling voice. "My uncle did not burn all the way."

With visions of a half-burned corpse dancing across my mind, morbidly wondering what parts had been consumed, I repeated her words. "Your uncle didn't burn all the way? What does that mean?"

Calmness abruptly replacing her previous angst, she stood and walked over next to me, saying, "Noojan is not ready to leave. There is something keeping him here. We knew this today when his eyes would not close. We knew it last night when he came to my sister. There is something bothering Noojan Phundet and we must solve whatever it is so he can have peace."

"But we don't know what it is."

She looked down at me lying on the patio. "Then we must find out."

"How do we do that?"

"We must go to Noojan's house."

"Right now?"

"Right now."

Leaving our half-filled glasses of beer, Supattra, her sisters, mother, and I ventured down the road and turned left, walking past our pickup truck and the thatched-roof hut. Following the dark perimeter road toward Noojan's house, I could see small lights flickering under the overhead canopy in front of his house as we carefully made our way across the small field to the red plastic chairs and folding tables. Only four or five friends and family sat under the canopy at the tables, laughing and drinking beer with one another, as if nothing had happened. Peeking through the front door, I saw all the orange-robed teenage boys lying on the floor in line against one wall, sleeping. Behind them another fifteen or twenty friends and family were crowded on the floor, also in various stages of slumber, keeping Noojan's spirit company. It was not the scene I had expected, considering the recent news of the un-burned corpse and Noojan's questionable departure.

I gestured inside and whispered to Supattra, "Do you think they could fit anyone else in there?"

"Noojan's spirit has still not moved on. They will sleep with him until that time comes."

My curiosity perked, largely because of the ten glasses of beer I had consumed before coming to Noojan's house, I then asked, "And how long will that take? How many days?"

"That all depends on whether we find out what's keeping him here."

Glancing back into the room at the crowd of villagers sleeping on the floor, I asked her one more time, "How will they know when Noojan leaves?"

"They will know."

I moved over to one of the tables. The red plastic chair wobbled slightly, its legs sorting themselves out on the uneven grass below, as I sat down. The top of folding table felt somewhat sticky against my elbows, undoubtedly from all the spilled food and drinks over the last two days. As Supattra's mother disappeared into the house, weaving her way through a labyrinth of prone bodies, by one of the women I had seen cooking in the kitchen the day before delivered a glass of beer to me. Supattra and her two older sisters sat down next to me and began a conversation with a woman sitting across the table. During a short break in their conversation, I asked Supattra where the woman was from because in this part of Thailand, where the woman have very little leg, arm, and facial hair, she seemed downright furry. With long, dark, wavy hair, the woman's eyebrows looked as if two massive black caterpillars had been glued to her brow and even in the dim light under the table I could see her legs were covered with thick black hair. Dressed in a floral long-sleeved silk blouse and a black skirt, there was something about her that seemed odd and unsettling.

Leaning close to me, Supattra answered in a muted voice, "She is from Yuan Kom City."

Taking a sip of beer, I said, "She doesn't look like she's from around here."

She is...how do you say?...someone who can see things

others cannot," Supattra whispered in the same hushed tone.

"A soothsayer?"

"What's that?"

"Someone who can tell the future."

When the hairy woman gave me an irritated glance, I realized she couldn't understand what I was saying to Supattra. Like many of the citizens of Isaan, she didn't understand English. I had witnessed that look many times over the years, the annoyance of not being able to understand everything that was being communicated. And, of course, I knew that feeling well, living in a country where I only had a loose grip on the language.

"She can see things but I'm not sure she can see the future," Supattra explained.

Suddenly the woman was looking directly at me. Her dark oily eyes seemingly penetrated through to my very soul. Scrutinizing me, the woman then looked at Supattra and said something in Isaan. Supattra replied in a cautious voice to which the woman quickly responded, the tone of her voice as trenchant as her eyes.

Growing up and residing in the United States, I never gave much credence to astrology or horoscopes, but having witnessed many unusual things over the years while living in and traveling around this wonderful country, I have found that I no longer immediately brush off claims of clairvoyants, unusual prophesies, or sightings of ghosts and phantoms. Living in a country filled with oracles and spirits, as a son of the sixth sign of the Zodiac, I have begun to open my mind to those things I once though ludicrous. However, on occasion, I feel the need to return to my roots, and with my feet firmly on the ground, assert my *farang* upbringing and education.

Looking the soothsayer square in the eyes, I asked, "What did she say?"

"She asked if we had any children and when I told her no she said it was because your seed is weak."

Laughing, maybe a little bit too loudly, I replied, "Tell her I've already spawned three children and my seed seemed to do just fine."

As Supattra translated my reply, the woman appeared to lose a little of her former piercing confidence as she glanced at her feet and then took a sip of beer, before looking back up at me and, in a less penetrating tone, responded to my proclamation.

Feeling my *farang* essence bubbling to the surface, keeping the wavy-haired soothsayer locked in showdown of eyeballs, oily black versus blue, I then asked, "Now what'd she say?"

Looking over at me with a questioning expression, as if she was trying to figure out what I was doing, Supattra said, "She says that maybe she was wrong, and it's me. We cannot have children because of me."

Chuckling at the woman's quickly changed envisage, in an internationally understood sarcastic tone, I commented, "So now your eggs are weak?"

Watching the woman, waiting for some reaction to my evident mocking tone, I noticed that when she raised her glass of beer to her lips, her hands wobbled. Looking into her oily black eyes, I detected a fogginess that I hadn't seen before. Listening to her speak to the three sisters in their native language, I could hear a nearly indistinguishable slur.

"Pat, what are you doing?" Supattra asked. "Be careful, she is very powerful."

"What's she going to do, cast a spell on me?" I asked, keeping the clear mocking tone in my words, which needed no translation. "Turn me into a frog?"

Tapping her fingers on the table top, breaking eye contact with me just long enough for her to say something else to Supattra, the woman turned her gaze back onto me. It was at that moment, putting together all of my minute observations, I realized the hairy purported-clairvoyant was drunk.

Supattra then asked me, "What day of the week were you born on?"

Still keeping a watchful eye on the drunken fortuneteller across the table who was vigilantly examining my every detail, I replied, "I don't know."

"She says you were born on a Tuesday."

Chuckling at the hairy woman's attempt to reaffirm her

prophet status, keeping the cutting tone in my voice, I said, "Well, let's see about that."

Taking my cell from my pocket, I began working back through fifty-six years of calendars, which I quickly concluded would take a good amount of time. As I clicked away on my cell, the hairy woman began speaking to Supattra's sister Aae, her former penetrating voice now taking on soothing tone.

When I finally reached 1958, attempting to keep any sound of triumph from my voice, I announced in a tone as flat as I could invoke, "Tell your drunken soothsayer that I was born on a Wednesday."

Abruptly turning to me, placing an index finger against her lips, Supattra said, "Please let her talk."

"But she's drunk," I retorted, somewhat surprised that she hadn't recognized it before me.

"Yes, she is very drunk. She is drunk every night. She is a village drunk. But you must let her talk."

"What's going on? Why are we listening to an intoxicated mystic who has been wrong about each of her declarations?"

"Pat," Supattra replied, "she knows why Noojan's spirit has not left."

"The woman has been wrong on both her recent claims and she's drunk. Now she knows why Noojan is not at peace? I'm not sure which is more surprising, that she still thinks we believe anything she says or that you actually believe what she's saying."

Ignoring my remark, Supattra continued to intently listen, as the hairy woman talked in caring tone to the three sisters. The three sisters nodded in acknowledgment to whatever the woman was saying. I drank beer with a bit more intensity; and the hairy woman talked in captivating and slightly slurred Isaan. It was an assembly of the believers and skeptics and, much to my chagrin, clearly the believers were winning. When the woman stopped talking, Aae stood up, turned, and walked into the house. Supattra patted me on the knee, as if all the family problems had suddenly been solved, and the hairy woman looked at me with a clear expression of conquest over her *farang* opponent.

Taking an exceedingly long drink from my glass filled with beer and ice, I asked in a somewhat defeated tone, "So what's going on?"

"The woman knows why Noojan has not left. She felt there was a problem between two family members and asked us what it might be. My sister explained about her argument with Noojan's daughter and how he came to her and held her hand when she wasn't sure she wanted to come. The woman asked if my sister had spoken with Noojan's daughter yet, and my sister said no. The woman said that until they talked and my sister forgave Noojan's daughter, he would not leave. That has been his unfinished business."

"And you believe her?"

"She knew there was a problem between two people in the family."

Leaning back in my chair, every fiber in my body screaming to apply my *farang* logic to disprove this drunken soothsayer, I considered what had just transpired. Taking another long drink from my beer, I pushed my *farang* judgments and beliefs back into that small closet in the back of my mind, where I've kept them incarcerated for so long, and quickly reverted back into my former Thai-trained accepting and nonjudgmental self. While I had won a momentary victory over the fortuneteller, it was a win only I recognized. I could never hope to change what had taken centuries for the Thai culture to create or ever think my beautiful partner and her family would alter their beliefs simply because I refuted one self-proclaimed visionary. Culturally taught, the daily lives of most Thais are seeped with mysticism and spirits, and as I sat under the canopy outside Noojan Phundet's house, a thin smile broke across my face as I wondered why in the world I ever let the *farang* in me out. One of the reasons I love Southeast Asia is that this country's spirituality and openness to the world is far more complex than what the Western Hemisphere accepts.

Gazing out from under the overhead canopy, I surveyed the moon and stars glimmering behind a thin sheen of slow-moving translucent clouds, turning the sky into a wondrous canvas painted in differing shades of gray. Beyond the village boundary, I examined the rice paddies sparkling under the same black and white work of art as a gentle and warm breeze brought with it the scent of freshly turned earth, stagnant water, tender rice stalks, and fragrant flowers. It was a soul-healing aroma unique to Isaan.

Sitting in the red plastic chair, next to the beautiful Buddhist woman I had spent the last eight years with, I considered my past and wondered about our future, realizing that I was taking a risk in bringing Supattra back to the US. Knowing that every nation and its associated culture has its perks and dissuaders and that Thailand was not the panacea to a perfect society, I wondered what effect a country populated by individuals whose world is limited by strict science, unwavering rules and regulations, and stanch cultural conventions would have on a Buddhist woman raised in poverty? Would an unforgiving society filled with materialism and stringent ideology triumph over the simplicity of growing up in Thailand? Who am I to risk the very essence of a rice farmer's daughter by taking her back to the United States?

Looking back up at the moon, now released from its former cloud veil, it dawned on me. Supattra's and my life are intertwined and we will always be together. We are like two hooves on the same buffalo moving along a common trail. We will always suffer together and be partners until the day our candles are blown out when we have reached perfect enlightenment. Who was I to fight destiny?

The table around me suddenly became hushed. Supattra, her older sister, and the soothsayer turning in chorus toward Noojan's front door broke me from my thoughts of that distant land I once called home. As if the women around me had a premonition, Supattra's sister appeared in the door with her mother and walked over to our table. In the dim flickering light under the canopy, with tear-stained cheeks, Aae nodded her head to silently inform her sisters and the village oracle that she had freed Noojan Phundet and forgiven his daughter. It was done. Noojan was released from this life, and we all could bid him a fond adieu and safe journey into his next.

Farewell, Noojan Phundet.

A Final Note from the Author

Recently asked why this story should be published, I replied, "The loneliness of posttraumatic stress can't be described in a sentence or two—nor can the reasons behind the decisions its sufferers make. However, that loneliness and those often unusual choices can be coherently scribed into a non-fictional narrative written by another sufferer. It would help other victims know they are not alone in their struggle."

I also believe that, while the causal factors may vary, the road to living with posttraumatic stress is common—understanding how to deal with its symptoms, creating a strong support system, and time. And finally, *A Distant Island* is a highly personal and honest tale, and it takes that kind of intense soul searching to overcome and control posttraumatic stress.

While having never formally studied posttraumatic stress, or any other medical subject, for that matter, I have lived with the consequences and possibly understand its life-altering properties better than many of those physiatrists and psychologists educated on the topic. What I have learned about posttraumatic stress is simply through experience—trying to figure out how to live a life inflicted with its daily penalties. And while I have never totally defeated the disorder, I have learned to manage its effects. Like that wise Bangkok monk so artfully pointed out to Supattra, after certain catastrophic events we will never be the same man or woman we were before. Given this conclusion, an attentive reader might ask, "So what was your awakening?" That is a very interesting question and one that I've given a lot of thought as I finish this manuscript. Simply written, my awakening from posttraumatic stress occurred when I candidly evaluated my life, completing a sincere and meticulous introspection or self-examination. For me, coming to terms with the disorder had to include recognizing the events that led me to posttraumatic stress, and the act of identifying and taking ownership of my follow-up mistakes.

My parents taught me that strength comes from within, and

to pursue the challenges and problems that arise from time to time on my own, only seeking help as a last resort. Managing to teach myself how to operate a restaurant on a Southeast Asian tropical island through trial and error, I took on the difficulties of posttraumatic stress with the same spirit. What I have learned is that beyond the unseen endocrinological and anatomical changes to the brain, posttraumatic stress affects an individual on several levels—dealing with the identifiable symptoms and adjusting oneself to a slightly new persona and different perspective. A professional might tell you there is a third—dealing with the underlying causes—but I would submit that comes with the awakening.

Everyone on this earth has or will struggle with sleep, anxiety, irritability, aggression, ruminations, concentration, and impulsiveness at some point in their lives. Commonly these disruptive qualities are the consequences of distressing events we all experience from time to time. The intensity of those behavioral issues will be commensurate with the catastrophic nature and duration of the event that created them. Extreme cases spawned on a battlefield, through sexual abuse, or growing up in intense poverty will inflict its victims with a number of these problems simultaneously in such a way that it outwardly affects their ability to function within society's norms.

Having personally struggled with sleep for a number of years, I have found that a lack of an adequate siesta easily unites with each of the other symptoms of posttraumatic stress and amplifies the effects. As a result, I have tried a plethora of unusual drugs and crazy techniques to resolve my sleep problems. Sadly, I have found that the use of alcohol has been the only reliable method to that end but, as you have learned in the pages of this narrative, over drinking has the tendency to increase my irritability and aggression—and therefore worth avoiding.

A second issue that posttraumatic stress has left me with is an untimely tendency to ruminate, losing focus on whatever task is at hand. By another title, my ability to concentrate has suffered. Projects that require a great deal of concentration aren't the issue. I spent hours glued to my computer writing this narrative, day after day. It's the mundane tasks we find necessary to function within the constraints of our society that are the problem. Conversations are problematic for me. The longer the dialogue, the more apt I am to find myself drifting through the cosmos of time and space, contemplating life's true meaning, reminiscing some past battle, or wondering whether I should change the bald front tires on my pickup truck before a potential blow out.

Three months after my return from Thailand, my two youngest children and I journeyed to visit with my oldest daughter who had recently graduated from the University of Colorado, and where I planned to meet with my extended family after an eight year absence. I considered reestablishing the connections with my brothers and sister, all of whom reside in the state, a necessary element of my recovery. After picking us up from the airport in Denver, my oldest daughter called my ex-wife and said she was angry because I wasn't communicating. To be honest, finding myself sitting in the passenger seat of a moving car is a guaranteed checkout from reality. Scenery gliding through car windows is like taking a strong prescription painkiller, and the added obligatory conversation clinches an untimely trip down memory lane. My oldest daughter had been right. I recall checking out and pondering something so important that I can't remember what it was in order to write it down on the pages of this story.

Depending on how deeply I am affected with posttraumatic stress on any given day, the final symptom I continually struggle with is impulsiveness. Arguably, that trait is unavoidably woven into our genetic material and, like my first wife, I have been slightly impulsive since the day I was born. Impulsiveness is a common human frailty or strength, depending on the monetary or personal results of exercising that particular trait. However, take a moment to imagine yourself standing in front of a commercial building on the beach of a tropical island located in a distant country that has a reputation for corruption and suddenly deciding on the spot to buy the property while having no idea what you were going to do with it. Imagine yourself flying to the corrupt country's capital three days later, even having had time to reconsider, and putting a hefty down payment on the property, still having no idea what you were going to do with the building. That is posttraumatic stress-style impulsiveness. While buying the building I own in the Gulf of Thailand is a good example of potentially self-destructive impulsiveness, there are more damaging versions. Reckless words, or behavior, to friends or loved ones that damage our supporting reeds can have even farther reaching consequences.

As a former combat veteran with numerous and incredible stories of courage and survival, a man who took the unbelievable risk of opening a business on the beach of a tropical island in a foreign country known for its beautiful and exotic women, many people look to me as a someone who has done what everyone else wishes they had, but lacked the audacity. They perceive my life as one filled with bravado and adventure. What they don't see is how my beginning and subsequent choices led to a good man finding himself out of control and hurting everyone within close proximity. They see the adventure and glory of combat, but not the consequences that the experiences of danger, death, and unfairness eventually create. They see the allure of living a life where one is not afraid of making adventurous choices and not the impulsiveness or regret that follows. I am not the man who looked into the mirror on the morning of September 11, 2001, nor will I ever be that person again. The sight of my reflected image now elicits a deeper pondering, wondering where that man has gone and whether I can ever reclaim the peacefulness and happiness of a bygone life.

Posttraumatic stress has created someone who feels oddly out of place, someone who has issues with sleep and difficulty concentrating, and someone who tends to be more than a bit impulsive. We spend our youth learning to understand how to avoid our weaknesses and use our strengths in order to survive a very unfair world. Victims of posttraumatic stress find themselves a different person from their youth, figuratively thrust back into their adolescence to learn who they are and how to survive all over again. We can always see that distant island on the horizon and remember who we were, but we will never walk its shores again. The trick is finding solace in that new person residing inside your skin.

During a recent conversation with my psychotherapist sister-in-law, she equated my time in Thailand to the wise man on the mountaintop. Like the wise man, choosing to live on a mountain in order to get away from the daily distractions of the civilized world to ponder the meaning of life, I chose to move to Thailand to escape the confusion and reminders of my posttraumatic stress and reflect on my life. She went on to say that my growing anxiety, now that I have returned, was normal and the only true path to recovery was with the aid of a trained professional. Having read this manuscript, she agreed, that most the psychiatrists and psychotherapists could never understand the loneliness and confusion of posttraumatic stress, before pointing out that some train for that profession because of an event in their past. Many psychotherapists who specialize in drug addiction are former drug abusers, those who train in posttraumatic stress might have a background tainted by some catastrophic event in their past.

Given my experience, one might ask: how do you manage or overcome posttraumatic stress? With the thoughtfulness and insight of my sister-in-law in mind, I would recommend you seek out a professional, schooled in the finer points of the disorder. If you choose not to seek out professional help, you will likely find yourself fourteen years into a posttraumatic stress struggle, suddenly "awakening" in some foreign country—having hurt all those you once thought important—to the realities affecting your very existence. While we would all like to believe that we are capable of extracting ourselves from the grips of calamitous events that occasionally interrupt our lives, it truly takes the art of a professional to lead us from the vicious and unrelenting tentacles of posttraumatic stress.

Secondly, find a good strong reed to lean against. Whether in the form of a woman, a family, or good friends, a sturdy and robust support system is the foundation for managing the chaos that seemingly engulfs the victims of posttraumatic stress. Don't discount the unusual ones, understanding that support may come in many forms, some of which we would never imagine. My rescuer came in the shape of a former bargirl who happened to be a devout Buddhist, with as many flaws as I had. With Supattra by my side, I reclaimed a portion of my previous self and learned how to manage the long term effects of posttraumatic stress.

Ultimately, realize and accept that you will never be the man or woman you were before, and, even though you can never walk its shores again, look to that distant island as a past achievement. Hold tightly onto your reeds, watching your former self glistening on the horizon, and feel that new island rise beneath your feet. Then take the time to learn the contour of its beaches, the texture of its sand, and angle at which the sun strikes your shoulders during the day. While you can always see your former life across the waters in the distance, know and accept that this new place is now your home.

On a different note, I once tried to explain to a woman of academia, who allegedly had earned more than one advanced degree from several reputable universities, that the truth lies between. Mistakenly receiving an email meant for a common acquaintance, I learned that she believed I was a complete moron and my theory on truth was unequivocally without merit. Even at risk of confirming my idiocy, I will attempt to explain my belief that the truth lies between because it is an important element of any story concerning posttraumatic stress.

I believe that the truth, to some level, is based on our perception of how events unfold around us. More witnesses may provide better accuracy as to exactly what happened, but it also creates more variance as to the details. For airline disasters there are black boxes and cockpit voice recorders that allow investigators to hone in on the truth but, even with those aids, at some point, human logic and emotions play a part. Witnessing Jeff Couch, Dan Adams, Phil Chapman, and Top Snell die in the helicopter accident over Calipatria, California, I knew what altitude they were flying when their helicopter began its initial descent—the UH-1N had no black boxes or cockpit voice recorders back in those days. I also had a good idea at what point the main rotor blades struck the tail boom and they began their free fall toward the farm fields below. Landing at the crash site, initially to provide security and later to give statements, as witnesses on the ground began providing their version of the story, I realized just how different their perspective was from mine. In matters of the heart with no precise electronic or visual records, human emotions at play, and personal prejudices in place, the truth becomes even more convoluted and difficult to pin down. The truth will normally be found between the participants' perceptions.

While I have attempted to place the bulk of the blame on myself, this story is based on my perception of how events unfolded during my struggle with posttraumatic stress and is undoubtedly filled memories tainted by swinging emotions and personal prejudices. This story is mine and mine alone. I imagine my second wife would write an entirely different narrative and the truth would lie someplace between her version and mine.

Finally, the epilogue was a short stand-alone story, containing some repetition, I created to keep my hands off this manuscript before the editorial process began and added much later. After completing *Farewell Noojan Phundet* I realized it was the perfect complement to *A Distant Island*. Having had this autobiographical narrative concerning my struggle with posttraumatic stress reviewed by several publishers, the common complaint was that the reader would want to know what happened between me and Supattra, and whether or not I returned to Thailand. For those who didn't read it between the lines, there now should be no doubt that I will die in the arms of beautiful Buddhist woman, many years my junior, as she whispers in my ear, "Please wait for me this time."

About the Author

Growing up in the Rocky Mountains and graduating from the University of Colorado, Patrick Ashtre chose a career in the military opposed to one slugging it out in the office cubicles of corporate America. After serving twenty-six years in the Marine Corps as both an infantryman and aviator he took a fancy to a horizon of water over that of mountains. Spending his final tour in Japan, Ashtre retired from the marines and moved to the small tropical island of Phangan, located in the Gulf of Thailand, where he owned and operated a popular beachfront pub.

After eight years of living, working, and traveling throughout Southeast Asia, he is now in the process of moving back to the Colorado Rockies. With a misspent youth and experiences from around the globe as a canvas, Ashtre will likely fill the pages of many more books before he closes his laptop for the last time.